People in

'This book is to be returned on or before

People in Organisations

Valerie Bell and John Harrison

Pitman

PITMAN PUBLISHING
128 Long Acre, London WC2E 9AN

First published in Great Britain 1987
Reprinted 1988 (twice)

British Library Cataloguing in Publication Data
Bell, Valerie
  People in organisations.
  1. Communications in organisations
  I. Title   II. Harrison, John
  302.3′5   HM131

  ISBN 0–273–02283–0

Text photoset in Times and Helvetica by
Tek Art Limited, Croydon, Surrey

Printed and bound in Singapore

Contents

Acknowledgements

The authors and publishers are grateful to the following for permission to reproduce photographs and illustrations.

Acco Company Ltd
British Telecom (Prestel)
Canon (UK) Limited
Dexion Limited
Flexiform Limited
Hewlett Packard Limited
IBM United Kingdom Ltd
The Institute of Administrative Management
Kodak Limited
Office Equipment News
Open BTEC/Macmillan (Updating for Business: The Design of Office Systems)
Pitney Bowes plc
Rotadex Systems Limited
Sasco Limited
Signal Business Systems Ltd
3M United Kingdom plc
Twinlock plc
Vickers plc

Introduction

This book has been written primarily to cater for the needs of students taking the BTEC National 'People in Organisations' double unit with its aim to equip students with an understanding of people in organisations, the ways in which they function, and their systems of communication. It will also develop the skills and knowledge which will increase their ability to communicate effectively in organisations. In addition, the book will meet many of the requirements of other intermediate-level examinations such as RSA Stage II Office Practice, Pitman Intermediate Office Practice and IAM Certificate in Administrative Management.

The approach is essentially practical and many of the assignments centre around four organisations which, though differing greatly in aims and size, together combine to encompass many of the problems, procedures and human relationships inherent in business and public administration. Case studies for these organisations are provided on the following pages. As students work through the tasks related to these organisations, which appear at appropriate stages throughout the book, it will become apparent that good administrative practices and good communications are essential for the maintenance of both internal and external equilibrium and that all organisations form part of a network in which weak links may have detrimental and far-reaching effects.

In working through the graded assignments, the student will not only be required to apply principles and theories to practical business-related situations, but will also be encouraged to develop problem-solving skills by individual and group work. The application of skills and knowledge within the students' own work experience is a feature of many of the assignments and the use of information technology and its impact on people and systems is stressed throughout. Students are also given every opportunity to develop their communication skills so that they can relate effectively to others as individuals, groups and within organisations.

Key facts are included in each unit to assist in reinforcing the main issues. Integrated core assignments are also included at intervals throughout the book to develop interrelationships between core units. Whilst the text provides much background information, it is important to supplement this in order to keep up-to-date with technology and the various services available to business.

Visits to firms and work experience are an invaluable means of providing the full-time student with realistic background knowledge; part-time students should draw upon their own job experience as much as possible to relate principles to practice.

In order to simplify the writing of this text, the masculine pronoun has been used in most cases, and we wish to make it clear that all references to men apply equally to women and a deliberate distinction between the sexes is not implied.

The case studies

The case studies relate to four organisations operating in the Westleigh areas of Midlandshire.

1 Joblinc Personnel Agency – a small partnership providing an employment and office work service.
2 Domilux (UK) plc – the UK holding of a multinational company manufacturing commercial and domestic appliances.
3 Westleigh District Council – a local authority.
4 ALBEC (All British Electrical Components) Ltd – a small manufacturer of electrical components.

Although the firms portrayed are fictitious, they are based on real organisations and the material used is authentic. The case studies are not, however, intended to represent any particular organisations, nor to reflect their policies.

Case 1 *Jobline Personnel Agency*

The Jobline Personnel Agency was set up as a partnership some six years ago by Janet Keele and Mary Webb. Janet was aged 33 and married with two children at school. Before leaving work to bring up a family, Janet had been employed as Assistant to the Personnel Manager of a large manufacturing firm. Once her children were at school, she decided to resume her career and obtained a job as a recruitment officer for the local branch of an international employment agency. After eighteen months, Janet realised the potential profits to be made in this type of business and decided to set up a staff agency of her own. However, a condition in her employment contract prevented her from setting up in competition within a 5-mile radius for a period of four years after leaving her present employment. In order to spread the risk and to provide additional expertise, she decided to take a partner, Mary Webb.

Mary was single and aged 28. She worked as an accounts supervisor for a large garage, but was disillusioned by the lack of career prospects and job satisfaction.

Stage 1

Six years ago, the two women, with a capital of £8000, secured the lease of two rooms situated above an office stationers in a busy commercial area 8 miles away from Janet's previous employer. The premises were within easy distance of two industrial estates, rail and bus stations, a college of further education and a government job centre.

The first year proved very difficult and the partners made a loss. Most of their time and money was spent on advertising. They distributed leaflets to possible employers and contacted prospective clients by telephone and advertised in the local press and Yellow Pages for temporary clerical and office staff. All the office work was shared between them – one manning the office and telephone while the other was out visiting clients. As the business grew, they could not cope and recruited a secretary/receptionist to deal with some of the routine work.

At the end of the first year of business the work was divided as follows:

Janet:	responsible for correspondence, publicity, interviewing temps and liaising with employers.
Mary:	responsible for accounts, wages, cash, also interviewing temps and liaising with employers.
Audrey Lamb (the new secretary):	responsible for secretarial work for both partners, reception, filing, handling the mail and the telephone.

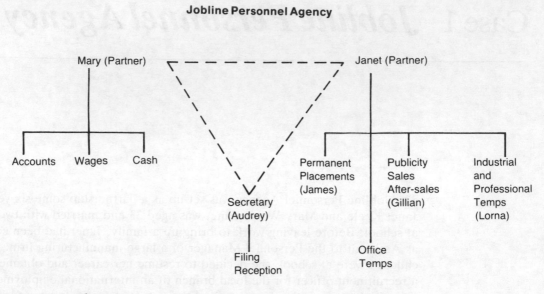

Figure 1

The following year a sales representative was recruited to visit employers on a regular basis, both to acquire new business and to provide a follow-up service when assignments were completed. This proved so successful that the partnership was able to expand further. They opened a new section to deal with placement of professional, technical and industrial staff. As the business expanded, Janet recruited an ex-colleague, James Leigh, to look after all the permanent job placements. The organisation chart in Fig. 1 shows the firm's organisation at this stage.

Case 2   *Domilux plc*

Domilux (UK) plc is a subsidiary of Baroche International, New York, which has worldwide interests in the manufacture and distribution of commercial and domestic appliances.

Domilux operates as an independent company controlled by a board of directors under the chairmanship of Sir Harry Paton, who is also the managing director. The company's Head Office is at Westleigh, Midlandshire, where its main production plant (manufacturing washing machines and tumble dryers) is also situated. Other plants are in operation at Hull (making commercial and domestic refrigerators), Glasgow (making vacuum cleaners and upholstery cleaners) and Cardiff (where small appliances such as kettles, coffee percolators, etc. are produced).

The overall policy and control is exercised at Head Office, which keeps central records and statistics; provides management services such as work study, organisation and methods, share registration, legal advice and systems analysis; undertakes the marketing of products by research and advertising, controls the regional sales teams and provides central training facilities for staff at all levels.

The four production plants are run as semi-autonomous units, each with its own plant manager and departments for personnel, purchasing, production, sales, accounts and office administration. Each plant manager is accountable to Head Office, but has wide authority for decision-making. He can hire and dismiss staff, negotiate with unions and utilise production resources (i.e. labour, materials and machines) to the best advantage according to local conditions. However, he must keep in close contact with Head Office, who can quickly identify units making a loss and take appropriate action.

The sales force is organised on a regional basis, each team being supervised by a regional sales manager who is accountable to the Sales Director. The salesmen send customer orders direct to Head Office, who distribute them to the appropriate plant (e.g. the factory manufacturing the item requested). When the factory has despatched the item to the customer, it informs Head Office of the amount to charge and Head Office then sends out the invoice to the customer.

The organisation chart in Fig. 2 shows the firm's organisation.

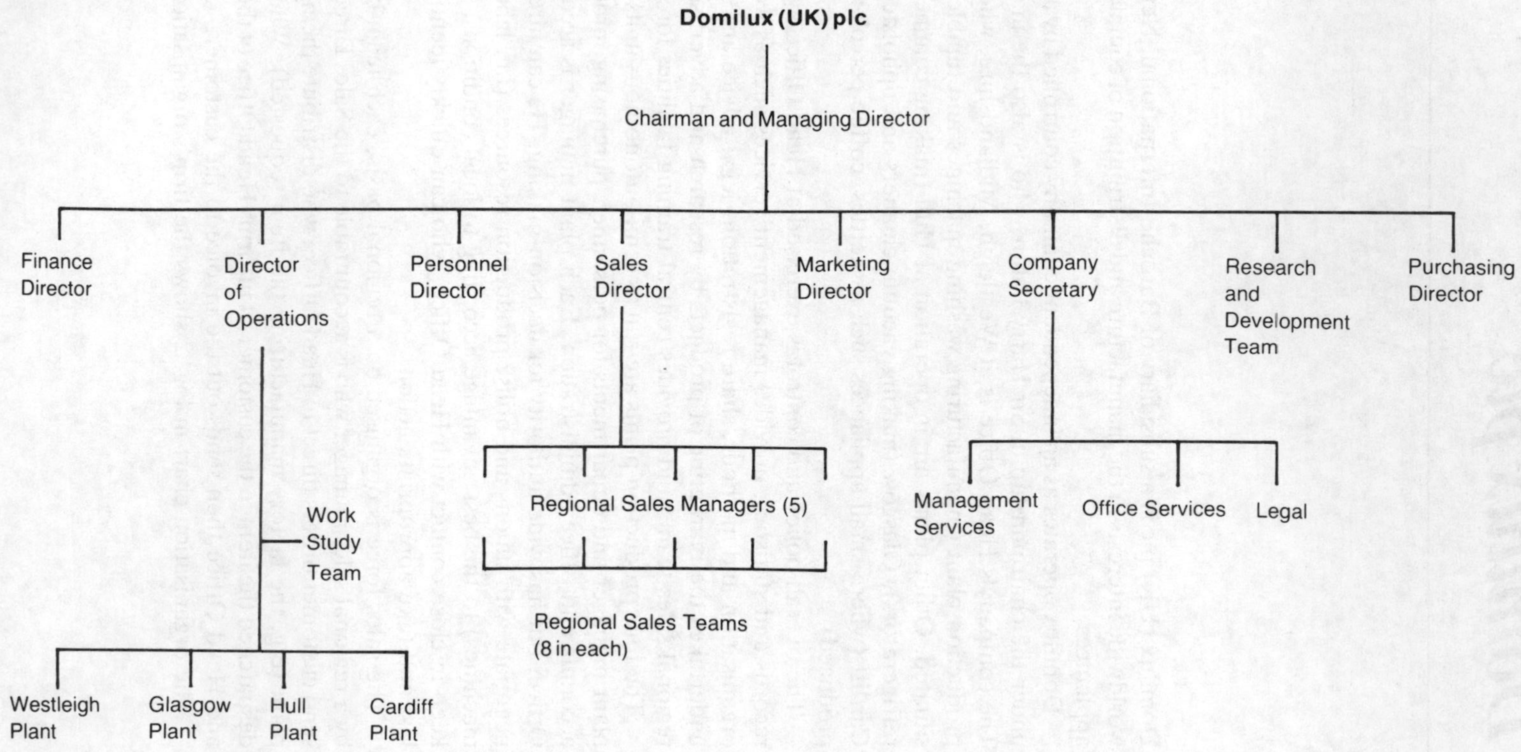

Domilux (UK) plc

Chairman and Managing Director

- Finance Director
- Personnel Director
- Director of Operations
  - Work Study Team
  - Westleigh Plant
  - Glasgow Plant
  - Hull Plant
  - Cardiff Plant
- Sales Director
  - Regional Sales Managers (5)
  - Regional Sales Teams (8 in each)
- Marketing Director
- Company Secretary
  - Management Services
  - Office Services
  - Legal
- Research and Development Team
- Purchasing Director

Figure 2

Case 3 *Local government – Westleigh District Council*

History

Westleigh District Council was created by the 1972 Local Government Act, which rationalised the whole system of local government on a basis of two tiers – county and district councils. The division of functions between county and district councils in non-metropolitan areas is shown in Fig. 3.

Whilst many major services, including education, social services, highways and strategic planning, are carried out by the county council, Westleigh District Council is still responsible for many significant local services, including housing, refuse collection, district planning, parks and recreation (leisure) and environmental health. In addition, it carries out highway work as agents of the county council.

Function	County Council (e.g. Midlandshire)	District Council (e.g. Westleigh)
Clean air	–	✓
Community services	–	✓
Consumer protection	✓	–
Education	✓	–
Environmental health	–	✓
Fire Services	✓	–
Highways	✓	–
Housing	–	✓
Libraries	✓	–
Museums and art galleries	✓	✓
Parks and recreation	✓	✓
Personal social services	✓	–
Planning	✓	✓
Police	✓	–
Refuse collection	–	✓
Refuse disposal	✓	–
Transport	✓	✓
Youth employment	✓	–

Figure 3

5

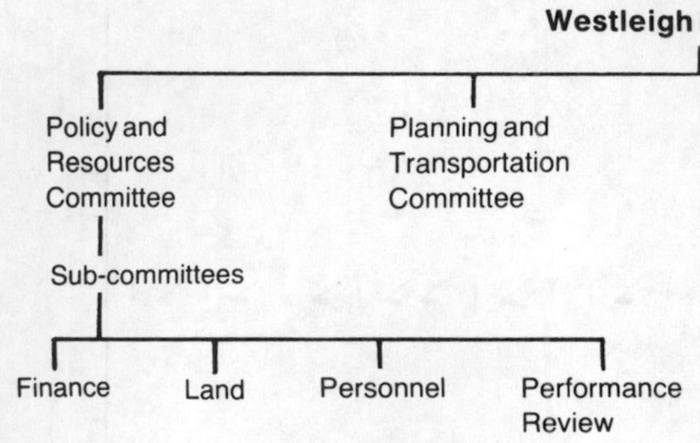

Westleigh District Council

Figure 4

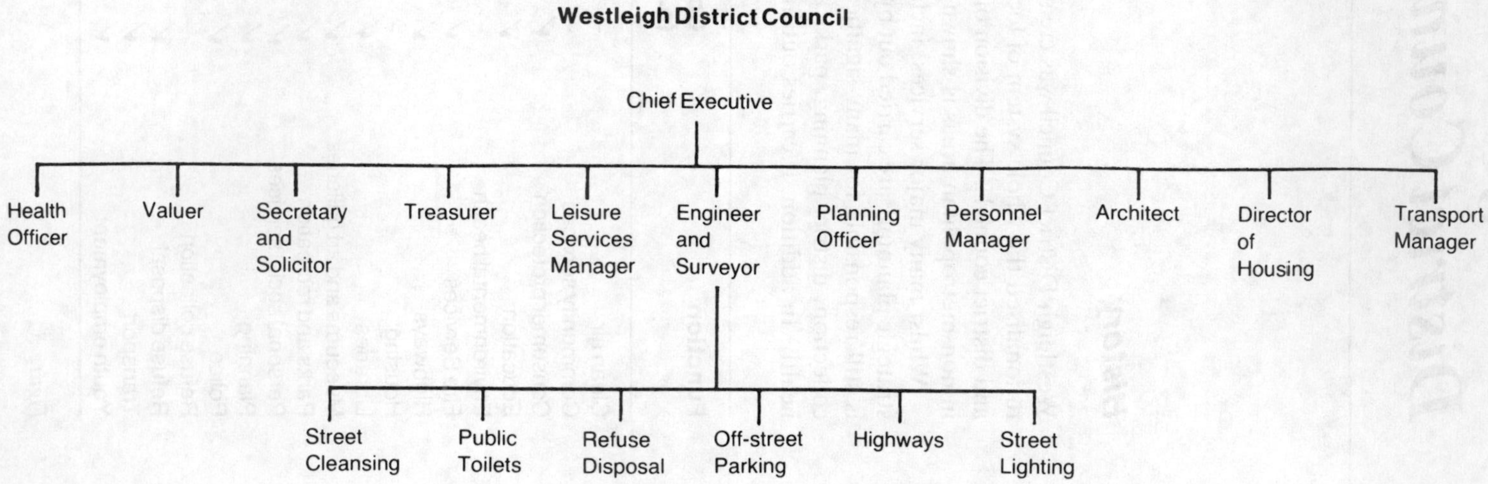

Westleigh District Council

Figure 5

Responsibility for some services, e.g. planning, is shared between the county and district councils.

Control

Policy-making at Westleigh District Council is carried out by the 35 elected councillors, representing 11 wards, in the current ratio of 20 Conservative, 10 Labour and 5 Independent members. These councillors are paid a small allowance plus expenses and usually have a job in addition to their public career. Each councillor is normally elected for a period of four years, one-third retiring annually in May, except in every fourth year when county council elections are held. A number of district councillors also serve as county councillors.

In order to cope with the large volume of work, the council (i.e. the elected members) delegates decision-making through a framework of committees, as illustrated in Fig. 4.

Membership of the various committees is normally based on interest or expertise in relevant fields and is in the same political ratio as that of the full council.

Most committees deal with a group of services, e.g. community services, and this has helped to reduce the number of committees and, *inter alia*, the number of meetings which councillors have to attend. The Policy and Resources Committee is a co-ordinating committee which is composed of the chairman of all the other committees and which is responsible for budgeting, forward planning, performance review and the work of all the other committees. Its decisions and recommendations are very rarely overturned by the full council.

Administration

The policy decisions of the council are implemented by paid employees, under the direction of the chief executive, who co-ordinates the work of the various departments, liaises closely with the council and attends council meetings, together with executive staff responsible for the matters under discussion. Because each committee covers a range of services, several departments may be represented at any particular committee meeting. The organisation chart in Fig. 5 illustrates the executive structure of Westleigh District Council.

Case 4 *ALBEC Limited*

History

Three years ago Bob Jones, a married man of 35 with three children, suddenly found himself facing redundancy. For the past twelve years he had worked for Remco, a large multinational firm manufacturing electrical components for the 'white goods' industry, which had a large factory in Easthampton. Bob had originally been employed as a design draughtsman and was now chief sales engineer. Remco had decided to trim down its UK operations and concentrate its main activities on its more profitable operations in Germany where the emphasis was on the manufacture of electrical components for cars.

Apart from the fact that this decision would involve selling off UK assets and dismissing the workforce, Remco was also placed in the embarrassing position of letting down longstanding customers with whom it had built up good relationships over the years. Some of these customers had long-term contracts with Remco and, moral considerations apart, could well sue for breach if their contracts were not honoured. Despite these difficulties, the firm decided to go ahead with its rationalisation plans and circulated its employees accordingly.

Bob, being an enterprising person, saw the chance of doing something he had always wanted to do, i.e. start up business on his own. He approached four other men from Remco who were also to be made redundant and whose skills and expertise he respected. Together, they formulated a plan to launch a new company financed mainly from their redundancy money, which would virtually fill the gap left by Remco's withdrawal. They approached Remco management with their scheme which involved taking over existing customer contracts and buying the firm's machinery and equipment in order to start production.

They argued that although Remco had found this area of their operations unprofitable, a small firm with fewer overheads and more efficient use of labour and equipment could make a success of it. Remco was delighted to be given such a workable solution to their problems, and not only sold the machinery to the men at a very reasonable price, but co-operated to the extent of giving them the patents of some of the components which the new company would now be manufacturing instead of Remco. The existing customers were happy with the arrangement because, in fact, although ownership had changed, they would still be dealing with the same men they had always dealt with – Bob had negotiated many of the contracts himself whilst employed as sales engineer for Remco.

After obtaining a small factory unit at the Boyatt Wood Industrial Estate, the five men went into production, initially with very few extra staff. They worked 12 hours a day, 7 days a week, with wives and friends supplying free labour until they became established.

Organisation was very gradual and haphazard but after two years, the company, in addition to its directors, employed nineteen staff, and the work was organised as follows:

Bob Jones
(Managing Director)

Commercial
Staff: 1 sales representative
1 buyer

Andrew Baxter
(Director)

Accountant and Office Manager
Staff: 1 accounts clerk dealing with wages, petty cash, sales and purchase ledgers, cash book, day books

1 secretary/receptionist (Sandra Smith) dealing with secretarial work for all directors; helping accounts clerk when necessary; and in charge of:

1 clerk/typist (Ann Barratt) typing orders, invoices, statements, filing; helping buyer chase up suppliers

Kevin Adams
(Director)

Packing and Distribution
Staff: 2 van drivers
1 warehouseman

David Parkes
(Director)

Production
Staff: 10 production line staff
1 maintenance/odd job man

Larry Symmonds
(Director)

Design Draughtsman
No other staff

Learning and studying skills

The way you approach your learning and studying will greatly affect the degree of success you achieve not only on your course but in your chosen career. Many of the skills needed are the same for both purposes. The acquisition of sound and systematic work habits will be an invaluable aid to your progress, enabling you to absorb knowledge faster, retain it longer, understand it and use it to tackle and solve problems in your personal and business life.

It is important to regard learning as a long-term – even lifelong – process. Skills may not always be mastered quickly, and it is easy to be daunted by tasks which you think are beyond you. When you are faced with such tasks it helps to break them down into small manageable parts before attempting them. Remember that each skill mastered, each piece of knowledge acquired and understood, is another brick in the building of your future.

As you work through the activities in this book and in other areas of your course, you will build up your skills and knowledge through practice. The following guidelines will help you to start developing the correct approach from the outset.

1 Plan ahead
Establish appropriate goals and review them regularly:
* long-term goals – what you aim to achieve within the next 2 or 3 years:
    in your career
    in your education
    in your personal life
* short-term goals – what you aim to achieve:
    this year
    this month
    this week
    today
* Are these goals realistic in terms of
    relevance to your needs?
    the time you have available?
    your own ability?

2 Identify the questions to ask when faced with a task or problem
* **What** – is the problem (underline *key* words)
    are you trying to achieve? (look at the terms of reference)
    facts do you need? (make a list)
    format is required? (report, oral presentation, etc.)

- **Why** – has the problem arisen? (find out the background)
- **Where** – can you obtain information?
- **When** – is the information required? (note the date in your diary)
- **Who** – requires the information?
     else is involved? (you may need to consult, liaise or work in a team)
- **How** – are you going to organise your time?

3 Select relevant information for the task in hand
   - only use the information you need (too much information may confuse the issue)
   - people may not have time to read long reports
   - you do not need to waste time on irrelevant information

4 Use a range of information sources
   - books, handouts, newspapers, publications, reports, statistics
   - radio, television, audio, video, electronic databases and viewdata (e.g. Prestel)
   - people who can offer advice and assist you in your task

5 Use a range of techniques to help you assimilate information
   - skimming – picking out key points by reading very quickly
   - sifting – discarding irrelevant or unwanted information
   - note-taking – noting down the main points as you read, listen or watch

6 Manage your time effectively
   - make a list of tasks to be done
   - list them in order of priority – revise the list regularly
   - set realistic time targets
   - tackle difficult tasks when you are fresh (e.g. in the morning)
   - be prepared to readjust your plan to meet changing situations
   - allow yourself time for leisure activities to prevent you becoming stale or unfit
   - keep a diary to monitor your work schedule and remind you when tasks are required and update the diary regularly

7 Review your own work
   - proof-read to check for mistakes or omissions
   - edit if necessary

8 Use an efficient filing system
   - file your material under subject headings
   - compile an index so that you can find information quickly

9 Working in a group
   If you are required to work in a group:
   - discuss together the problems to be tackled
   - divide tasks by mutual consent
   - keep a record of who is doing what
   - report back to the group at agreed intervals
   - keep to deadlines so that you are not holding up other people's work

- accept criticism and be prepared to modify your views
- put the group's needs before your personal needs

10 Advice and counselling
- seek advice from peers, lecturers, work colleagues or other experts when necessary
- accept criticism and be prepared to modify your views
- if you have personal problems, it is usually best to consult your course tutor, college counsellor or supervisor at work before the problems become too large

Unit 1 *Organisational structure*

What is an organisation?

Throughout our lives we belong to various organisations. As young people we join youth groups and sports clubs; as adults we belong to trade unions, charities and social clubs. Most of us will eventually be employed by an organisation, whether it is a commercial enterprise carried on for profit, a government department, or the office of a charitable or non-profit-making concern.

One definition of an organisation is 'a group of people working together over a period of time to achieve a common goal or objective'. This definition can be applied to all of the organisations mentioned above, and it is generally true of those described in the case studies at the beginning of this book and on which our studies will be based.

Objectives

Every organisation is formed for a reason and it is important for its objectives to be clearly known at the outset so that everyone involved in policy-making, administration and implementation is able to work towards the 'common goal'. The corporate objectives of an organisation are decided at board level, are set out in the objects clause of the Memorandum of Association (the document which sets out the company's name, registered address, objectives and liability of shareholders, etc.) and are often quoted in a firm's annual report and accounts, especially in large organisations. It is worth remembering that while the profit motive is high on the list for commercial firms, it is not the only objective.

The following extract has been taken from the annual report of a large biscuit manufacturer:

The long-term corporate objectives which our company strives to achieve are:
- security of employment and the highest possible standard of living for our employees
- the best possible value for money to the consumer
- consistent reward to the investor (shareholder) at a level which fully recognises the element of risk
- ensuring that the business remains internationally competitive

Short-term objectives of a firm could include plans to expand, to diversify its products, to cut back size etc.

Task 1.1

1 Read Case Study 1 – Jobline Personnel Agency – and list its possible corporate objectives.
2 How might this organisation dispose of its profits?
3 What would be the objectives of:
(a) a firm's sports/social club
(b) a charity such as OXFAM
(c) the Citizen's Advice Bureau?

Designing the organisation structure

It is useful when setting up a new organisation or redesigning an existing one to establish guidelines by asking the following questions:

- What activities are necessary to achieve the corporate objectives?
- Should division or departmentation be:
  by function, e.g. buying, selling, production
  by product, e.g. where a firm makes several products
  by process, e.g. painting, welding, assembly
  by geographical location of units
  or by some combination of these?
- What use can be made of centralisation, e.g. office services such as typing, filing, reprographics?
- To what degree can specialisation occur?
- How many levels of supervision will there be?
- Have clear objectives been set for each division to define its contribution to the overall objectives?

These questions are considered more fully in the following pages.

Division of activities

The division of activities will be decided by top management who will take into account many factors, such as:

Objectives – the main divisions/departments will be geared to achieving the corporate aims and will vary in size according to their importance, e.g. the largest department in a manufacturing firm is production, followed by marketing and finance.

Size – the number of personnel employed may determine to what degree specialisation can occur, e.g. a sole trader undertakes most of the activities himself, whereas a large firm has many departments each of which specialise in a different activitiy.

Nature – the nature of a business demands particular types of organisation, e.g. food-processing firms require depots at strategic locations throughout the country to ensure rapid distribution of their products and a pharmaceutical manufacturer may divide its activities by product such as medicines, tablets, cosmetics.

Geographical location – some firms, such as car production plants, operate in scattered units many miles apart. In this type of organisation it is convenient to give each plant manager wide decision-making authority so that he can respond quickly to local conditions, although he is still accountable to Head Office for the profitability or otherwise of his unit.

Automation – where, for example, automation has integrated data-processing systems, departments such as order processing, stock control, wages, accounts, etc. may be considerably reduced in size, whilst the computer department will emerge as a department in its own right.

Some of these factors can be appreciated by examining the case studies at the beginning of the book.

If you look at Case Study 1 (Jobline Personnel Agency) you will see that the largest department is Personnel. This is because the primary objective is to provide skilled labour for clients. In order to satisfy clients, staff must be recruited and placed with integrity. If staff supplied by the agency are unsuitable, clients will be dissatisfied and business will suffer. The service must be promoted by mailshots, advertising and personal contact, and complaints followed up promptly in order to maintain good customer relations. The marketing function is, therefore, also important. Lastly, there must be an administration section to process information, pay wages, settle accounts, keep records and maintain security.

Domilux (UK) plc (Case Study 2) is a very large organisation in the private sector. Its activities have been divided by a combination of function, product and geographical location. The present structure has evolved over a period of years and will probably change again if circumstances require it. No company can afford to be static and structures must be constantly reviewed to ensure that they are appropriate.

Westleigh District Council (Case Study 3) is a local authority. Because it provides a wide range of services to the local community, it has many departments each dealing with a specialist function, e.g. planning, leisure services, etc. A unique feature of this type of organisation is that it is controlled by various committees composed of elected councillors rather than a board of directors. This can make administration difficult as policy tends to be dominated by politics and can change overnight if a different political party gains a majority at the council elections. The paid executives have no choice but to carry out the council's policy, even if they do not agree with it.

Division by function

Although no two organisations are the same, many firms find it convenient to divide their activities into the following functional areas:

finance
production
marketing
administration

In small firms, one person may be responsible for all these activities, whereas in large firms there may be many more divisions than this, with specialist departments for personnel, purchasing, data processing, etc. The most common functional areas are explained below.

Finance

In order to make decisions to expand, contract, diversify or modify, an organisation needs to be aware of its financial status. The finance function is necessary to ensure that the business is able to pay its debts and make a profit. It does this in the following ways:

- by costing its products accurately, i.e. taking into account both direct production costs and overheads such as administration and distribution costs
- by ensuring that departmental budgets are not overspent
- by recording all financial transactions
- by providing for depreciation of equipment and machinery
- by credit control
- by auditing its accounts

Production

The production function is to produce goods in the quality and quantity required at the right time. This involves:

- close liaison with the marketing and purchasing departments in order to synchronise production schedules with the order book
- keeping accurate records of materials, labour and overheads for costing purposes
- keeping abreast of consumer preferences and technological developments
- planning for seasonal fluctuations

Marketing

Marketing is a broad term covering research into consumer preferences, advertising and selling. In some large firms these functions are carried out in separate departments. In order to maximise profits, the marketing department should seek to:

- anticipate demand
- predict trends in fashion
- advertise its products to the right people
- deliver goods on time
- provide an efficient after-sales service

The information it provides to the production department is vital for production planning.

Administration

Although the prime objectives of an organisation are to produce and market its goods (in the broadest sense), it could not exist long without a sound administration. This function provides a backup for the other departments with services such as typing, filing, reception, communications (including telephone and mail systems) and security.

Personnel

The personnel function consists of:

- forecasting manpower requirements
- utilising labour efficiently
- recruiting staff of the right calibre for the job
- providing a healthy and safe environment at work
- promoting good industrial relations
- providing training for staff
- fixing salary grades and career structures commensurate with responsibilities and expertise
- keeping manpower costs down

Purchasing

This function is essential to the production and marketing departments with whom it must liaise constantly to ensure that materials, products and components are available when required. The purchasing function is concerned with:

- researching new sources of supply
- monitoring trends in fashions, prices and delivery times
- obtaining the best possible terms from suppliers
- ensuring that adequate stock levels are maintained

Management services

Large firms generally have a management services department providing management with accurate and up-to-date information by using modern techniques and technology. This department's functions could include the following:

- an organisation and methods section which reviews office systems with a view to improving efficiency and productivity
- a computer section which carries out routine data processing, e.g. wages, invoicing, accounting; compares and analyses statistical data by the use of spreadsheet programs; provides fast and reliable printouts of debtors, cash flow, predicted profits/losses, etc.: this helps management to make decisions regarding diversification, rationalisation, etc.
- a research and development section which constantly researches and develops new processes, techniques or products in order to keep up with or overtake competitors

Division by product

Some large manufacturers producing several products find it convenient to group activities according to product. Examples of this include canned food-processing firms, vehicle manufacturers and makers of washing detergents and soaps. In this type of organisation, brand or product managers are responsible for the marketing and sales of their particular product. Salesmen operate on a national rather than a regional basis and are involved in much more travelling.

Firms organised in this way usually have functional (specialist) departments as well.

Task 1.2

1 Divide into groups and make a list giving as many examples as possible of firms divided by:

function
product
process
geographical location of units

2 Suggest reasons why they operate in this way.

Specialisation

Just as the functions of a firm are divided into specialist departments for greater efficiency, so the activities within departments are divided in order that workloads can be grouped and allocated. The activities undertaken by the various departments of Domilux plc (Case Study 2) are illustrated in Fig. 6. In a large firm like this, experts can be appointed to carry out each of the various activities, e.g. typing, filing, work study, accounts, personnel etc. In a small firm such as Jobline (Case Study 1), one person will have to carry out several activities; and where a person is in business as a sole trader, he may have to do everything himself.

Task 1.3

Refer to Case Study 1 (Jobline)
1 What information does the organisation chart (p. 2) in the Case Study give you?
2 Describe the division of activities as shown in the chart at the end of the first year of operation.
3 Do you think the partners have divided the work fairly? Comment, with reasons.

Task 1.4

1 Discuss in groups the advantages and disadvantages of specialisation from the following aspects:

(a) use of people's expertise
(b) productivity (quantity and quality of output)
(c) recruitment of staff

(d) job grading and salary structure
(e) career development
(f) job interest
(g) covering for absent colleagues

2 Suggest how any disadvantages could be overcome.
3 Report your findings to the rest of the class.

Department	Functions	Activities
Company Secretary	Advising and liaising with board of directors Controlling administration Communicating with shareholders	Legal matters; patents; legal contracts; insurance; company meetings; share registration Office services: telephone, mail, reprography, filing, secretarial, data processing, stationery Office planning and layout
Finance	Financial control Budgeting Forecasting	Financial accounts; reporting to management; costing; credit control; payment of wages; payment of suppliers; preparation of statements; petty cash; auditing of accounts; budgeting and forecasting; loans and investments; taxation (VAT, corporation, PAYE)
Marketing/Sales	Sales promotion Consumer research Good public relations	Home and export sales; advertising; customer records; market research; transport; after-sales service; employment of agents and representatives; preparing catalogues/price lists, invoices and credit notes
Purchasing	Buying of materials and goods on the best possible terms and ensuring that delivery dates are met	Researching suppliers; monitoring market trends; keeping supplier records; placing orders; synchronising deliveries to meet production schedules
Personnel	Recruiting and engaging staff of the right calibre for the job Providing effective training for staff Maintenance of good relations between management and workforce Health and safety at work	Recruitment, employment and dismissal of staff; welfare; safety; training; personnel records; job grading; staff appraisal; labour relations
Production (Operations)	Planning and control of factory operations	Production planning; quality control; management of plant and equipment; design and development; work study; materials control; despatch of goods
Research and Development	Development of new products and improved techniques	Work study; product research; testing of products; technological innovation

Figure 6 Chart showing the activities of Domilux (UK) plc

Levels of responsibility

When a person sets up business on his own he often cannot afford to employ staff and carries out all the activities himself, i.e. buying, selling, book-keeping, etc.

As the business expands, he may take on extra staff, either to bring in more expertise or simply because he cannot cope with all the work himself. Once he does this, he is handing over responsibility to someone else: this is called delegation. The person to whom he delegates the work is still accountable to him for any action taken but has the responsibility for the duties allocated to him.

In a small business, such as a garage, there will be few levels of responsibility, as in Fig. 7.

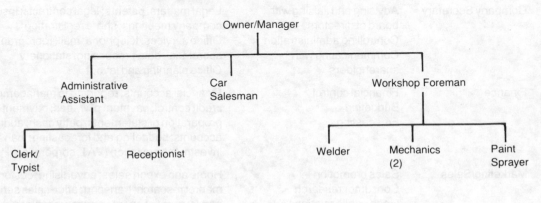

Figure 7

The larger the organisation, the more levels of supervision will be necessary so that any one person does not have too wide a span of control. An example of the levels of supervision in a large organisation is given in Fig. 8.

Span of control

The span of control is the number of people a person is required to supervise. The span will vary according to the duties carried out by the people being supervised. It is often said that a person can only effectively control four to six people, but where jobs are routine or similar, a supervisor can control many more than this. This is illustrated in Fig. 9.

Just as one person can only be expected to supervise a limited number of people, the staff being supervised should only be accountable to one superior. If, for example, a general clerk is employed with no specific job description, that person may be given tasks by a variety of superiors and become overworked, inefficient and confused as to which tasks have priority. This will cause job dissatisfaction and the employee will probably leave. Secretaries, in practice, are often required to work for more than one person and must, therefore, exercise initiative and diplomacy in deciding priorities.

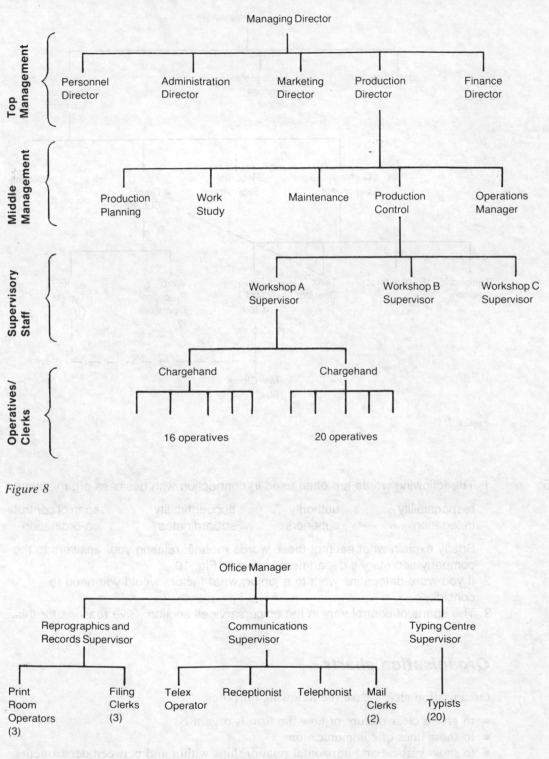

Figure 8

Figure 9

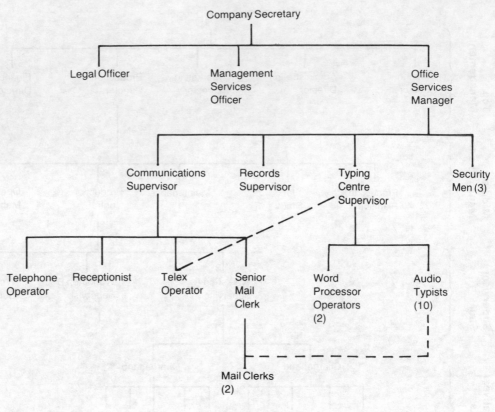

Figure 10

Task 1.5

1 The following words are often used in connection with business organisation:

responsibility	authority	accountability	span of control
delegation	superiors	subordinates	co-ordination

Briefly explain what each of these words means, relating your answers to the company secretary's department shown in Fig. 10.

2 If you were delegating work to a junior, what factors would you need to consider?

3 The spans of control vary in the office services section. Give reasons for this.

Organisation charts

Organisation charts have the following purposes:

- to give a clear picture of how the firm is organised
- to show lines of communication
- to show vertical and horizontal relationships within and between departments
- to show levels of authority and responsibility

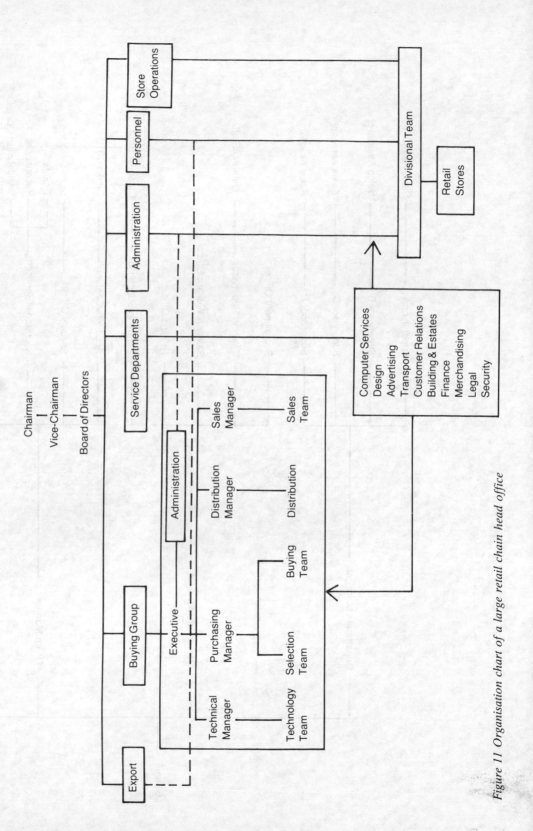

Figure 11 Organisation chart of a large retail chain head office

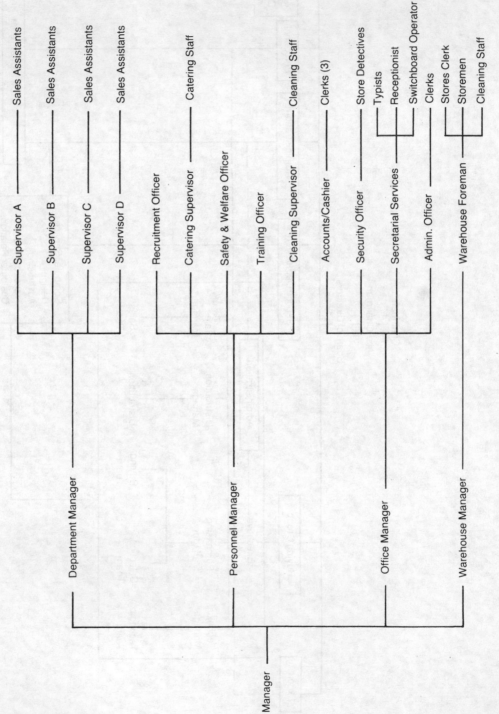

Figure 12 Horizontal organisation chart of a local department store

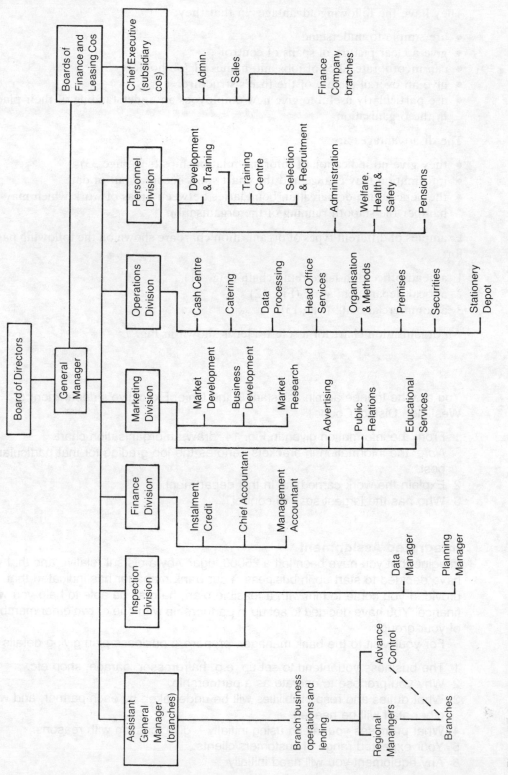

Figure 13 Organisation chart of commercial bank

They have the following advantages in that they:

- are simple to understand
- give a clear picture of spans of control
- can incorporate titles of jobs and names of job holders
- give an overall picture of the firm's structure
- are particularly useful to give new employees an understanding of their place in the organisation

The disadvantages are:

- they give no indication of informal relationships (see page 33)
- information may change and the chart soon becomes out of date
- they encourage demarcation boundaries between areas of work which may hamper the smooth running of the organisation

Examples of different types of organisation chart are shown on the following pages for:

1 a head office of a large retail chain (Fig. 11)
2 a local department store (Fig. 12)
3 a commercial bank (Fig. 13)

An organisation chart for a sole trader is shown in Fig. 7.

Task 1.6

You are the trainee admin assistant in the Chief Executive's department of Westleigh District Council.

1 From the information given in Fig. 14, draw an organisation chart.
Note: the information in brackets denotes the job grading for that particular post.
2 Explain the work carried out in this department.
3 Who has the largest span of control?

Task 1.7

Integrated Assignment
Imagine that you have been left a £5000 legacy by a distant relative and that you have decided to start up in business. Your bank manager has indicated that, provided you come to him with a feasible plan, he may be able to help you with finance. You have decided to set up in partnership with one or two other members of your group.
For your visit to the bank manager, prepare a business plan giving details of:

1 The business you intend to set up, e.g. hairdresser, garage, shop etc.
2 Why you propose to operate as a partnership.
3 What duties and responsibilities will be undertaken by each partner, and what other staff will be needed.
4 What premises you intend using initially – give location with reasons.
5 Your expected range of customers/clients.
6 Any equipment you will need initially.

Post	Post No.	Accountable to
Chief Executive Mr J Boynton	CE1	Leader of the Council
Secretary/Mayor's Secretary (AP3) Miss S Trudgett	CE4	Chief Executive/ Mayor
Information/Public Relations Officer (SO2) Mr R Kimber	CE14	Chief Executive
Personnel/Management Services Officer (PO2) Miss H Budden	CE2	Chief Executive
Admin Asst/Secretary (AP1/2) Mrs S Wallis	CE15	Information/PR Officer
Asst Personnel Officer (SO1) Ms N Perkins	CE3	Personnel/MS Officer
Work Study Officer (SO1) Mr H Carrington	CE8	Personnel/MS Officer
Senior Asst Work Study Officer (AP5) Mr D Roberts	CE7	Work Study Officer
Admin Assistant (AP2) Miss K Fennell	CE9	Work Study Officer
Personnel Assistant (AP2/3) Mrs P Jennings	CE6	Assistant Personnel Officer (CE3)
Admin Assistant (AP1/2) Mr L Clark	CE5	Assistant Personnel Officer (CE3)
Assistant Work Study Officer (AP3) Mr A Robinson	CE10	Senior Assistant WS Officer (CE7)
Assistant Work Study Officer (AP3) Mr S Masters	CE11	Senior Assistant WS Officer (CE7)
Bonus Clerk (C1) Mr P Wright	CE12	Admin Assistant (CE9)
Bonus Clerk (C1) Mr W Rushton	CE13	Admin Assistant (CE9)
Trainee Admin Assistant (AP1/2)	CE16	Personnel/MS Officer *and* Information/PR Officer

Figure 14 Staffing establishment of chief executive's department

7 A financial plan giving an estimate of income and expenses for the first 6 months.

Note: Information can be obtained from local authority handbooks on industries in the area; estate agents for details of commercial property available; business location handbook for details of finance available; and banking leaflets.

Key facts

Principles of good organisation

Objectives	should be determined and made known to all parts of the organisation so that activities can be co-ordinated to achieve them.
Span of control	should be limited to a reasonable number – maximum of six for varied work.
Line authority	a clear line of authority should exist throughout the organisation so that responsibility can be fixed.
Accountability	each person should be required to report to only one superior.
Delegation	authority and responsibility should be delegated as far down the line as possible.
Centralisation and	of office services.
Specialisation	of labour should be used wherever possible.

Unit 2 *Interrelationships within and between departments*

Lines of communication

Formal relationships of staff within a firm are usually described as line, functional, staff and lateral.

Line relationships

Traditionally, organisations are based on the hierarchical principle in which authority and responsibility flow in a direct line from the top to the bottom of the organisation. Department heads have sole control over their departments, as in Fig. 15.

Each person is accountable to his immediate superior up the 'line', providing a vertical relationship. The advantage of line organisation is that it makes clear to people to whom they should report and for what staff or areas of work they are responsible. If there are too many levels, though, communications may be delayed (upward communications suffer most).

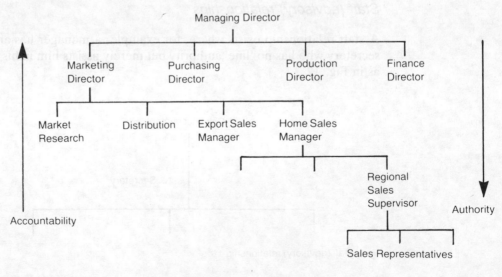

Figure 15

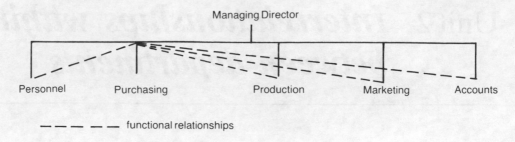

Figure 16

Functional relationships

In most organisations, specialist departments are set up to deal with specific functions throughout the organisation, as illustrated in Fig. 16. Here, the purchasing department carries out buying activities for all the other departments. The purchasing manager would have authority over the other departments. This is called a functional relationship and relies entirely on expertise. Whilst this type of organisation makes the best use of specialisation, it can be confusing for employees who may have one set of instructions from their 'line' (or departmental) superior and another set from the 'functional' expert. A department may, for example, wish to purchase a particular wordprocessor, but be overruled by the purchasing department on the grounds that there should be standardisation of this type of equipment throughout the firm.

There is normally a combination of line and functional organisation within a firm, for even where a department carries out a function for the whole organisation, the staff within departments still have direct line relationships with superiors and subordinates.

Staff (advisory) relationships

A staff relationship exists where, for example, a manager has an assistant or secretary who has no 'line' authority but merely assists him in his day-to-day work, as in Fig. 17.

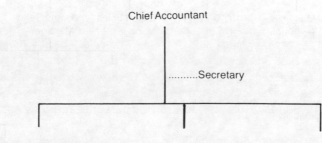

Figure 17

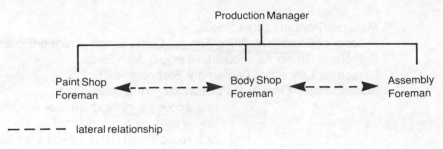

Production Manager

Figure 18

If a line manager needs expert advice from a functional expert, such as the office manager, this is also a staff relationship as the functional expert has no authority over the line manager.

Lateral relationships

Where several employees at the same level of responsibility need to co-operate or co-ordinate their activities, they are said to have lateral (or horizontal) relationships, as in Fig. 18.

Difficulties can sometimes arise where people do not 'get on' and supervisors are often required to exercise tact and diplomacy in getting people to work together.

Informal (diagonal) relationships

In addition to the formal relationships which are recognised as part of the organisation structure, many informal relationships develop between employees within and between departments. They usually result from frequent contact in the performance of their work, e.g. a stores supervisor in the production department may frequently need to check with an order clerk in the purchasing department on the progress of orders for components needed in the manufacturing process. Such relationships are important and necessary to the smooth running of an organisation as they speed up communications and alleviate the constrictions of a rigid 'line' structure.

Task 2.1   This assignment relates to Jobline Personnel Agency (Case Study 1). The original structure of the company is shown in Fig. 1 (see p. 2).

Situation: A year ago the lease of the office stationer's shop on the ground floor expired, and the partners purchased it to open an office services bureau. It was decided that Janet would run the personnel agency and Mary the office services bureau.

The present organisation of Jobline is as follows:

Partners: Janet Keele and Mary Webb
Secretary: to both partners – Audrey Lamb

Personnel Section:
Manager/Partner: Janet Keele
Personnel Officer for Office Temps: Lorna Smith – responsible for one assistant
Personnel Officer for Industrial Temps: Alan Betts
Personnel Officer for Permanent Staff: James Leigh
Administrative Officer: Ron Dawkins – responsible for:

> one accounts clerk (full-time)
> one wages clerk (part-time)
> one receptionist (who liaises with Secretary)

Publicity and Sales Officer: Gillian Lark

Office Services Section:
Manager/Partner: Mary Webb
Sales Supervisor: Wendy Jones – responsible for:

> one sales assistant (full-time)
> one sales assistant (part-time)

Reprographics Operator
Telex/Word Processing Operator (who liaises with Secretary)
Computer Operator

Task: You are required to draw an organisation chart showing the present structure. Illustrate in your chart examples of functional, line, staff and informal relationships.

Task 2.2   You are working as an accounts clerk at ALBEC.

1 Draw a chart of ALBEC from the information given in Case Study 4 showing functional, line, staff and informal relationships.
2 You have noticed that there is sometimes friction between Sandra Smith and Ann Barratt. Ann complains that Sandra always finds jobs for her to do when she is helping the buyer. You feel that Sandra could help you more with the accounts. Is it all due to personality clashes or has it anything to do with the organisation structure? Discuss.

Flow of information between departments

No department can work in isolation. It is the responsibility of management to plan, organise, direct and control activities so that they are synchronised and integrated to achieve the corporate objectives. This is relatively easy in a small business because of the number of staff involved, the ease of communications and the absence of complex systems. In a large firm with many departments, however, co-ordination becomes much more difficult and can only be achieved if there is an effective network of communication channels going across sections and departments, as well as up and down within them.

Task 2.3   Refer to the organisation chart given for Domilux (UK) plc in Case Study 2 (p. 4). Departments which rely particularly on each other for up-to-date information are

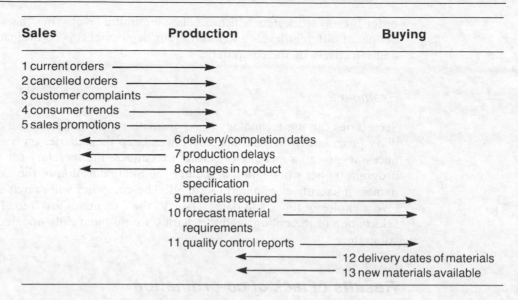

Sales	Production	Buying
1 current orders ⟶		
2 cancelled orders ⟶		
3 customer complaints ⟶		
4 consumer trends ⟶		
5 sales promotions ⟶		
	⟵ 6 delivery/completion dates	
	⟵ 7 production delays	
	⟵ 8 changes in product specification	
	9 materials required ⟶	
	10 forecast material requirements ⟶	
	11 quality control reports ⟶	
		⟵ 12 delivery dates of materials
		⟵ 13 new materials available

Figure 19 Flow of information between sales, production and buying departments

sales, production and buying. The chart in Fig. 19 illustrates some of the information which flows between these departments. Explain why liaison is necessary in each case, e.g. sales informs production of current orders so that production can allocate labour, materials and machines most effectively to meet demand.

Alternative task for day-release students in employment
Make a list of information (1) which your department provides to other departments and (2) which other departments provide to your department, explaining why this information is required in each case.

The effects of technology on co-ordination

Traditionally, organisation structure is based on vertical relationships where orders and instructions go down the line and reports and requests go up the line.

Technology, including data processing, has developed in what might be called a horizontal plane, i.e. the machine process cuts across superior/subordinate relationships, affecting people's jobs in different areas, departments and work groups. This aids co-ordination by bringing together people affected by a particular project or subject, irrespective of rank or department.

Example 1

A large vehicle manufacturer has a computerised data-processing section. When an order is received from a customer, it is passed to this section, where a clerk enters the details into the computer via a keyboard. The computer automatically creates a customer account; prints out an invoice; prints out a list of the materials/ components required to make the vehicle; adjusts stock levels; generates a new order for any stock item which is below minimum level. Thus the work of several people at different levels and in different departments is co-ordinated efficiently and effectively by the computer.

Example 2

Secretaries can use technology to co-ordinate meetings by the use of electronic diary programs. In large firms, executives keep their diaries on computer. If it is necessary to call a meeting of certain executives, the secretary can call up the program on her workstation and enter the likely duration of the meeting and the names of executives required to attend. The computer will search the diaries and give a choice of times and dates when all the executives are free. The secretary selects one of the options and the diaries are automatically updated by computer.

Results of lack of co-ordination

An analysis of companies that fail reveals that one of the chief factors responsible is lack of co-ordination, resulting in bottlenecks, duplicated effort, heavy and unnecessary costs, loss of time and output, misunderstanding and irritation amongst employees and dissatisfied customers.

Task 2.4   Think of as many examples as possible of situations where lack of co-ordination would cause difficulties, delay or financial loss. You may relate answers to the case studies at the beginning of the book or, if you are employed, relate them to your own organisation.

Example: When the despatch department is delivering goods to customers, it plans a delivery route, then loads the van so that parcels are in the right order for unloading at each stop. If this is not planned properly, time will either be lost at each stopping point whilst the parcels are sorted and reloaded, or the van will have to take a roundabout route, again losing time and money.

Causes of poor co-ordination and co-operation

Some of the common causes for lack of co-operation are:

- weak management
- poor communication channels
- low morale
- inadequate supervision
- inefficient procedures or systems
- rivalry between people, sections or departments
- inappropriate organisation structure
- lack of training

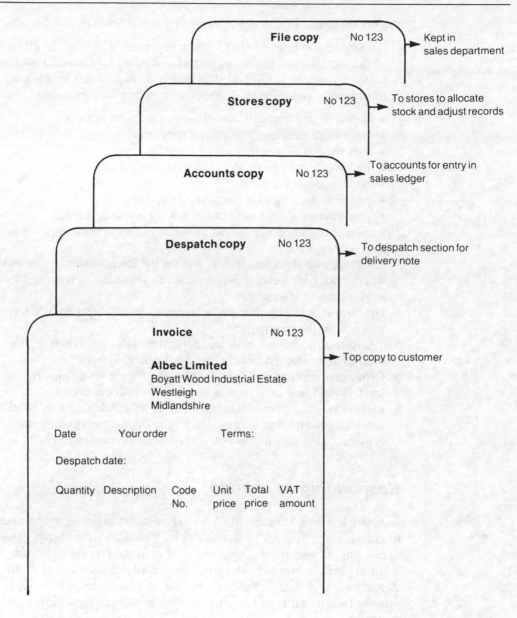

File copy	No 123	→ Kept in sales department
Stores copy	No 123	→ To stores to allocate stock and adjust records
Accounts copy	No 123	→ To accounts for entry in sales ledger
Despatch copy	No 123	→ To despatch section for delivery note

Invoice   No 123

→ Top copy to customer

Albec Limited
Boyatt Wood Industrial Estate
Westleigh
Midlandshire

Date   Your order   Terms:

Despatch date:

Quantity   Description   Code   Unit   Total   VAT
                        No.   price price   amount

Figure 20 Liaison by documentation

Ways of achieving co-ordination and co-operation

The successful manager achieves co-ordination by creating an appropriate
organisation structure, selecting skilful employees, and training and supervising
them effectively. He provides and explains the integrated plans and programmes
that subordinates will carry out and checks whether they are being done properly

and on schedule. Practical ways in which co-ordination can be achieved are:

1 Arranging meetings of staff – these represent a deliberate effort on the part of the superior to consult with staff and bring into contact all those concerned with a particular subject so that they are encouraged to integrate their efforts to achieve a common goal. Types of meeting may include:

- heads of departments' meetings to co-ordinate policy
- safety and accident prevention meetings
- cost reduction meetings
- development, design and technical committees
- departmental meetings
- progress meetings on particular projects
- consultative meetings between management and staff

2 Encouragement of 'cross-talk' between different sections as opposed to vertical communication.

3 Development of project teams, e.g. for the introduction of computer techniques, where staff from several departments or sections are required to work together irrespective of status.

4 Uniform training methods which lead to similar approaches to problems throughout the enterprise.

5 Transfer of personnel between departments or job rotation. This increases mutual understanding of the needs of other sections.

6 Office procedure manuals and codes of practice which ensure standard practices are followed and help to eliminate errors and omissions.

7 Liaison through documentation. This is an invaluable way of ensuring that essential information is provided to the departments concerned. An example is given of the distribution of copies of an invoice in Fig. 20.

Responding to change

In order to remain competitive, an organisation must be able to respond quickly to changes in consumer preferences and technical innovations. This may involve expanding its operations, reducing staff or restructuring departments.

In organisations where the free flow of information is not restricted by departmental or hierarchical boundaries, management will be able to encourage a more flexible attitude towards changes in job responsibilities and work systems.

Key facts   Co-ordination involves:

Creating a suitable organisation structure with lines of communication clearly defined.
Limiting each person's span of control to a manageable number of functions.
Balancing work groups so that they work in harmony.
Allocating appropriate workloads to members of the team.
Encouraging 'cross-talk' between individuals, sections and departments.

Adequate training and supervision.
Devising suitable procedures and documentation systems.
Ensuring that staff know

- what the organisation is trying to do
- how to achieve it
- who does what in the organisation
- to whom they should report

Unit 3 *People in the office*

Introduction

The range of personnel employed in an organisation varies considerably with its nature, i.e. whether it is manufacturing goods or providing a personal service; the type of business such as a sole trader compared with a government department; and the size of its operations.

Whereas large organisations are able to employ many specialist staff, this is impracticable in small firms where employees may be required to carry out several functions. In fact, one of the attractions of working for a small concern is that it can provide people with a wide variety of experience which may enhance their career prospects and provide increased job satisfaction.

The chart in Fig. 21 shows the range of people employed in a typical manufacturing company.

Proprietors – The shareholders, represented by the board of directors, own the firm and make the major policy decisions.

Executives – The managerial staff are the paid executives who implement the policy of the board of directors. They make important decisions, give the orders and accept the responsibilities. People in management are normally professionally qualified, e.g. accountants, company secretaries, engineers etc.

Administrative staff – They are concerned with implementing the policies of management in detail, usually acting in supervisory roles or as personal assistants to managers.

Clerical staff – These staff provide the day-to-day office services and report to the supervisors. They include secretaries, typists, clerks, receptionists, office machine operators etc.

Technical staff – Like office staff, technical staff provide a support service to the rest of the organisation and may be involved in maintenance, design, engineering etc.

The role of the office

It is apparent from the case studies that the staff who are of primary importance to the organisation are those engaged in producing its goods or services, e.g. the factory workers, the salesmen etc. In the sense that they are not actually involved in making or selling things, office workers are 'non-productive' and could therefore

41

Proprietors: Shareholders — Board of Directors — General Manager

Executives	Staff	Functions/records
Financial Controller	Chief Accountant, Chief Cashier; Ledger Clerks, Wages Clerks, Cashiers, Cost Clerks, Credit Control Clerks	Financial affairs, Recording invoices, credit notes, cheques in accounts, Preparing statements, cheques etc., Preparing wages, Budgetary control, Credit control, Costing, Petty cash
Company Secretary	Office Manager, Data Processing Manager; Receptionists, Telephonists, Computer Operators, Filing Clerks, Telex Operators, Mailing Clerks, Caretakers, Cleaners, Security Staff, Data Preparation Clerks	Legal matters, Share registration, Company meetings, Insurance, Shares, Office Services: telephone, mail, reprography, filing, secretarial, data processing, stationery, Organisation & Methods
Marketing Manager	Home Sales Manager, Export Sales Manager, Advertising Manager, Transport Manager; Invoice Clerks, Transport Clerks, Shipping Clerks, Sales Representatives, Drivers	Home and export sales, Advertising, Customer records, Market research, Transport, After-sales service, Employment of agents and representatives, Preparing catalogues/price lists, invoices, credit notes, etc
Chief Buyer	Buyers; Order Clerks, Stock Control Clerks	Purchase of goods and materials, Preparing orders, Stock records, Suppliers' records
Personnel Manager	Employment Manager, Training Manager; Welfare Officer, Nurses, Canteen Staff	Recruitment/employment and dismissal of staff, Staff records, Welfare, Training, Industrial relations including negotiations with unions
Production Manager	Chief Engineer, Chief Designer, Work Study Engineer; Engineers, Technicians, Factory Operatives, Despatch Clerks, Production Control Clerks, Draughtsmen	Production of goods, Quality control, Design and development, Work study, Stores, Despatch of goods, Maintenance of equipment, Preparing goods received notes

Figure 21

be thought of as an unnecessary expense.

Yet even the smallest organisation must pay wages, keep accounts, receive and send correspondence, chase up debtors, pay suppliers and preserve its records for future reference. In other words, whilst the office may be *secondary* in importance to the 'productive' departments, it nevertheless provides an essential *complementary* service to them by acting as a communication and control centre ensuring that information is processed and distributed as and when required.

Examples of office jobs are shown in the advertisements in Fig. 25 (*see* p. 49).

Task 3.1   Make a list of all the types of work you can think of which go on in an office.

The types of work which you have just described will all fit into one of the following categories:

- receiving information
- recording information
- processing information
- storing information
- disseminating information
- safeguarding assets – records/cash/stock/people/property

} Functions of the office

Office skills

Although much of the repetitive and routine work of the office has been reduced or taken over by new technology, human skills are still needed to:

Draft memos, letters and reports	Units 5 and 6
Proof-read and edit text	Unit 9
Extract, transfer, interpret and analyse information, e.g. from computer output	Unit 15
Summarise information for reports, minutes, etc.	Unit 5
Communicate by telephone	Unit 6
Organise and plan work	Unit 13
Communicate face-to-face with other people as individuals or in groups	Unit 12

The acquisition of these skills will form a major part of your learning experience, and guidelines are given in the relevant units to enable you to practise the right techniques.

Job descriptions

Each employee at Domilux is issued with a job description which specifies his areas of responsibility and accountability and sets out his main duties (see Fig. 22).

JOB DESCRIPTION

Department: Personnel
Section: Training and Development
Post: Personnel Assistant No: PA 09/10/19
Grade: Scale 2/5
Accountable to: Personnel Manager
Responsibilities: General personnel and administrative support for training and development, employee relations, conditions of service and health and safety

Main duties:

1 To organise in-house training courses, including induction courses.
2 To keep records of external training courses and disseminate information to relevant staff.
3 To maintain individual training and development records for each member of staff.
4 To assist in liaison with trade unions on employee relations.
5 To maintain records of accidents and ensure follow-up action is taken.
6 To assist in health, safety and welfare matters as required.
7 To assist in the drawing up of Contracts of Employment and conditions of service for new employees.
8 To undertake other duties as required.
Job received: 1 May 198–

Figure 22

The job description can be used as a basis for

- deciding what qualities and qualifications are needed for a particular post
- determining the grade or rate of pay
- inducting new staff and informing them of their duties and the work of others
- identifying training needs

Task 3.2

The business you proposed in Task 1.7 is now operating successfully but you and your partner(s) have decided to appoint a clerk to deal with orders, general clerical work and book-keeping duties.

1 Draft an advertisement for the post described above giving *brief* details of the job, specifying the qualities and qualifications/experience required, and stating to whom enquiries for an application form should be made.
2 Find out how much it would cost to place the advert in a local newspaper using three different types of display.
3 Design an application form which could be used by candidates, using the guidelines on page 263 and make 4 copies.
4 In groups of four, compare your forms and allocate a maximum of 3 marks for each of the points listed in the guidelines.
5 Dictate a message to be left on an answering machine asking enquirers to leave their name and address and saying that you will send them an application form.

Grade I   Routine, unskilled work requiring little or no training and carried out under close supervision.

Grade II   Supervised work requiring basic mechanical skills or clerical work requiring some aptitude.

Grade III   Skilled work requiring a longer period of training/experience and some degree of responsibility/initiative.

Grade IV   Responsibility for a group or work requiring semi-professional training.

Grade V   Responsibility for a department or complex work requiring specialist or professional training.

Grade VI   Control of a wide range of people and activities, requiring wide experience and specialist training/qualifications.

Figure 23

Note: Remember that the caller *cannot* ask questions, so you must give him all the information he needs.

6   Imagine that you are one of the applicants and leave a recorded message asking for an application form to be sent to you.

Job gradings

In small firms, such as Jobline Personnel Agency (Case Study 1), salaries are fixed by the owner/manager and are assessed according to the value placed upon a particular employee to the business. The profitability of the firm will also have some bearing on the matter. Any increments, i.e. wage increases, are discretionary and there is no apparent career structure.

Large organisations usually pay salaries according to the type and grade of work being done, and there is normally a range of increments within a particular salary scale. For example, in Westleigh District Council, as in all local authorities, there are separate salary scales for manual workers, clerical staff, administrative and professional staff, technical staff, senior officer and principal officer grades.

The Institute of Administrative Management has published a suggested scheme for grading office workers and a simplified version is shown in Fig. 23.

Task 3.3   The following staff are employed by Domilux (UK) plc (Case Study 2):

1   Carol Jones – the training officer at Head Office responsible for organising all training programmes, both internal and external. She liaises with all departments and with personnel staff at the various plants.

2   Enid Williams – a data preparation clerk who inputs batches of data via a keyboard for processing by computer, e.g. from timesheets for wages, details of production costs, etc.

3   Peter Colenutt – personal assistant to the managing director.

4 Ken Jones – regional sales supervisor for the Midlands area supervising 8 salesmen.

5 Brian Phillips – a qualified work study officer.

6 Kate Archer – the senior telephonist at Head Office who supervises two other staff.

7 Jane Tranter – secretary to the sales director.

8 Claire Wheeler – a word processor operator who has been employed by the firm for 2 years in the typing centre.

9 John Hubert – a computer programmer who writes complex programs for use by the firm.

10 Elaine Wright – the telex operator at Head Office.

11 Ann Adams – in charge of the reprographic section, a print room with four assistants.

12 Adrian Boult – a filing clerk.

13 Jim Painter – one of six buyers who buy all the materials required for production.

14 Alan Smith – the cost accountant.

15 Stephen Kennedy – the office junior in the mailroom.

16 David Watson – a clerk in the customer relations section who deals with complaints and queries.

17 Rona Williamson - a legal officer in the company secretary's department.

18 Amy Forbes – a clerk in the accounts department who checks all expenses claims from staff before authorising payment.

You are required to suggest suitable grades for each of the above staff.

Task 3.4   Refer to the staff list for Domilux (UK) plc, supplied in Task 3.3 above. State the person who could deal with or provide information in the following situations:

1 A request has been received from a local college of further education asking if some business studies students can attend a board meeting as observers.

2 A secretary wishes to know the quickest way of sending some documents to Amsterdam.

3 A switchboard operator at Head Office has asked for permission to take her annual holiday during the first two weeks in August.

4 One of the sales representatives requires a quotation to be prepared for a customer.

5 Several new employees have joined the firm and have applied for day-release at local colleges.

6 A letter has arrived from a customer asking for a replacement for the defective steam iron he bought recently. The guarantee is enclosed.

7 The sales department urgently requires 2000 copies of a 6-page advertising leaflet to be produced internally.

8 A sales representative complains he is not receiving the correct mileage allowance.

9 Because of a strike at their factory, a supplier is unable to deliver materials required for current production. An alternative supplier must be chosen.

10 Productivity has fallen at the Westleigh plant. The manager would like the present systems to be reviewed to see if improvements can be made.

11 A query has arisen regarding the patent for a new type of vacuum cleaner to be launched later this year.

12 A sales campaign has to be planned for the promotion of the new vacuum cleaner in the Midlands area.

Applying for a job

Whether you are applying for a part-time job, work experience or a full-time job, it is worth taking trouble over your letter of application, following the general guidelines for letter-writing in Unit 6.

The letter – which should enclose your curriculum vitae or application form – should

*   refer to the advertisement where you read about the job
*   explain why the job appeals to you
*   convey that you are the right person for the job

Examples of sentences you could use are:

> This job particularly interests me as I have always enjoyed figurework.
> I am pleased to note that there would be opportunities for foreign travel as I enjoyed using my French and German during work experience at a travel agency.

Curriculum vitae

If an application form is not required, it is a good idea to submit a neatly written or typed CV containing the information outlined in Fig. 24.

Task 3.5

1 Write a letter of application enclosing a curriculum vitae for the post of publicity assistant advertised on page 49.

Refer to Unit 6 for information about letter-writing.

2 In groups of four, assess each other's letters of application awarding a maximum of 3 marks for *each* of the following factors:

presentation – handwriting, neatness and layout
style   – fluency of expression, vocabulary
content   – relevance to requirements of job as specified in the advertisement

Task 3.6

You will need to work in pairs for the following assignment. Before you start, read the guidelines on telephoning in Unit 6.

Curriculum vitae

Name
Address
Telephone number
Date of birth
Secondary and further education – include the names of schools and colleges with dates
Qualifications – include dates, grades, subjects, special awards, medals etc.
Past experience – include previous employment and work-experience attachments, emphasising relevant aspects to post being applied for, e.g. figurework, dealing with public etc.
Present employment – include name and address of employer and brief description of post held. Normally your present employer will be asked for a reference if you are called for an interview
Hobbies and interests – give details of clubs, hobbies etc.
Other relevant information – e.g. if you hold a current driving licence

Figure 24

When you attend for interview for the job of publicity assistant (advertised in Fig. 25), you are required to carry out the following tests.

Test 1 – Receiving a telephone call
The interviewee (Student 1) is required to deal with a telephone call from an irate customer (Student 2) who complains that the advertisement for which you have invoiced him is incorrect. The customer refuses to pay the bill.

Test 2 – Making a call
The interviewee (Student 1) is required to make a telephone call to a local printer (Student 2) asking if they can print some advertising leaflets by next Friday. Student 2 is adamant that this cannot be done. Student 1 must persuade the printer to change his mind as otherwise it might mean losing an important client.

Key facts Categories of people at work: proprietors
executives
administrative staff
clerical and secretarial staff
technical staff

Accounts Clerk

International Computers is one of Britain's leading computer companies offering a total computer service encompassing hardware, software, distribution and repair. To ease pressure in our expanding accounts department we now require an experienced person to supplement our existing team.

This demanding position involves maintenance and reconciliation of all cash books, detailed monitoring of group sales ledger cash receipts and reconciliation of all nominal ledger control accounts. Duties will also include responsibility for the fixed asset register, deputising for the cashier as necessary and preparation of nominal ledger input.

Candidates must have a good working knowledge of computerised accounting systems together with the ability to work in close liaison with other group departmental personnel.

The benefits of working for this successful public company include an excellent working environment and a salary which reflects our commitment to attracting high calibre personnel.

If you can function with minimum supervision and wish to extend your career you are invited to telephone or write to

SECRETARY RECRUITMENT CONTROLLER

THE COMPANY: We are well established as one of the foremost employment agencies

THE RESPONSIBILITIES: You will be responsible for control on our busy temporary secretarial division entailing interviewing, selection and work delegation.

THE ATTRIBUTES: You will be sales orientated with a good telephone manner, able to converse easily with our many clients and temporary staff and to absorb and work under pressure. A clean driving licence is also required.

THE REWARDS: A basic starting salary of £6,000 and a profit sharing scheme are the initial rewards for this challenging position.

Please send c.v. to:

PERSONAL ASSISTANT TO SALES DIRECTOR

Applications in writing are invited for this position.

Secretarial skills, an enquiring and retentive mind together with customer and personnel relations experience will be a positive requirement.

In return, we offer an interesting and varied career, scope for personal initiative and progression, an attractive salary and benefits, together with the opportunity to succeed with this successful Company.

Please send full details to:

Management Trainee

Europe's leading Trailer Rental Organisation requires a Management Trainee

The successful applicant, responsible to the Branch Manager, will be trained in customer liaison, handling of rental arrangements, credit control, trailer inspection, supervision of maintenance and all documentation associated with the operation of a large and varied fleet. In order to fully develop career potential, applicants should be prepared to travel when required.

Applicants (male or female) should be 16-19 years of age and have a good general education.

Please apply in writing giving personal history and telephone number to:

SALES ADMINISTRATOR

A vacancy has arisen at our modern distribution centre in Southampton for a Sales Administrator.

The successful applicant will join a busy sales / distribution team, involved in customer contact by telephone, computerised stock control and all other associated administration / distribution work.

Applications are invited from persons aged 19/27 years who have a pleasant personality, a sense of humour and an interest in telephone sales.

Clerical experience would be an advantage but not essential as training in all aspects will be given.

Conditions of service are excellent, the starting salary will depend upon age and experience.

Please telephone for an application form:

PUBLICITY ASSISTANT

Junior Assistant wanted by bustling PR/Advertising Agency, to help us produce and distribute Press releases and other marketing communications. Good telephone manner required. We're based in the lively Shamrock Quay complex in Northam.

Figure 25 Job advertisements

Role of the office:
  complements production by: receiving information
          recording information
          processing information
          storing information
          disseminating information
          safeguarding assets
  Job descriptions give: job title
          job grade
          areas of responsibility
          accountability
          main duties

Unit 4 *Sources of information*

Introduction

Information is the lifeblood which flows into, out of and within an organisation. It forms the basis of decisions and stimulates action. The success or otherwise of a business may depend on the accuracy and timing of the information supplied or the effective use made of it.

Developments in computer technology have brought about a major information 'explosion'. If the advantages offered by this accessibility are to be exploited to the full, it is essential to know what types of information are or could be of use to your organisation and to be able to obtain such information quickly when required.

Why is information needed?

An organisation needs information:

- to provide up-to-date records of sales, purchases, assets and liabilities so that its financial position can be ascertained at any time
- to co-ordinate activities within and between departments to meet the objective, e.g. supplying a customer's order (refer to Fig. 19 in Unit 3 and Task 2.3 (p. 34) which illustrate why information is needed by various departments)
- to analyse trends so that appropriate action can be taken, e.g. sales can be analysed by product to identify unprofitable lines
- to monitor performance against forecasts so that adjustments can be made if necessary, e.g. if production is slower than predicted, additional labour/machines can be employed or sales reduced
- to comply with legislation, e.g. Companies Acts; health and safety legislation; employment law; consumer legislation
- to enable employees to carry out their duties efficiently and effectively, e.g. a shipping clerk will need shipping guides, import/export regulations, etc. at hand.
- to keep abreast of political and economic trends which may affect the organisation, its suppliers or competitors, e.g. government policy on youth training schemes; stoppages or closure of other businesses; scarcity of fuel or raw materials

Where can information be obtained?

Much of the information relating to the day-to-day running of a business is available within the organisation itself. Where you need to use external resources, it will save you a great deal of time if you know where to telephone, write or visit.

For convenience, the main information resources available are grouped under the following headings:

- internal sources (excluding reference books)
- reference books
- external sources – general
- external sources – specialist

Internal sources of information

1 Colleagues have a wealth of knowledge and experience which can save you valuable time and costly mistakes – the best way to learn is to be observant, listen and ask questions.
2 Company handbooks, noticeboards and staff magazines supply information for employees on various aspects of company policy and activities, as well as social events.
3 Departments provide specialist information and advice – make sure you know who does what in your organisation.
4 Management database systems – where company information is computerised, it is possible to access various files and records via terminals. The use of passwords prevents unauthorised access to information.
5 Personal systems, e.g. diaries, checklists, indexes, statistics, etc. can be a useful and quick reference source devised to suit the individual's needs.
6 Procedure manuals set out standardised methods of carrying out particular tasks, e.g. use of machines; committee procedures; procedures for passing payments.
7 Records and files provide background information on subjects and people.
8 Reference books – see below.
9 Reports, minutes and circulars are intended to keep people up to date – they should always be read and circulated as soon as possible.

Reference books

The range of reference books kept will reflect the size and nature of the business and the duties of personnel employed. It is important to be familiar with the contents of books you may need to use in your job. A visit to your local reference library will pay dividends. A selection of reference books is given below under topic areas.

Current affairs

- *Monthly Digest* and *Annual Abstract of Statistics* contain statistical tables relating to social and economic matters including trade, health, population and production. Published by HMSO.
- *Britain: An Official Handbook*, published annually by HMSO, describes the current status of Britain in political, financial, social and economic terms.
- *Hansard*, published by HMSO, is a verbatim record of proceedings in both Houses of Parliament.
- *The Europa Year Book*, a world survey of international organisations and countries, contains a wealth of information about every country in the world – including economic and statistical surveys, constitution, government, religions etc. Published annually.
- *Keesing's Contemporary Archives* is a weekly diary of world events in the form of news-sheets which can be bound together in a special case to form a reference book. The information is compiled from the world's press and information services.
- *Municipal Year Book* gives information about local authorities in England and Wales. The area, population, rates and names of chief officers are given for each county council, district council etc.
- *Pear's Cyclopaedia* is a compact and useful handbook, with sections on events, gazetteer, office compendium, prominent people, synonyms and antonyms, legal data etc. Published annually.
- *Whitaker's Almanac* gives facts and figures about world affairs, government, industry, finance, commerce, the arts etc. and also provides names and addresses of associations, societies and government offices. Published annually.

English usage

- A good dictionary, such as the *Concise Oxford Dictionary* or *Collins English Dictionary*, is essential.
- Books on English usage, grammar and style include *Fowler's Modern English Usage and Abusage*.
- *Dictionary of Acronyms and Abbreviations* gives the meaning of initials and abbreviations in common use.
- *Roget's Thesaurus of English Words and Phrases* arranges words according to their meaning rather than alphabetical order.
- Technical dictionaries are useful for particular trades, e.g. *Authors' and Printers' Dictionary, Black's Medical Dictionary, Dictionary of Scientific Terms* etc.

Foreign languages

- Berlitz, Collins and Hamlyn all publish excellent pocket dictionaries and phrase books useful for travellers.
- If your work involves translation and correspondence in foreign languages, or if you travel abroad a lot, then you will require a large reference dictionary such as those published by Harraps, e.g. *Harraps French Dictionary*.

Literary

- *British Humanities Index/British Technology Index* are useful for tracing magazine and newspaper articles.
- *British National Bibliography* is a weekly publication listing British publications.
- *Oxford Companion to English Literature* is a dictionary of authors, literary works and fictional characters.
- *Oxford Dictionary of Quotations* and *Stephenson's Book of Quotations* list quotations alphabetically according to authors' names.

People

- *Black's Titles and Forms of Address* sets out the correct way of addressing people and introducing them.
- *Burke's Peerage* and *Debrett's Peerage* are the most reliable guides to peers and their families.
- *British Qualifications* is a useful guide to educational, technical, professional and academic qualifications in the UK giving descriptions of qualifications and the addresses of professional bodies.
- *Directory of Directors* is published annually and gives a detailed record of all directors and their joint stock companies.
- *Who's Who* contains biographies of living eminent people.
- *Who Was Who* provides a record of eminent people who have died. The *Dictionary of National Biography* is the most comprehensive reference book of noteworthy people from the British Isles and the Commonwealth dating back for several centuries.

Certain professions and occupational groups publish directories of their members. These directories include:

The Times Guide to the House of Commons
The Diplomatic Service List
Vacher's Parliamentary Companion
The Air Force List
The Army List
The Navy List
The Bar List
The Solicitor's Diary
Crockford's Clerical Directory
The Medical Register
The Dentist's Register

- *Croner's Reference Book for Employers* is designed to provide employers with information on employment legislation. A monthly amendment service is provided in order to keep the information up-to-date.

Postal and telecommunications services

- British Telecom publications:

  Telephone Directories and *Yellow Pages* are published for all areas.
  Europages is a classified telephone directory for the six major EEC countries, listing company names, addresses and telephone numbers.
  Telex Directories gives details of telex numbers and answerback codes.
  Leaflets on various telecommunications services and equipment can be obtained on request.

- Post Office publications:

  Post Office Guide gives details of inland and overseas postal services; import regulations for foreign countries; savings schemes and National Giro.
  Inland and overseas compendiums provide current rates of postage and these can be obtained from local post offices free of charge.
  Post Code Directories give correct postal addresses and post codes.

- *Thomson's Local Directories* contain local community information, a classified trade directory and a postcode directory for the area.

Trade, finance and industry

- *Banker's Almanac and Year Book* is the standard international banking reference work; the *Building Societies Yearbook* is the handbook of the Building Societies Association.
- *Business Location Handbook* contains information for business on relocation areas, transport, financial aid available, comparative property and salary levels, sources of finance (other than grants). A very useful book for new businesses or organisations thinking of relocating premises.
- *Civil Service Year Book* details functions of government departments and lists top personnel.
- *Directory of British Associations* lists the addresses, activities and publications of trade and professional associations, societies, research organisations, chambers of trade and commerce, and trade unions.
- *Insurance Blue Book and Guide* gives information about insurance companies.
- *Kelly's Manufacturers and Merchants Directory* lists manufacturers and suppliers alphabetically under the headings of goods and services.
- *Key British Enterprises* (Dun and Bradstreet) provides a profile of the top 20,000 companies in Britain.
- *Personnel and Training Management Year Book and Directory* supplies details of courses, conference centres and related services, and reviews developments in training and personnel management.
- *Stock Exchange Official Year Book* gives financial information on firms, securities, investments etc.
- *UK Kompass* is a comprehensive register of British industry and commerce. Volume 1 provides names and addresses of suppliers of products and services, listed by industrial groups. Volume 2 contains information about companies,

listed geographically by town and county. It includes company structure, names of directors and senior executives, number of employees and nature of business.

- *Yellow Pages* and *Europages* group names, addresses and telephone numbers according to trades or professions.

Travel

It is useful to keep some reference books on travel information in the office, even if you regularly use the services of a travel agency. A basic selection could include an atlas, timetables, maps and a guide to hotels and restaurants.

- Atlas – there are several good atlases currently published, e.g. *Times Atlas of the World*, the *Oxford Atlas*.
- *Good Food Guide* is published annually by the Consumers Association, and covers hotels and restaurants in the UK.
- *Hotels and Restaurants in Great Britain* is published annually by the British Tourist Authority.
- *Hints to Exporters* is a series of free booklets on different countries giving advice about travel, visas, import regulations, hotels, etc. They can be obtained from the Export Services and Promotions Division of the Department of Trade at Export House, 50 Ludgate Hill, London EC4M 7HU.
- Maps – various maps are published by Ordnance Survey, Bartholomews and petroleum companies.

Timetables:

Air   – *ABC World Airways Guide*
        ABC Guide to International Travel
        ABC Air/Rail Europe

Rail   – *ABC Rail Guide*
        British Rail Passenger Timetable
        Passenger Timetable International
        Cook's International Timetable

Road – *AA* or *RAC Handbooks*
        ABC Coach and Bus Guide
        National Express Service Guide

Sea   – *ABC Shipping Guide*

External sources – general

In this section are included press, periodicals, radio, television, libraries and computerised databanks. Some of these also, of course, provide specialist information.

Libraries

Although some very large organisations have their own library, the majority keep only a few reference books directly relevant to their line of business.

- Public libraries contain a wide selection of reference works including dictionaries, almanacs, encyclopaedias, atlases, daily newspapers, periodicals and technical books. The British Library is one of the most comprehensive in the world and books can be borrowed from it through your local library on payment of a fee.
- Specialist libraries exist in universities, polytechnics, and a large number of professional institutions and government organisations. You can obtain details from the Association of Special Libraries and Information Bureaux (ASLIB) who publish a directory of specialist and technical libraries.
- Commercial libraries are found in most large cities and contain major trade and professional directories, newspapers, trade periodicals and technical and specialist business publications. They form part of the public library.
- Film libraries such as the Central Film Library hire and sell informational and training films on subjects such as telecommunications and health and safety at work. Some of the films may be hired free of charge.

Newspapers

It is a good idea to get into the habit of reading a newspaper every day:

- to develop a broad appreciation of political, economic and current affairs
- to deepen your understanding of the business world, particularly of matters relevant to your own organisation.
- to keep abreast of topics of general interest such as social, sporting or cultural events
- to help you formulate opinions and take part in discussions with confidence and interest

Your choice of newspaper may be influenced by the style or political slant, but it is best to select one which is reliable and informative. You would be well-advised to read and analyse several newspapers over a period before deciding which is most appropriate for you.

Periodicals

There is a wide range of periodicals, magazines and trade journals available covering both general and specialised business interests. Most professional bodies also publish their own journals for members.

Details of newspapers and publications relating to any particular trade can be found in *Willing's Press Guide* or *Benn's Press Directory*.

You will probably come across some of the periodicals listed below in the course of your work as well as more specialised and technical publications applicable to your own particular trade or profession.

Business Equipment Digest
Business Systems and Equipment
Data Processing
Industrial Society
Management Today
Marketing
Mind your Own Business
New Scientist
Office Equipment News
Office Magazine
Personnel Magazine
Reprographics
The British Journal of Administrative Management
The Economist
The Listener
The Spectator
Which Word Processor

Radio and television

Documentary and news programmes can furnish you with useful specialist and general background information on many subjects. The use of video-recording facilities should not be overlooked, although copyright restrictions must be observed.

Televised information services (videotex)

Quick access to a wide range of information stored on centralised computer databases is available via teletext and viewdata systems, using specially adapted TV sets or communicating data/word processing equipment.

- Teletext: Ceefax (BBC), Oracle (ITV) and 4-TEL (C4) present information in a characteristically journalistic format covering news; arts and entertainment; business and financial matters; weather and travel information; TV guides and reviews.
- Viewdata (public): British Telecom's public viewdata service (Prestel) is a two-way information system accessed via telephone lines. It provides a much fuller range of reference material than teletext and is therefore more useful to the businessman. The Prestel equipment is illustrated in Fig. 26.
- Viewdata (private): Private viewdata systems supply specialised information to restricted user groups, e.g. farming, travel, stock exchange, law, local government etc. Access may be via Prestel or directly through the public telephone network.

Figure 26 Prestel viewdata

Task 4.1

For this assignment you will need to visit your college or local library.

Answer the following questions, quoting the reference book used, page number and library catalogue number (if applicable).

1 Who is your local MP, does he hold any ministerial post and is he a director of any companies?
2 Name two of the main items discussed in Parliament last week.
3 Find a word opposite in meaning to lethargic.
4 What is the population of Holland?
5 What is the address of the Institute of Administrative Management?
6 Who is the Minister for Trade and Industry?
7 Who is the Chief Executive of your local authority?
8 What is the meaning of 'nomenclature'?
9 Find a word similar in meaning to phlegmatic.
10 What do the following initials stand for: SEATO; FAO; RICS?
11 What is the meaning of the phrase 'pari passu'?
12 How would you address a mayor who is a married lady?
13 Name two directors of Marks and Spencer plc.
14 What is the telex number and answerback code of your local chamber of commerce?
15 What is the correct postal address, including postcode, of your local DHSS offices?

16 What was the annual sales turnover of British Leyland last year?
17 What is the capital city of Sri Lanka?
18 Name two 3-star hotels in Birmingham.
19 How far is Bristol from York? Which route would you take by car?
20 What are the conditions covering maternity leave for employees?

Task 4.2   Assume that you are an administrative trainee in the head office of an organisation of your choice.

Over the next few weeks, compile an annotated folder of press/magazine cuttings relevant or useful to the organisation chosen. Your folder could contain articles on such items as:

1 matters relating to the organisation, its products or services, its interests or competitors
2 new technology applicable to the organisation
3 changes in legislation relating to the organisation
4 general business matters, e.g. bank rate, government economic policy etc.
5 reviews of relevant books, conferences, broadcasts, etc.

Note: If you are in employment, you should relate the folder to your own line of business.

External sources – specialist bodies and agencies

Chambers of commerce

Most organisations belong to their local chamber of commerce which offers a wide range of services for business, including the provision of statistical data, advice on international trading regulations and translation services.

Central Office of Information

This is the government's central source of information which produces a large variety of statistical, political and general national information.

Daily Telegraph *Information Bureau*

This bureau provides a telephone information service on general matters and current affairs. It does not advise on specialist or technical matters.

Embassies and consulates

Information concerning particular countries can be obtained from embassies, consulates or trade delegations in this country. Some will also provide interpreters.

Government departments

Government departments, many of which have local offices, will supply information either free of charge or for a nominal fee. Addresses can be found in *Whitaker's Almanac* or local telephone directories.

HM Stationery Office

There are several branches throughout the country supplying copies of government legislation and publications.

Local council offices

Local authorities will provide information on any local matters, e.g. planning regulations, development proposals, environmental health etc. There is often a public relations department which provides literature on issues of public interest such as industrial development, road planning, leisure facilities etc.

Professional and trade associations

These bodies exist primarily to supply technical and specialist support and advice to members and provide a forum for the exchange of views. However, they will also supply information to organisations and members of the public. Examples of these bodies are the British Medical Association, the Electrical Trades Association, the Bus and Coach Council, the Food Manufacturers' Federation and the Association of British Travel Agents.

Specialist agencies and consultancy services

In most local areas, there are agencies which specialise in staffing, advertising, public relations, travel, accommodation etc. There will also be local firms of accountants and solicitors. It is often cheaper in the long run for a firm to use these services rather than set up its own specialist department.

Task 4.3   If you are a full-time student, refer to Jobline Personnel Agency (p. 1) or the business which you set up in Task 1.7 (p. 28).

1 Make a list of essential reference books this company would need, explaining for what purposes they would be used.
2 What external sources of information other than reference books do you think the company might need to use? Give reasons for your answer.

If you have a part-time job, a full-time job or are on work experience, compile a folder listing sources of reference which would be useful to you in your work.

Task 4.4   You work in the Personnel Department at the Hull plant of Domilux plc.
Some Saudi Arabian businessmen are to visit your plant to discuss a contract

and it is proposed to take them on a trip to the Wedgwood factory at Barlaston. You have been asked to make arrangements, for which you will need the information listed below.

1 Where exactly is Barlaston?
2 Prepare some brief notes on china marks.
3 Name two good hotels or restaurants in the vicinity which could provide lunch.
4 Obtain details of the life of the founder, Sir Josiah Wedgwood.
5 Josiah Wedgwood was a member of the Lunar Society. What does 'lunar' mean? What was this society and who were its members?
6 Are there any dietary rules to be careful about when booking the meal for your visitors? Does the visit coincide with any dates of religious observance – the visit to the china factory is on a Saturday?

Supply the answers to these questions and also state where you could obtain the following information:

1 The names of two local firms who could provide transport.
2 The name of a firm of translators.
3 Details of air flights to the Middle East.

(Adapted from RSA paper)

Task 4.5 ALBEC Limited is engaged in a campaign to extend its sales abroad and is considering appointing an agent in France. The agent would be responsible for marketing the firm's products in France and possibly assembling parts shipped from this country in a knocked-down condition.
The next monthly meeting of directors will be considering this matter in detail.
You are required to prepare a memo containing the following information which may be used at the directors' meeting:

1 The current rate of exchange of francs against pound sterling.
2 The total population of France.
3 The population, position and industries of the port of Le Havre.
4 How much it costs to telephone, telex and send a telegram to France.
5 The address and telephone number of the French embassy in London.
6 The address and telephone number of the French Consulate in your nearest town.
7 The name of the government department that is able to assist in this project and any government publications that may be helpful.
8 Local sources which can be used for engaging a French translator.
9 Any other information which you consider might be useful for discussion of this matter at the meeting.

Key facts

Information is needed:

- to provide financial records
- to co-ordinate activities to meet the objectives
- to analyse trends
- to monitor performance against forecasts
- to comply with legislation
- to enable people to work efficiently
- to aid decision-making

Information can be obtained from:

- within the organisation, e.g. departments, files, people
- reference books
- external sources, e.g. the media, libraries, computer databases, public and private sector organisations

Unit 5 *Internal communication*

Introduction

The importance of effective communication as a means of co-ordinating the activities of individuals and departments within organisations has already been discussed in Unit 2.

Good communication has an equally important role in fostering harmonious relationships and boosting morale. While people at work often complain that too much paperwork is generated or there are too many meetings, they are just as frequently heard to say that 'no-one ever tells me anything' or 'I'm always the last to know'. It is always important to ensure that information is communicated to the right people at the right time, and to err on the side of giving too much rather than too little. This not only enables staff to do their work properly, but helps them to feel part of a team.

What is effective communication?

It is simply the transmission of a message to another person in such a way that the recipient interprets it exactly as the sender intends and receives it at the right time. This involves correct timing, logical thinking, fluent expression, careful reading and listening, and sensitivity to the circumstances so that the most appropriate media, tone and style can be used for the situation. It also involves obtaining feedback to check that the message has been understood.

Media

The main methods used to communicate within organisations are as follows:

Verbal
Personal exchanges (face-to-face)
Meetings
Telephone

Written/visual
Memos
Reports
Abstracts
Summaries
Documentation
Notices/bulletins
VDUs/computer printout
Charts, graphs
House journals

The choice of media will be affected by the degree of urgency, the type and nature of the information transmitted, whether discussion or persuasion is required, the need for a permanent record, security aspects and the number of people involved.

Tone and style

People in organisations are required to deal with many different individuals in the course of their work. The nature of these relationships will greatly influence the tone and style used in any particular situation. For example, communications with superiors and subordinates will tend to be more formal than with peers.

The circumstances and content of the communication will also have a bearing, e.g. asking a favour may need persuasiveness; disciplinary action demands formality and objectivity; personal problems require a sympathetic and less formal approach.

Courtesy should always be used – the use of 'please' turns an order into a request and thanking colleagues for their co-operation indicates appreciation of their efforts.

Guidelines for effective communication

- Organise your thoughts before you speak/write
- Present your ideas logically
- Use simple, concise sentences and avoid unnecessary jargon
- Use the most appropriate media – if necessary, follow up verbal exchanges with a written confirmation
- Obtain feedback by checking that the recipient has understood your message
- Make sure you listen to assimilate what the other person has to say
- Always be courteous
- Say what you mean, and mean what you say!

Personal exchanges

Direct personal contact takes place informally many times during the working day to relay messages, give directions or advice, make requests etc. It is always the best method to use where discussion or persuasion is needed and where personal or confidential matters are to be discussed.

Although face-to-face contact is time-consuming, it has the advantage of instant feedback. There is opportunity for questioning, elaboration and explanation, and mistakes can be rectified immediately. The use of facial expression, tone and gesture lend emphasis and convey the feelings of the participants in a way that the written word cannot. However, if the conversation contains information which may be referred to or queried later, it is wise to confirm it in writing for the record.

Meetings

Meetings provide an excellent way of keeping people up-to-date with developments, discussing diverse views or obtaining a consensus of opinion. Provided they are not called unnecessarily and are controlled properly, they save time by bringing several people together at once for face-to-face consultation.

Procedures and formalities of meetings are discussed in detail in Unit 14.

The telephone

The telephone is the best method of oral communication after face-to-face contact, providing the advantages of convenience and instant feedback. It is less time-consuming than face-to-face exchanges, particularly where distance is concerned (e.g. in a large organisation) and the fact that facial expressions and gestures cannot be seen is often an advantage! Where urgent communication is necessary, it is frequently possible to talk to a busy member of staff on the telephone, even if he has someone in his office, whereas to burst in on him would appear rude. On most modern telephone systems, several extensions can be linked simultaneously so that a group of people can confer.

Telephone techniques are discussed on page 78.

Memoranda

Memos provide an extremely efficient means of communicating written information up, down and across the organisation. They are usually handwritten or typed on a printed form (size A4 or A5) similar to the example shown in Fig. 27.

The name of the organisation does not normally appear on a memo for internal use. No salutation or complimentary close is necessary and it is usually initialled rather than signed. If copies are distributed to third parties, this should be indicated both as a record for the file and for the information of the recipients. The attachment of enclosures should also be indicated.

Uses of memoranda

- to transmit ideas and suggestions for consideration or approval
- to confirm oral communication
- to keep people informed of developments
- to clarify or seek information
- to request help or co-operation from other staff or departments
- to introduce new procedures or policies
- to give or seek instructions or advice

Tone and style

Whatever the circumstances or content of the message, it is wise to remember that the written word is permanent and difficult to retract later. Therefore, care should

MEMORANDUM

To: A Baxter (Chief Accountant)   Ref DP/PB 1824

From: D Parkes (Production   Date: 8 October 19...
               Director)

Subject: Payment of Wages to Production Staff for Short-time
Working

As agreed at the Board meeting yesterday I have notified
production staff that they will not be required to work on
Thursday and Friday next week because of the cancellation of
a major order. Stores staff and goods inward/outward staff
will be working as normal.

I should be grateful if you would arrange to pay production
staff wages on Wednesday instead of Friday.

A list of the staff affected is attached.

                                                    D.P.

Enc

Figure 27

always be taken to avoid ambiguity and emotive or provocative language. Sentences should be simple and concise and ideas grouped into paragraphs, if necessary under appropriate headings. To reduce paperwork, instead of a covering memo, an action slip can be attached to documents asking for comments, approval, draft reply etc. An example is illustrated in Fig. 28.

```
┌─────────────────────────────────────────────┐
│  ┌──────────────┐                            │
│  │ ACTION SLIP  │                            │
│  └──────────────┘                            │
│                                              │
│    To:                        URGENT  ☐      │
│                                              │
├─────────────────────────────────────────────┤
│                                              │
│         Please:                              │
│         ☐  Draft a reply for my signature    │
│         ☐  Give comments required            │
│         ☐  Circulate and return to me        │
│         ☐  Note and return to me             │
│         ☐  Take appropriate action           │
│         ☐  Note for your information         │
│                                              │
├─────────────────────────────────────────────┤
│    REMARKS                                   │
│                                              │
│                                              │
├──────────────────────┬──────────────────────┤
│    From:             │   Date:              │
│                      │                      │
└──────────────────────┴──────────────────────┘
```

Figure 28

Task 5.1   You work in the Accounts Department at ALBEC Limited.

Refer to the memo from D Parkes (Production Director) (Fig. 27) and draft a memo to production staff saying you will pay them at 1130 hours next Wednesday. Absentees will receive a cheque by post. Send a copy to D Parkes for his information.

Summaries

If the busy executive is to manage his time effectively, he has to keep himself properly informed without wasting time on minutiae. He achieves this by encouraging staff to present ideas, reports and feedback in a condensed form that leaves out superfluous detail and is easy to assimilate.

Summarising is necessary for many oral and written communications and may involve any of the following skills or techniques:

- ability to comprehend a wide range of information and data presented in various formats and styles
- ability to identify key points
- ability to analyse complex issues
- objectivity in reproducing the essence, tone and attitude of the original
- knowledge of formats of various types of written documents

Uses of summarising

- preparation of reports for meetings
- reporting of meetings and discussions
- passing on messages
- delegating work
- briefing workgroups
- drafting notices, press releases, articles, circulars, advertisements
- drafting letters and memos which convey information or ideas
- composing telegrams, electronic mail and telex messages
- completion of forms, e.g. accident reporting, machine breakdown reports

Methods of summarising

Summarising may take the form of

- a summary – condensed version of selected points as required by brief
- a précis – condensing whole passage to about one-third of its original length
- an abstract – selected parts of long article or report condensed to required length

Format and style

The choice is between schematic layout or continous prose, but format and style are normally dictated by the purpose and circumstances. A summary is usually used in minutes to record the proceedings at a meeting.

Guidelines for summarising

1 Make sure you know what is required – e.g. a summary, précis or abstract.
2 Read the item through twice to make sure you understand the general meaning and terminology – use a dictionary if necessary.
3 Use a title which conveys what the summary is about.
4 Identify the key points and compare them with the title to check that they are relevant.
5 Determine the format and style required.
6 Compose a rough draft in your own words, then edit it, checking for length, accuracy, logical flow of expression and ideas, grammar, spelling etc.
7 Produce a final version in the format required, adding details of source, date written and your own name.

Reports

Reports are normally written in order to provide a record of the communication but are sometimes presented orally. Their main purpose is to keep management up-to-date with relevant developments within and outside the organisation so that they can make decisions based on accurate facts, expert advice and well-considered opinion. Where reports are to be considered at a meeting, they should be distributed to participants in advance to give them time to read the contents before discussion.

Uses of reports

Reports may be used:

- to summarise investigations into causes and effects of problems or trends and to recommend solutions, e.g. why there has been an increase in absenteeism, the reason for a fall in sales
- to provide statistical or financial summaries, e.g. monthly sales report, annual accounts
- to record decisions made at meetings
- to supply information for legal purposes, e.g. accident report, annual report for shareholders
- to monitor progress, e.g. in negotiations, in building work, in the implementation of a new system
- to look into the feasibility of introducing new procedures, making new products, changing company policy

Format and style

A report must be accurate, clear, concise and logically arranged. It should be concise to the extent that there is no 'padding' or irrelevant details. The writer should 'telescope' phrases wherever possible and avoid using long, involved sentences.

If the report is an individual one from the administrative assistant to the manager it should be written in the first person, but formal reports or reports of meetings should be written wholly in the third person to indicate their objectivity.

1 Short informal reports may be written as a memo or set out in report form. In either case, they are normally presented in the following format:
   (a) title
   (b) introduction (explaining the background)
   (c) body of report (containing the findings)
   (d) conclusions
   (e) recommendations
   (f) action required

2 Formal reports are more schematically laid out and are normally presented as follows:
   (a) title page containing the name of the organisation, the subject of the report, the name and post of the writer, the name of the commissioner, distribution list (this may appear at the end)
   (b) list of contents, index
   (c) terms of reference explaining the reason for the report, e.g. who commissioned it and why
   (d) procedure, i.e. how the writer went about the task, names of people interviewed etc.

REPORT

CONFIDENTIAL

To: B Collins, Production Director

Ref: S 1923.

REPORT ON ABSENTEEISM OF PRODUCTION STAFF

1 Terms of Reference: As a result of the increasing rate of

   absenteeism amongst production staff, the Production Director

   requested an investigation to be made and recommendations

   suggested for an improvement.

2 Procedure: The following procedures were adopted to ascertain the

   amount of absenteeism, the causes and the remedies

   2.1 Records of individual absences were analysed

   2.2 All employees who had been absent more than three times during

        the past 6 months were interviewed

   2.3 The flexitime system of time-keeping was evaluated and compared

        with the clock-card system used at present.

3 Findings:

   3.1 Analysis of absences revealed that

        3.1.1 2500 man hours had been lost during the last year at a

               cost to the company of £8000

        3.1.2 In the current year:

                                                    Last year
               60% were absent 2 days or less (Cat 1)   22%

               20%   "   "   2 - 14 days   (Cat 2)   2%

               20%   "   "   longterm   (Cat 3) no change

Figure 29

3.1.3 48% of Cat 1 and 10% of Cat 2 had been absent more than 3 times during the last 6 months

3.1.4 Total day absences since self-certification was introduced had increased by 40%

3.1.5 40% of Cat 1 were absent on Mondays

3.2 At interviews staff gave their reasons for absence as:

stomach illness - 40%

cold associated illness - 30%

headaches - 20%

other - 10%

3.3 Evaluation of time-keeping systems

3.3.1 Flexitime was considered unsuitable for the factory because of the need for standard hours to keep production lines running

3.3.2 The present system of clock cards appeared to be efficient

4 Conclusions: The incidence of 'casual' sickness since self-certification increased by 38% whilst normal sickness rates remained approximately the same.

5 Recommendation: In cases of repeated sickness, i.e. more than 3 times in any 6-month period, individuals should be interviewed by the Personnel Officer and then referred for medical advice.

A Miller

Finance Director

10 December 198-

(e) findings, i.e. what the writer discovered

(f) conclusion, i.e. a summary of the findings

(g) recommendations – if appropriate

(h) signature of the writer and date

The layout of a formal report is given in Fig. 29.

Where draft reports are typed on word processors, the information may be stored and retrieved again later as required. Corrections, insertions or deletions can be made to the original without having to retype the whole report. It is also possible to include sections from other reports which cuts down the amount of re-typing and proof-reading needed. The use of emboldening for titles, sub-titles etc. improves the appearance and adds emphasis.

Use of language

The language used should be appropriate to the audience, e.g. the vocabulary and sentence construction should be of the right level and technical terminology should be reserved for specialists.

Key facts

In preparing reports
- check the terms of reference, i.e. what you have been requested to do
- plan the information in a logical sequence
- decide what format is required
- consider the language and style to be used, bearing in mind the circulation list
- consider if statistics or other data should be presented as a separate appendix or in another format
- prepare the draft and check it against the terms of reference
- if the report runs to several pages, consider the presentation of the cover and binding
- if the report is confidential or secret, make sure this is indicated on the front cover

Task 5.2

You are working at the head office of Domilux plc.

The director of operations was asked at a recent meeting with the various plant managers about the possibility of installing cellular radio telephones in the delivery vans to provide constant communication between plants, van drivers, head office and customers.

Prepare a report comparing cellular radio with private mobile radio, taking into account costs, convenience, versatility etc. so that the director of operations can report to the next meeting of plant managers.

The article given in Fig. 30 will provide background information and help you to prepare a summary of relevant facts. Your report should not exceed 300 words.

Figure 30

Transport News
Communications on the Move

James Colyton talks to Peter Bryant

Introduction

'By the early 1990s, there will be about 500 000 mobile phones in Britain, not only in cars, taxis and trains, but also in the briefcase, the handbag or pocket. You may even be wearing one on your wrist like a watch so that you can be in contact with other phone users wherever and whenever you wish.' This is the view of Peter Bryant, Managing Director of the Banning Telecommunications Group.

He goes on to say, 'At present, about 80 per cent of cellular phones are fixed in cars or other vehicles. Over the next few years, though, there will be a change towards the purchase of transportable phones for use either in the car or out of it. Data is becoming easier to transmit and more manufacturers are producing "hands-free" cellular phones which make it safer for drivers to make calls while driving. The car user simply talks into his microphone and the requested number is dialled automatically for him.'

Cellular Radio

'How does cellular radio work?' I asked. He explained, 'The service area is divided up into smaller areas (cells) each with its own radio base station. A central computer switches radio-telephone calls from one aerial to another as the mobile units (the users) move through the call areas. At the moment the cells are clustered around major commercial areas, motorway and trunk routes, but they will eventually cover the whole of the UK.'

'I can understand the benefits to fleet owners,' I said. 'But what about when you need to make phone calls to other companies on the public telephone network? Surely, you will have to stop at a public call-box?' 'Not so!' he explained. 'The big advantage of the cellular system is that users can call ordinary subscribers on the PSTN (public switched telephone network) at home or internationally as opposed to being restricted merely to other users of the system.'

'Suppose a call comes through for you when you are temporarily away from the car?' I asked. Peter was ready with the answer as I knew he would be. 'The cellular system companies have developed extra services for their subscribers such as voice messaging, radiopaging and payphones. For example, British Telecom's Voicebank Service enables subscribers to ring up and leave a message in a mailbox (rather like an answering machine) and retrieve messages. If the mailbox is linked to a BT radiopager then the subscriber is automatically bleeped and retrieves the message by dialling the Voicebank as soon as he returns to his car. So you see, it's the complete answer for travelling executives, engineers, sales reps and distribution staff. It's catching on fast now – some of the large taxi firms are on cellular and even offshore boats are using it. The latest development is the airphone in which you can make calls while flying across the world in a jumbo jet – imagine that!'

We then got down to the nitty-gritty of cost and, of course, cellular radio is not cheap although prices are coming down all the time. The options available are as follows:

- cord connected mobiles mounted in car with 'hands-free' option

  Cost £800 – £1200
- transportables – powered by rechargeable batteries (can be used in or out of the car)

  Cost £1500 – £2000
- hand portables – powered by batteries (can be used virtually anywhere)

  Cost £1500 – £2000

It is worth looking at the features provided before purchasing equipment. These may include:

- memory for storing often-used numbers
- electronic lock to stop other people using the phone
- last number recall (will automatically redial the last number called)
- volume adjustment – useful in heavy traffic
- call barring to prevent long-distance calls being made
- time and cost monitoring – displays cost and time of call while in progress

Running costs include a quarterly subscription of around £75, plus the cost of calls (about three times as much per minute as a conventional telephone call). Many companies prefer to lease equipment rather than buy it as leasing costs are fully tax deductible and have the advantage of spreading payments to aid the company's cash flow. Typical charges are £100 per quarter per £1000-worth of equipment over three years and £70 per quarter over five years.

Band 3 Radio (Private Mobile Radio)

I asked Peter whether there were any alternatives to cellular radio for firms wishing to operate a private service.

'Band 3 – an advanced two-way radio service – is ideal for medium or big organisations such as distribution chains or transport firms. As with cellular radio, drivers will have handsets in their vehicles but will not be linked to the BT network, except for 999 calls. Instead, they will talk to their base and to other operators or drivers in their particular network. Operating costs are just over half those for cellular radio.'

Conclusion

The choice depends mainly on whether firms' mobile phones need to be linked to the public network or not. Peter forecasts that Band 3 will create a market twice as big as cellular radio and that this will provide more growth for the industry than has been experienced in the last 20 years. One final word of advice, though – shop around for the best deal before buying. Prices are coming down all the time!

Documentation

Documentation provides an invaluable means of co-ordinating activities and standardising the format and style required for particular purposes. Data systems are discussed in Unit 10.

Notices and bulletins

Notices and bulletins are used to publicise forthcoming events, changes in company policy and items of general interest to personnel.

Notices are usually short and relate to one item only whereas bulletins often contain several items in the form of a factsheet. Although both can be posted onto the noticeboard, it is often safer to distribute individual copies to staff if the information is important.

It will encourage staff to read noticeboards if material is well-displayed and contains current information only. The use of labelling highlights items of special interest.

House journals

These provide a more extensive range of information about the company than bulletins and are often published by large organisations two or three times a year in the shape of an attractively-produced colour magazine. They are often distributed to customers as well as to staff to promote the company's image.

VDUs

Screen-to-screen messages may be sent between computer and wordprocessing terminals via the central computer. Messages sent through the network are usually brief and informal and take the place of telephone calls or memos (see Unit 11).

Task 5.3 You work in the Personnel Department at Domilux plc (students in employment may use their own organisation).

1 Draft a notice to staff about a new suggestions scheme to be introduced for which cash prizes varying from £100 to £20 will be awarded depending on savings or efficiency brought about by implementation of ideas suggested. Use appropriate style and language.
2 Draft a bulletin containing about five items which you think will be of general interest to staff. Invent details.

Unit 6 *External communication*

Introduction

External communication exists to tell people outside the organisation:

- why you are there
- what you can do for them
- when you can do it

Promoting good relations with the public, customers and clients is essential if the organisation is to be successful. This involves advertising its services or products and building up good personal business relationships. Responding promptly and honestly to customer/client requests will inspire confidence in your organisation and encourage business. Some of the ways in which this can be achieved are outlined in this Unit.

Media

The main methods used to communicate externally are as follows:

Verbal	*Written/visual*
Telephone	Letters
Personal exchanges	Telex
Meetings	Electronic mail
Radio/television interviews	Telegrams/cables
	Press releases
	Notices/posters/leaflets/handouts

Choice of media will depend on urgency, cost, the need for a written record, whether influence is required, distance, the time of day, legal requirements, prestige, security, equipment available, convenience etc.

The telephone

The telephone is still the most universally-used method of oral communication in business. It is convenient, direct and cheap when used sensibly and often reduces the need for lengthy correspondence. It reduces the number of meetings required and speeds up decision-making. If necessary, several people in different organisations can be linked by telephone simultaneously via teleconferencing systems (see pages 99–100 for details).

As the telephone may be the first contact a person has with the organisation, it is imperative that calls are dealt with efficiently to give a good impression. Remember that the person at the other end of the line can only hear you and cannot see your facial expressions or gestures and it is, therefore, easy for him to misinterpret what you say. Care should be taken to adopt a helpful and courteous tone, to be tactful and diplomatic, to give your whole attention to the caller and not to be distracted by others around you.

British Telecom produce many excellent booklets on telephone techniques and also run training courses for operators. However, the following guidelines may be helpful to office staff.

Switchboard techniques

The majority of incoming calls are routed through the operator (in large organisations) or the secretary.

Calls should be dealt with as follows:

1 Answer calls promptly.
2 Greet a caller with 'Good morning/afternoon' followed by name of firm.
3 If a call cannot be connected, keep the caller informed of what is happening.
4 Be pleasant, courteous, helpful and patient at all times.
5 Remain calm even when under pressure and try to deal with calls in the order received.
6 Be prepared to take messages.

Extension techniques

Receiving calls

1 Always answer the telephone promptly.
2 Announce your name, department or extension number.
3 Have paper and pen handy in case you need to take notes.
4 Be prepared to take messages for colleagues.
5 Listen carefully and do not be afraid to ask for points to be repeated – it is embarrassing to have to ring back for clarification.
6 If you need time to obtain information, arrange for either you or the caller to ring back at a certain time.

Message taking

Calls and messages should never be entrusted entirely to memory. The following details should be written down while the call is in progress:

1 Date and time of call.
2 Name of person for whom the call is intended.
3 Caller's name, address and telephone number.
4 Precise details of message – repeat it back to the caller to ensure accuracy.

After the call has finished, you should complete a telephone message form, sign it and pass it to the recipient at the earliest opportunity. If the matter is urgent and the recipient is unlikely to come back to the office on the day the call is received, inform his deputy or deal with the matter yourself if possible.

Making calls

1 Plan the call by having the necessary information ready, e.g. files, notes etc.
2 Make a note of the telephone number before dialling in case you have to re-dial (if the call is made by the operator, it is your job to look up the number).
3 Make sure you know the name of the person you are calling (if possible).
4 Be prepared to leave a message if necessary, possibly to an answering machine.
5 Announce your name before you start speaking.
6 Speak clearly and be patient if asked to repeat information.
7 Try to make calls in the afternoon when they are cheaper.

Personal exchanges and meetings

Face-to-face contact is used externally where:

- persuasion is needed, e.g. for selling
- the organisation supplies a personal service to customers, e.g. engineers, architects, accountants
- members of the public are frequent visitors, e.g. local authorities, retail establishments
- negotiation of terms with suppliers is necessary
- candidates for job vacancies are interviewed

Tone and style

This usually depends on the relationship between the parties concerned, but the following general guidelines should be observed:

1 Visitors to the firm should be treated courteously and routed efficiently to the correct department/person (see also Reception, page 131).
2 The customer/client is always right! Remember that you are there to provide a service and must remain calm and in control of your emotions even if aggression or anger is displayed by the visitor.
3 Refer situations which you cannot handle to a colleague who is in a position to assist.
4 Make allowances for people who may be nervous and ill-at-ease, e.g. candidates for interview, people who are unfamiliar with the organisation.
5 Make your points clearly and, if necessary, support them with written information.

The main points of business meetings or discussions should always be recorded for future reference. This applies even where informal conversations take place during social functions or business lunches. Many brief notes have been made on the back of envelopes or menus when the executive has forgotten to take a notepad or diary with him!

Letters

Letters are still the most widely-used form of business communication as they provide a written record and can be used to convey almost any type of information at a reasonable cost.

Letters may be used to:

- request or provide information
- acknowledge receipt
- confirm details
- complain or apologise
- request, make or adjust payment
- check credit-worthiness
- advertise goods or services
- seek or tender quotations/estimates
- place an order
- apply for or resign from a job
- seek references
- convey personal messages, e.g. congratulations, commiseration etc.

Format

Layout and style are important as they give the reader an impression of a firm's efficiency. Business letters are usually typed on A4 or A5 headed paper. Letters are usually displayed in the blocked layout as in the examples given in Figs 31 and 32.

Many letters are routine and lend themselves to the use of form letters which can be stored in a wordprocessor. The operator simply retrieves the form letter when required, displays it on the VDU and then enters variable information via the keyboard before printing it automatically. This enables personalised letters to be sent without typing out the whole text each time.

The following salutations and complimentary closes are normally used for business letters:

Where name is not known:	Dear Sir/Madam	Yours faithfully
Where name is known:	Dear Mr Jones	Yours sincerely
Where writer is on first-name terms with recipient:	Dear David	Kind regards/Sincerely

Enclosures should always be indicated at the bottom of the letter in the same way as they are on memos.

Content and style

The writer must have a clear idea in his own mind of the message he wishes to convey or the questions he wishes to ask and know exactly how to say it simply

DOMILUX (UK)
—— plc ——

Registration No: 103874
Registered Office: 128 Hannington Lane WESTLEIGH Midlandshire WM5 4AX
Telephone: Westleigh 225945 Telex: 594928 Cables: DOMILUX WESTLEIGH 4AX

Our Ref: TM/JH

Your Ref:

3 November 198–

Mr D Parkes
Production Manager
ALBEC Ltd
Unit 5
Boyatt Wood Industrial Estate
Westleigh
Midlandshire
WM6 9ST

Dear Mr Parkes

SUPPLY OF WATER PUMPS - YOUR PART NUMBER H359421

We wish to complain about the faulty workmanship in the last two
consignments of water pumps which you supplied to us with your
delivery notes 1359 and 1582.

It was unfortunate that both consignments had to be returned to you
as our testing procedure revealed that they did not meet our
specification. This caused a hold-up in production which resulted in
the delay of a shipment of washing machines to a customer in Holland.

Can you please assure us that future consignments will be rigorously
inspected before despatch to avoid a recurrence of the problem? We
should be reluctant to withdraw our custom from you after so many
years of trouble-free dealings.

Yours sincerely
DOMILUX (UK) PLC

T. Martin

T Martin
Quality Control Manager

Directors: Sir Harry Paton MD   B Collins   A Miller   G de Ville   P Harmer

Figure 31 Letter of complaint

ALBEC
ALL BRITISH ELECTRICAL COMPONENTS LIMITED

Telephone Westleigh 28195

Telex 281942

Registered Office: Unit 5 Boyatt Wood
Industrial Estate
WESTLEIGH
Midlandshire
WM3 2PD

Registered England No 181000

10 November 198–

Mr T Martin
Quality Control Manager
Domilux (UK) plc
128 Hannington Lane
WESTLEIGH
Midlandshire
WM5 4AY

Your Ref: TM/JH

Our Ref: DP/SB

Dear Mr Martin

SUPPLY OF WATER PUMPS (OUR PART NO H359421)

Thank you for your letter dated 3 November 19.. concerning the supply
of defective water pumps.

Naturally we accept complete liability and have adjusted your account
accordingly – by the enclosed credit notes 195 and 282. It is
unfortunate that our own inspection procedures did not discover the
fault at source and so avoid the inconvenience which has been caused
to a valued customer.

We have now introduced a new statistical quality control system to
ensure that mistakes such as this will not occur in the future. You
may rest assured that our reputation for producing quality products is
of first importance to us and we do not intend to let our high
standards fall.

Please accept our apologies for the inconvenience caused.

Yours sincerely

D Parkes

D Parkes
Production Manager

Encs

Directors   B Jones (MD) A Baxter C White E Monk L Symonds K Adams
D Parkes

Figure 32 Reply to letter of complaint

and concisely so that the reader can grasp the contents instantly. No room should be left for doubt. Care should be taken that the recipient's title and name are correct and that the tone is appropriate for the situation.

Letter-writing should be approached in the following way:

1 Plan the letter, noting down points to be included in logical sequence, checking that nothing essential is omitted.

2 If you are replying to a letter, quote the reference.

3 Use simple and unambiguous language, avoiding pompous terms, slang and technical jargon.

4 Divide the letter into paragraphs, each dealing with one point only and arranged as follows:
(a) opening sentences
(b) the body of the letter (further subdivided into paragraphs)
(c) closing sentences

5 Check spelling, grammar and punctuation as mistakes create a poor impression.

When determining the length of the letter, the writer must ensure that courtesy of tone and exactness of meaning are not sacrificed to brevity.

Use of language

This involves adopting the right tone, vocabulary and style for the situation and appreciating the impact it will have on the recipient.

Some examples of good and bad letter-writing style are illustrated below.

	Not this	*But this*
Keep it simple	I am in receipt of yours of the 10th of this month	Thank you for your letter dated 10 May 198-
Avoid slang	I daresay you've guessed In a couple of weeks	You probably know Within the next 2 weeks
Be courteous	I can't understand why you haven't telephoned	As I have not heard from you
	If you don't pay by next Friday	I look forward to receiving your cheque by the end of next week
Avoid being pompous	Assuring you of our best attention at all times	We hope to be of help to you in the future
Be impersonal	I was disgusted to receive yet a third statement	This is the third time this error has occurred
Be tactful	Mr Shifty is not really good enough for the post	I do not think Mr Shifty is suitably qualified
	I don't care what your problems are – I need the goods!	I appreciate your difficulties but the delay in delivery is holding up production

	Not this	But this
Use complete sentences	Reference your letter of 3 November *or* Referring to your letter of 3 November	I refer to your letter of 3 November
	Hoping to hear from you	I hope to hear from you
Use correct grammar	Neither of the partners were present at the meeting	Neither of the partners *was* present at the meeting
	Who did you speak to?	*To whom* did you speak?
	The supervisor agreed to him having a day-release course	The supervisor agreed to *his* having a day-release course
	A list of the outstanding orders have been sent to the Chief Buyer	A list of the outstanding orders *has* been sent to the Chief Buyer
	It is kind of you to invite Joan and I to attend	It is kind of you to invite Joan and *me* to attend
	I rung you up last week	I *rang* you up last week
	I would like you to quickly finish this letter	I would like you *to finish* this letter quickly

Key facts

When writing business letters:

- plan the letter in a logical sequence
- check the name, title and address of the recipient
- be concise, without omitting essential information
- use style and language appropriate for the situation and recipient
- indicate closures at the foot of the letter
- make sure the letter is clear and unambiguous

Task 6.1

Redraft the badly written letter from a small trader to Westleigh District Council (Fig. 33).

Task 6.2

You are employed in the personnel department of Westleigh District Council. Compose standard letters for use on a wordprocessor.

1 to invite applicants for interview;
2 to tell unsuccessful candidates they have not been selected for the post advertised.

Task 6.3

Draft a letter of complaint to Jobline Personnel Agency saying that the temporary shorthand/typist they supplied, Mrs Pat Collins, was unsatisfactory. She was late most mornings, much of her work had to be retyped and she had not respected the confidentiality of her work. Seek an assurance that future temporary staff will be properly selected.

Dear Sirs

We acknowledge receipt of yours of the 20th in connection with us not paying our rates for the half-year preceding this one.

Will you please accept our most sincere apologies for the delay which was caused because the girl who was dealing with this matter was suddenly taken very ill and was hospitalised. We had not realised that this rate demand had not been cleared, but we are now in the process of settling all our overdue accounts and have pleasure in sending you our remittance for £208.10 which we trust will settle our debt. We rung you last week to let you know but the person who was dealing with this wasn't there to speak to.

We would assure you most sincerely that we had no intention of avoiding payment as we always endeavour to meet our obligations, but hope you will understand notwithstanding that this was an entirely unforeseen situation beyond our control. Please forgive us for any inconvenience we have caused.

Yours sincerely

Tan Jones

Figure 33

Task 6.4   You are working in the offices of the Jobline Personnel Agency.
  Draft a circular letter which can be distributed to all companies in the locality advertising the firm's services.
  You should adopt a manner and style which will encourage firms to do business with you.

Task 6.5   You work in the public relations section of Westleigh District Council, assisting Mr R Kimber (see Fig. 14).

Trainee
This won't do our image any good! How can we improve situation? Pl. draft a reply to letter.
RK. 4/1/8

22 Abbot's Way
LUTON
Beds
30 January 198.

Dear Sir

I am writing to complain about the poor treatment I received when I visited your offices recently.

Having just obtained a job in the area, I came to enquire about houses in the district. As I would like to live in a fairly quiet locality, I wanted to find out about proposed developments in the town, shopping facilities, schools, playgroups and rates payable.

When I explained this to your receptionist, she directed me to the Housing Department who said they couldn't help me as they only dealt with Council Houses. I was then sent to the Finance Department who were only prepared to give information on rates. After that I gave up.

It has been difficult for me to find the information I require from other sources and the attitude of your staff has put me to considerable inconvenience.

Surely it is not too much to expect a local authority to have such information readily available for the public and to employ properly trained receptionists?

Yours faithfully
Alan Clarke.

Figure 34

Read the letter from Mr Clark (Fig. 34).

Investigation of the matter reveals that the receptionist on duty has only been employed for 3 months and does not know the proper procedure for dealing with inquiries or what is dealt with by the various departments. She is also overworked as she has to man the switchboard as well as deal with callers.

1 Discuss in groups the implications for the receptionist, the organisation and the general public and suggest how to improve matters.
2 Reply individually to Mr A Clark's letter, including a paragraph expressing the number of complaints received as a percentage of total inquiries (see below).
3 Draw up a training scheme for the receptionist.

Analysis of inquiries dealt with

Department	No. of visitors	Telephone calls	Letters	Complaints about service
Technical Services	982	1500	1200	200
Finance	1500	1000	800	30
Administration	850	1250	1000	40
Planning	761	890	650	35
Housing	692	682	759	50
Environmental Health	480	595	850	25
Chief Executive	1251	1479	1460	45

Telex, telegrams and electronic mail

Sometimes it is necessary to send urgent written messages to branches, customers, agents or other organisations. The widespread use of telex, computers and wordprocessors has been accelerated by the development of international communications standards to facilitate compatibility between machines and equipment manufactured by various suppliers. However, the ease with which messages can now be transmitted electronically should not disguise the fact that these methods are still costly compared with others. Information should therefore be presented as concisely as possible.

Telex messages

The advantages of telex are described in detail on page 101.

Telex messages may be used to confirm orders, dates and instructions and to provide or request information of a routine or urgent nature.

Modern telex machines allow messages to be edited and stored before being transmitted at high speeds to other telex machines on the worldwide network.

```
Recipient's
Answerback ──────▶        281942   AL PN R

                          FOR ATTENTION OF B JONES
                          CONFIRM ACCEPTANCE OF QUOTATION
                          FOR 5000 FIVE THOUSAND PROGRAMMERS
Message ──────▶           AT 20 TWENTY POUNDS STERLING EACH
                          STOP PLEASE ADVISE DELIVERY DATE
                          OF FIRST 500 FIVE HUNDRED

Sender's Name ──────▶     MINOLTA   ITALY

Recipient's
Answerback ──────▶        281942 AL PN R
```

Figure 35 Layout of telex messages

Before sending a telex message, check that the following details have been included:

1 the message commences 'FOR THE ATTENTION OF . . .'
2 the body of the message has been checked for accuracy (spellings and figures) and content
3 the message is concise
4 the message ends with the name of the sender – the telex message in Fig. 35 illustrates the format

To send a message:

1 look up the telex number and key it in
2 wait for the answerback code to appear (this tells you the remote machine is ready to receive your message)
3 key in your own firm's answerback code
4 key in the message
5 key in your own answerback code again (this tells recipient you have finished)
6 wait for the recipient's answerback code to appear (this indicates your message has been received)

Electronic mail

Messages sent direct from one computer terminal to another are usually brief and the same routines for checking should be observed as described for telex messages.

The procedures for sending the message will depend on whether the recipient

Receiver's
telegraphic address ⟶ RAMOD

Message ⟶ CARGO SPACE SS ELISE AVAILABLE STOP
CONFIRM SHIP SAILS DEC EIGHTH STOP
DELIVER CONSIGNMENT WITH
DOCUMENTS SOON

Sender's
telegraphic address ⟶ DOMIL

Figure 36 Layout of telegrams and cables

can be contacted direct via the normal telephone system or whether you are using an electronic mailbox service such as Prestel (see page 104 for details).

Telegrams, cables and telemessages

International telegrams and cables are used for conveying urgent written messages to someone who is not a telex subscriber or who cannot easily be contacted by telephone.

As charges depend on the length of the message, brevity is essential. The normal rules of syntax can be ignored, e.g. complete sentences are not necessary but sufficient information should be included to avoid misinterpretation. Sentences are broken up with the word STOP and figures are usually spelt out in full. The word REPEAT is often used to emphasise an important detail, e.g. DO NOT REPEAT NOT SEND CONSIGNMENT. (See the example in Fig. 36).

Telemessages are used to send urgent written messages within the UK and to the USA. These should also be brief but, as the minimum charge covers up to 50 words, proper sentences can be used.

Further details are given on page 98.

Advertisements/notices

Advertisements are normally used to attract customers, suppliers or candidates for jobs.

The display and layout should be attractively designed, important points being emphasised by emboldening and enlarging text and interest provided by varying the type style. The language should be simple and brief.

As advertising is expensive, consideration must also be given to cost factors, size and length, the need for graphics, the selection of appropriate publications and the number of entries required.

22 Kingswalk
Fairoak
WESTLEIGH
Midlandshire
SO5 2PH

9 June 198.

Dear Sir

I am writing to complain about the treatment my son received when he came to the Leisure Centre last Friday.

He and a group of friends were in the cafe and one of your officers swore at him and forcibly threw him out. Your officer said that they had been there too long, — they were only drinking coffee and talking. He said unless they bought something else, they should clear off and let people using the Leisure Centre have the tables. Honestly, where else is there for them to go?

As a ratepayer, I object to your policy. You operate a public service and you should not be allowed to pick and choose who you let in.

Unless you can give me some satisfactory explanation of this incident, I shall write to my MP and inform the press.

Yours faithfully

T.R.O.D. Underfoot

Figure 37

Notices may appear in the press, on public hoardings or be posted through doors. They are often used to publicise forthcoming events such as a road closure, a planning inquiry or a public meeting.

Radio/television interviews

Local radio can be a very useful medium for publicising a firm's activities. When being interviewed, you should have a clear idea of what you mean to say and make your points or opinions simply and concisely, in as natural a style as possible. It helps if interviewers provide a list of questions in advance so that you can prepare the essence of your answers.

Task 6.6

You have been seconded temporarily to work in the Leisure Centre run by Westleigh District Council as an administrative assistant.

You receive a letter from Mr Underfoot (Fig. 37). This refers to an incident last Friday evening when Mr P Trotter, the Recreation Officer on duty, ejected a group of youths who were causing a disturbance. After twice asking them politely to leave, he ejected them. He denies swearing at the boys but admits raising his voice.

1 Draft general guidelines for staff to follow when dealing with members of the public.
2 Reply tactfully to the letter from Mr Underfoot.

Press releases

Press releases are provided to encourage the media to publicise important events, successes or changes in company policy or structure. See the example in Fig. 38.

When preparing press releases, particular care should be taken to check that:

1 the heading is clear and indicates what the story is about
2 the subject is in the first three words and preferably in the first. If an organisation's name is the subject, it should be written as simply as possible, e.g. Domilux rather than Domilux (UK) plc
3 the opening paragraph summarises the main points of the whole story
4 facts are accurate and presented logically
5 style, content, vocabulary and length are appropriate to the audience and overall requirements of the publication chosen, e.g. consider whether use of technical jargon is appropriate.
6 supporting photographs, diagrams, etc. are available
7 the final paragraph gives the name and address of the organisation
8 the deadline date for copy is met
9 the press release has the name of the author and is dated

Task 6.7

Assume that a student attending your course has been notified as the national winner of a competition in investment organised by the Stock Exchange.

PRESS RELEASE

NEW ALBEC FACTORY TO DOUBLE PRODUCTION CAPACITY

ALBEC's recent acquisition of additional factory premises

in the Boyatt Wood Industrial Estate will double the

company's production capacity during 198-.

Last year ALBEC achieved record sales for their electrical

components and Managing Director Mr Bob Jones reports that

there is every indication that the greatly increased demand

will be maintained this year. New methods of packaging the

component parts have been well received in the retail outlets

and have been instrumental in increasing sales.

The new factory at Boyatt Wood will contain a complete

production line with machine shops, welding shop, assembly

and test facilities, as well as fully equipped offices.

ALBEC began manufacturing electrical components in Westleigh

in 1982 and have since acquired several retail electrical

shops in the locality.

A photograph of the new factory is enclosed.

Press enquiries to: Issued on behalf of:

Andrew Baxter   ALBEC Limited

Tel: Westleigh 28195   16 January 198-

Figure 38

Supply details of this successful achievement in a press release for your local newspaper. Take the opportunity to provide details of the course you are attending and draw attention to the relevance of the skills the students are acquiring on the course for their successful employment in modern offices.

Key facts

To consider in selection of communication media

- cost
- need for written record
- availability of equipment
- need for personal influence
- distance
- convenience
- image required
- security
- audience
- length of message

Unit 7 *Telecommunications*

Introduction

The fast pace at which commerce and industry move today is largely due to technological advances in the field of telecommunications. It is now possible for the businessman to contact people and organisations all over the world within a few seconds by telephone; he can even hold telephone conferences with groups of people located in different cities and if their telephones are linked to television they can see each other as well. Typed messages can be sent and received instantaneously by telex; copies of documents can be transmitted to distant locations within seconds by facsimile copiers linked to telephone lines. Remote branch terminals can communicate with mainframe computers at Head Office; inter-office mail can be sent electronically from one wordprocessor to another without the need for paper copies.

With such a range of equipment to choose from, it is important for administrative staff to keep up-to-date with developments so that they can influence the acquisition of equipment and systems which best suit their own and their organisation's needs.

Telephone equipment

Switchboards

Modern private electronic (digital) branch exchanges have push-buttons and are computer-controlled. Many functions are carried out automatically by a computer and this has brought about a drastic reduction in the number of telephonists needed in a large organisation as well as minimising the amount of office space required to house the equipment. Facilities provided by digital exchanges may include some of the following:

- direct dialling and connection from extensions
- storage of last number called – reconnects at the press of a button
- holding and transferring of calls
- storage of regularly-called numbers in memory for automatic dialling
- simultaneous connection with several extensions
- interruption of calls to convey urgent messages

- queueing system for incoming calls
- call logging to record all outgoing calls
- ring back when free – engaged extension rings caller back when the current call is finished

Private Datel Exchanges are similar to electronic switchboards but are used to control the transmission of digital data between computers and terminals or between computers.

Telephone answering machines

These machines are particularly useful for organisations which receive urgent calls at all hours or for small concerns where there is frequently no-one to man the telephone, e.g. at lunchtime. It should be remembered, though, that an answering machine is no real substitute for personal contact and may be offputting for customers.

The two main types of equipment in use are:

1 Answering machines which give callers a pre-recorded message, e.g. to tell them the office is closed or to ring an alternative number.
2 Answering/recording machines which allow the caller to leave a message to be dealt with as soon as staff return to the office. An interrogator may be fitted to this type of machine which enables businessmen to 'phone in from remote locations and listen to messages left on their answering machine. Sales representatives and service engineers often save time and wasted journeys by using this device.

A recent development is voice-mail – a central computerised-answering system which works like an electronic mailbox. Each extension user is allocated a box number – usually the same as his extension number. Incoming messages are stored in the person's 'box' and can be retrieved either when he returns to his office or from a remote telephone. If the person is away, his messages can be diverted to another box number.

Videophones

It is possible for a telephone to be connected to a TV monitor so that callers can see each other, but the cost of calls is at present too high for it to be in general use.

Accessories

Callmakers
Callmakers are devices which enable preselected telephone numbers to be dialled automatically, thus saving time in looking up codes and numbers and eliminating human errors in dialling. They usually have an electronic memory.

Charge clock
Metering of telephone calls is possible by connecting a charging unit to a telephone.

The cost and duration of the call is shown on a liquid crystal display panel while the call is in progress.

Call logging

Logging devices may be connected to telephone systems to monitor calls made on each extension. A printout can be obtained giving details of date, time, number and exchange called, duration and cost of call.

Loudspeaking telephone

The advantage of this equipment is that the built-in microphone and loudspeaker dispense with the need for a handset, leaving the user free to take notes, search through files etc. Other people in the room can hear and join in the conversation if desired. The loudspeaker automatically cuts out when the handset is lifted for private calls.

Internal telephone systems

These systems are quite separate from the external switchboard. Extensions are linked by multi-cord cable enabling up to 30 internal stations to communicate with each other, freeing the switchboard for external traffic.

Facilities offered by these systems may include:

- individual communication between stations
- linking of several stations simultaneously for communication of the same information to different people
- one-way communication to or from a master set
- built-in microphone and loudspeaker to allow 'hands-free' conversation to take place

Small systems are frequently installed to communicate between adjoining offices, e.g. boss and secretary; doctor and receptionist.

Public telephones

Payphones

Where organisations wish to discourage staff or customers from using the telephone at the firm's expense, they may install payphones at strategic points, e.g. in the reception or restaurant areas.

Cardphones

These have been introduced by British Telecom to replace coinbox telephones. Instead of cash, they accept plastic cards – which can be purchased from post offices – on which prepaid units are encoded holographically. When the caller inserts the card in the slot, the information is read by a microprocessor and the balance of credit remaining is displayed in a window panel. During the call, the display shows the reducing balance as units are used and audible signals warn the caller when the credit is running out so that a new card can be inserted.

This system saves British Telecom the cost of collecting cash from telephone boxes and is a deterrent to vandals and thieves as well as being convenient to the user.

Telephone services

Many of the special services provided by British Telecom are described in the telephone directory.

Services available through the operator

1 Alarm calls could prevent you missing early appointments or trains. You book the call in advance and the operator rings you at the appointed time. An additional fee is payable.

2 ADC (advise duration and charge). This service is useful if you are using someone else's telephone and wish to pay for the call. The request must be made to the operator before the call is connected. An additional fee is payable.

3 Credit cards enable users to make calls via the operator without paying at the time. The cost of the calls are charged to the subscriber's account. Organisations often issue these cards to sales representatives or employees who travel a great deal. Calls can be made nationally or internationally (see also cardphones on p. 97).

4 Fixed-time calls can be booked in advance with the operator who will connect you at or near the time requested. It is a popular method of making international calls. An additional fee is payable.

5 Freefone calls are paid for by the organisation you are ringing as a way of encouraging business. To make a freefone call, you dial the operator and quote the freefone number. In some areas, calls can be made direct by dialling a special prefix first.

6 International telegrams can be dictated to the operator for delivery to most other countries and charged to your account.

7 Personal calls can be booked if there is likely to be difficulty in contacting the person you require, e.g. where the person is out of the office a great deal or staying at a large hotel. Although the operator will keep trying to contact the person, you do not start paying for the call until you are connected. Only one fee is payable irrespective of the number of attempts to place the call during a 24-hour period. It is really only worth using this service for long-distance calls.

8 Telemessages are 'telegram-style' printed messages which can be sent to any address in the UK or USA. To achieve delivery the next day, they must be telephoned/telexed to the operator before 2200 hours. Greetings for special occasions are printed on attractively-designed forms. The cost is charged to your account.

9 Transferred charge calls are used when you wish the cost of the call to be paid

for by the person you are calling, e.g. if you have no money on you. The person called must agree to accept the call before the operator will connect you. The fee is paid by the person receiving the call.

10 Other operator services include faults reports, directory inquiries, international operator services and emergency services.

Direct dialling services

Calls can be dialled direct to almost anywhere in the world – see your telephone directory for details. In addition, certain other direct dialling facilities are available:

- business news
- motoring information
- time
- tourist information in several languages
- weather information

Telephone directories

Every extension user should have quick access to telephone directories used frequently. British Telecom provides each subscriber with a copy of the local telephone directory and yellow pages free, but charges for additional copies or directories for other areas.

Teleconferencing

Audioconferencing

Audioconferencing makes it possible for two or more groups of people located anywhere in the UK and in some countries abroad to be linked simultaneously by telephone. It is an economic and flexible way to run meetings, update staff or run training courses without the expense and disruption of face-to-face meetings. Organisations can either install their own equipment or use the Confertel Bureau operated by British Telecom. Where technical matters are being discussed, simultaneous transmission of graphic information, engineering data or pictures can be achieved by the use of slow-scan TV, facsimile equipment or computer terminals.

Videoconferencing

Videoconferencing is the linking of groups of people in different locations by sound *and* vision. Although an expensive method of communication, it provides the advantages of a face-to-face meeting without the wear-and-tear of travel. It also saves travelling and accommodation costs and makes better use of people's time. Any documents, models or technical drawings being discussed can be shown in close-up on the TV monitors installed at each location.

The two main services currently available from British Telecom are:

1 Confravision. It is possible to rent two or three closed-circuit television studios – located in seven major cities in the UK – to hold videoconferences. Participants simply travel to their nearest studio, where they are linked to whichever other studios have been hired for the meeting. Groups of up to five people can participate at each location. At least 2 hours' notice is required.

2 Videostream. This service can be used by firms with their own camera and monitoring equipment. New digital technology enables colour video signals to be transmitted economically over telephone lines, making this a viable means of communication for large organisations.

Note: Costs of both these services – based on time and distance – can be minimised if the meeting is well-prepared in advance to avoid time-wasting.

Paging systems

Many large organisations use paging systems to locate staff quickly. The choice of system depends on its suitability for the particular circumstances, but those most commonly used are public address, radio paging and coded signals in the form of bells, buzzers or lights.

Public address

Messages can be broadcast over loudspeakers connected to a central microphone – usually situated in the switchboard area. Clarity of speech is essential if messages are to be understood. Although a quick and effective way of making emergency announcements in the event of fires, bomb-scares etc., over-use of the system can be irritating and distracting for staff who may ignore it altogether. PA systems are commonly used in factories, warehouses, public transport terminals and superstores, but seldom in offices.

Radio paging

Staff who are constantly on the move may be issued with pocket-sized radio receivers controlled from a central base unit – usually the switchboard. There are three types:

1 'Bleeps' emit audible signals when activated from the base unit – which prompt the carrier to report to the nearest telephone. These devices are widely used in hospitals and large organisations where the use of public address systems would be disruptive. Some radio pagers can display and store brief written messages (up to 70 characters) which saves the receiver having to telephone the office for instructions.

Note: Private systems operate only within a limited radius of the base unit. The British Telecom radio-paging service caters for the needs of customers requiring to operate outside this range.

2 One-way radio is similar to a 'bleep', but has the additional facility of being able to transmit spoken messages directly from the base unit to the radio receiver.

3 Two-way radio requires a special licence and the allocation of a wavelength.
   It is used mainly by transport fleet operators, farmworkers, security staff, large
   building firms, service engineers and the emergency services.

Transmission of text/data

Teleprinters

A teleprinter is an automatic typewriter which is capable of reproducing messages
transmitted from a distant teleprinter over telephone lines, thus combining the
speed of the telephone with the authority of the written word.

The telex service

British Telecom's telex service offers a 24-hour service to over 1½ million
subscribers worldwide. As incoming messages can be received by unattended
teleprinters – provided they are left switched on and loaded with continuous
stationery – differences in international time zones present no problem. If the
machine has a punched-tape attachment fitted, messages can be typed and proof-
read before transmission to ensure accuracy. Messages can also be prepared off-line
on typewriters, wordprocessors and telex pads fitted with tape-cutters, for automatic
transmission later at 70 wpm.

The new electronic teleprinters have many additional facilities which include:

- memories which store messages and send them automatically when required
- ability to keep calling an engaged number until the line is free
- advanced editing facilities similar to wordprocessing
- optional disc storage and visual display unit

The advantages of telex are:

- speed
- reliability of written communication
- 24-hour service
- ability to receive messages outside office hours
- foreign languages can be translated at leisure before replying
- most businesses are telex subscribers

Private teleprinter circuits

These are not connected to the telex exchange, but are used to link branches or
split sites within an organisation.

Telecopiers

Facsimile (FAX) machines are desk-top copiers which use the telephone to transmit
copies of documents to compatible receivers located anywhere in the world. The
sending machine scans the original and converts it to digital signals for transmission
over the telephone line to the receiving machine which then produces an identical
black and white copy. A conversation can be held before and after the copy is

sent (it takes only a few seconds) or copies can be received by unattended machines.

The Post Office provides facsimile transmission services (Intelpost and Bureaufax) for firms or individuals without the necessary equipment. Applications include distribution of engineering drawings to branches; transmission of export documents to ports of destination; sending advertising and news copy (including photographs) to printers; gaining access to records at Head Office.

Advantages of FAX machines over telex are:

- any originals can be sent, whether they are drawn, typed or photographed
- no lengthy training is required to operate equipment
- errors are eliminated as no intermediate treatment is necessary
- overall cost is cheaper because of fast transmission speed (scanning device 'skips' white areas of original)
- small portable machines are available which can be plugged into any telephone
- it is possible to transmit a signed copy of the original document to give it authenticity

Figure 39 Desk-top facsimile transceiver

The digital transceiver illustrated in Fig. 39 can memorise up to 50 documents destined for a maximum of five locations and transmit them when telephone rates are at their lowest.

Telephone writers

Electronic systems transmit handwritten messages and sketches to any number of receiving stations over any distance via an electronic jotting pad connected to an ordinary telephone. Whatever the caller writes on his pad is instantly reproduced

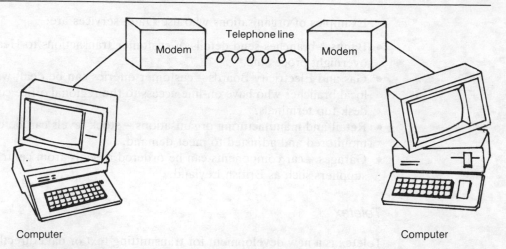

Figure 40 The Datel service

on the receiver's electrowriter. The equipment is normally used to communicate between departments on large sites or between branches of a firm, e.g. to transmit quality control data between laboratories and processing departments; to transmit prescriptions from wards to the hospital pharmacy; airline administration; to co-ordinate bookings between groups of hotels. The main advantage is that an authorisation signature is obtained immediately.

Datel

Facilities are provided by British Telecom for transmitting data/text between computers or between terminals and a central computer.

The medium used for transmitting the data/text is the ordinary public switched telephone network (PSTN). As the telephone was originally developed for voice transmission and only recognises analogue speech signals, the digital data signals produced by the computer have to be converted to analogue signals by a modem before being transmitted over the telephone network. Another modem at the remote location converts the signals back to digital data for input to the computer terminal, as illustrated in Fig. 40.

Data can be:

- prepared off-line on punched-tape for automatic transmission later
- prepared off-line and stored in the local modem for sending automatically later at cheap-rate times, e.g. at night
- transmitted to an unattended modem where it will be stored and retrieved at a later date for processing
- transmitted directly (on-line) between the computer and remote terminal if instant information/processing is required

Where branches need constant access to a central computer, private circuits can be rented from British Telecom. International datel services are also available using the packet switch stream service.

Examples of organisations who use Datel services are:

- Banks – branches send details of customer transactions to Head Office for overnight processing.
- Gas and Electricity Boards – customer queries can be dealt with instantly by local branches who have on-line access to the regional office computer via their desk-top terminals.
- Retail and manufacturing organisations – stock levels can be constantly monitored and adjusted to meet demand.
- Garages – car components can be ordered directly from central computers of suppliers such as British Leyland.

Teletex

Teletex is a new development for transmitting text or data directly from its source – a wordprocessor or computer – providing a system for electronic mail without using the postal service. It is an international electronic communications network specifically designed for use with automated text-processing machines, thus eliminating the need to convert digital signals into punched-tape form. Teletex is over fifty times faster than telex, can reproduce upper and lower case characters and all the symbols on a standard typewriter keyboard and its printouts are identical to a 'top copy' wordprocessed letter. Teletex can also be linked with telex so that the user can communicate with every terminal on the international telex network.

Viewdata systems

The use of viewdata and teletext systems as information resources was discussed in Unit 4. However, the interactive nature of viewdata – as opposed to teletext where communication is one-way only – makes systems like Prestel a valuable media for communication in the following areas.

- Electronic mail – each subscriber is given a mailbox number to which other subscribers can send messages from their own terminals. When the recipient logs on to Prestel, he retrieves the messages waiting for him and replies via his terminal.
- Telex – telex messages can be sent to telex subscribers even if they are not on the Prestel system.
- Gateway – many private viewdata systems can be accessed via 'gateways' in the Prestel system, e.g. the National Bus Company private viewdata system which links booking agents, bus stations and NBC regional offices. Only certain users are allowed access to such databases (closed user groups).
- Tele/transactions – travel bookings, teleshopping and telebanking are just some of the facilities available on Prestel, which is open 24 hours a day.

Nowadays many firms install integrated voice and data terminals which give simultaneous access to databases and telephones throughout the world. This means that users can respond to telephone queries with concise and accurate information instantaneously displayed on their screen whilst they are talking.

What of the future?

Now that British Telecom no longer has a monopoly in the provision of telecommunications equipment in the UK, a competitive market has emerged for a new wave of innovative products and services for business.

The telex system is already being updated by the faster teletex system. Electronic mail systems are expanding rapidly with services like British Telecom's 'Telecom Gold' enabling subscribers to use portable brief-case computers which can be plugged into any telephone to communicate with other subscribers. Viewdata systems are expanding and increasing their links with other databases.

Cellular radio communications could potentially eliminate the need for paging systems and office telephones. Once there is a cellular system in every area, it will be possible to make and receive calls 'on the move', wherever you happen to be, perhaps by means of a wristphone which could even incorporate a TV monitor.

The advent of cable television will also have a great impact on business as it will bring a much wider range of visual services to private individuals within their own homes via an ordinary television set, e.g. teleshopping, telebanking and even medical consultations!

The move will be towards

- integrating different technologies, e.g. voice/text transmission
- making various manufacturers' equipment compatible, e.g. enabling two different makes of facsimile equipment to communicate with each other

What will be the effects?

The effectiveness of an organisation depends to a large extent on the speed at which information can be processed, transmitted and acted upon. The new technology should enable either

- the same work to be achieved in less time giving people more leisure; or
- more work to be achieved in the same time, making the firm more effective and competitive

These aspects will be considered more fully in Units 11 and 20.

Task 7.1   You work for a telecommunications consultant. The following clients are at present seeking advice on the most suitable equipment to install for both internal and external communications.

1   A firm of travel agents with several branches.
2   A container line which imports/exports goods for firms in the UK and needs to transmit documents very quickly to agents and to be in constant contact with customers all over the world.
3   A firm of solicitors comprising: five partners each with their own office; one secretary, typist and clerk who share an office; two conveyancing clerks who share an office; and a receptionist/telephonist.

```
                              MEMO

To Trainee                          Ref:

From Office Manager                 Date:

Telecommunications

Since the new Company was set up, there have been a number

of complaints from customers and suppliers about our

telephone service. The main complaints are that

    1  our telephone is often engaged for long periods

    2  we take a long time to answer calls

    3  calls are handled inefficiently, i.e. callers are often

       transferred to the wrong person or kept waiting without

       explanation.

I am concerned that we shall lose customers if the situation

does not improve and would like to recommend to the Board of

Directors that we invest in some up-to-date equipment and

employ a full-time telephonist/receptionist. Will you please

investigate and let me have

    1  a report recommending suitable equipment which would

       (a)  cut down delays in handling calls

       (b)  allow us to communicate with customers at home

            and abroad both orally and in writing

       (c)  enable us to contact our directors quickly at any

            time

       (d)  reduce our telephone bill.

    2  a draft advertisement for the post of receptionist/

       telephonist

    3  a notice which we could circulate to staff on handling

       calls and keeping costs down.
```

Figure 41

4 A hypermarket shortly to be built in your area.
5 A service engineer who works from home without full-time office staff.
6 A new branch of a large bank which needs to be on-line to the Head Office computer.
7 A large printing firm where managers need to be contacted wherever they are in the factory.
8 A stockbroker and financial consultant who needs up-to-the-minute information on share and financial matters.
9 A road haulage firm.
10 The business you set up in Task 1.7 (page 27).

State what telecommunications equipment you would recommend in each case, giving reasons for your choice.

Task 7.2   Situation: new office manager has been appointed to ALBEC and you are employed as his assistant. He has just sent you the memo shown in Fig. 41.
    Reply to the memo as requested.

Task 7.3   Integrated assignment
Select a local organisation (full-time students may wish to use the firm where they are employed on work experience and part-time students could use their own organisation) and discover:

1 what links it has with the college, the local community, local government, central government and any organisations abroad
2 what methods of communication it uses to maintain these links and
3 what purposes are served by these links

Choose an appropriate format in which to supply the information required to your course tutor.

Key facts   Telephone equipment includes: switchboards
answering machines
videophones
callmakers
charging units
logging devices
loudspeaking telephones
internal intercom systems
paging systems
public address systems

British Telecom services include:	alarm calls
	ADC
	credit cards
	fixed-time calls
	freefone calls
	personal calls
	international telegrams
	telemessages
	direct dialling
Teleconferencing comprises:	audioconferencing
	videoconferencing
Transmission of text/data can be by:	teleprinters (including telex)
	telecopiers (FAX)
	telephone writers
	Datel service
	teletext (electronic mail)
	viewdata

Unit 8 *Records management*

Essentials for data storage and retrieval

A key activity in the administration of office work is the management of records, a process of arranging, classifying and storing documents so that they are readily accessible and can be found without delay as and when required. This process may also be referred to as information or data storage and retrieval, data processing or quite simply filing and indexing. If an organisation is to be competitive and capable of an efficient response to those who require a service from it, its records must be well-organised and systematically controlled.

The following checklist will help in keeping files accurate, complete and available when required:

1 ensure that all papers are passed (or authorised) for filing
2 keep a record of any documents removed from a file
3 keep a record when a file has to be removed from a cabinet (an absent file record)
4 file daily to ensure that files are always up-to-date
5 provide cross-references for files known by more than one name
6 adopt a file retention policy in order to thin out files regularly (see also page 112)
7 lock filing cabinets before leaving the office at night or for any length of time
8 adopt special safeguards for controlling the access to confidential files

Records are important to an organisation in providing:

- information during the process of a transaction, i.e. active/current records
- archival information, i.e. non-active files containing records of completed transactions
- information for statistical purposes
- information for audit purposes
- evidence for legal purposes
- information for government returns, i.e. VAT, income tax etc.
- data which has to be supplied to comply with the Companies Acts

Types and sources of records

Records can be preserved on paper, film or on computerised tape or disc. They are in different forms, such as:

- correspondence (incoming and outgoing letters, memos and messages)
- business documents (orders, invoices, stock cards, employee records)
- stock inventories
- reports and minutes of meetings
- mailing lists, record cards
- financial records (ledgers, journals, balance sheets)
- company documents (annual reports, memorandum and articles of association, shareholders registers)

The sources of information used to compile these records may include:

- catalogues, price lists and brochures
- quotations and estimates
- trade journals and newspapers (advertisements)
- reference books and viewdata services
- data retrieved from computer tapes and discs
- any of the business documents referred to above
- verbal exchanges and meetings

Analysing the requirements for filing

If there is a system already in use, its suitability should be determined by the following qualities:

- speed of access – delays may be attributable to unsuitable classification and/or equipment; location of cabinets too far away from users; misfiling of papers; documents removed from files and not being returned; too much correspondence retained in current files
- security – i.e. the provision made to safeguard documents and in particular confidential information
- availability of records – i.e. providing access to information when required by retaining the records for as long as is necessary
- efficient utilisation of space – this is affected by the equipment used, e.g. the type of cabinet, microfilming, computerisation
- ease of handling the materials filed – the choice here is between paper, film and computer disc/tape

The following factors will influence the requirements when setting up a new filing system:

- the quantity of records to be held at any one time
- the frequency of reference
- the speed of access required

} computer-aided retrieval would be beneficial for large quantities and for frequent and speedy reference

- the length of time documents must be retained – an important factor in determining the file retention policy
- the number and location of staff requiring access to the records – this has a bearing on the location of the filing cabinets, microfilm viewers or computer terminals
- the protection needed to guard against fire, theft and unauthorised reference – this influences the type of equipment used and security procedures such as locking cabinets, providing backup copies of discs and the use of passwords in computer systems
- The nature and size of the records and the requirements for working on them – petty cash vouchers may be filed in small loose-leaf binders, whereas large engineering drawings require storage in plan cabinets or copied on to microfilm; consider whether paper records are necessary for the users

Task 8.1   Select an organisation of your choice from those given in the case studies (day-release students should use the organisation in which they are employed) and (1) make a list of the records which are filed and the sources of information used to compile these records and (2) suggest reasons why documents may be temporarily lost and the changes that should be made to ensure greater efficiency in future.

Filing administration and management

Location

Filing can be located in an organisation at a central point or it can be dispersed in several departmental locations. As a general rule, when several departments require access to the same records it is advisable to adopt a centralised system, but if the records are of use to one department only they are better kept within that department. The points in favour of central and departmental filing are given below.

Central filing
- all files are kept and controlled together in one place
- filing staff can specialise in filing and be experts in it
- accommodation and equipment are more economically used in the central arrangement of filing cabinets
- a standardised system of filing can be maintained throughout the organisation
- more effective supervision is possible
- files are more complete as all aspects of a subject are filed together and fewer copies of correspondence are required for departments
- terminals can be used to capture computerised records held centrally

Departmental filing
- files are held in a department and are more readily available
- the type of filing system may be employed which is most suitable for the correspondence with which the department deals, e.g. an export department

would generally use a geographical system, whereas an advertising department would find subject filing more useful
- departmental staff will have a better knowledge of the work of the department and should be more expert in filing departmental papers
- it is more suitable for confidential files
- the filing system is not so large and therefore is easier to handle

Personnel

The responsibility for the overall administration of filing will normally be allocated to the office manager who will appoint a supervisor in charge of each filing unit. Where a centralised system is used, specialist filing clerks will carry out the work, but where the filing is dispersed to departments it may be undertaken by various members of staff whose duties may not be confined to filing. In some organisations it is the responsibility of the secretararies to file the correspondence they have typed.

File retention policy

If records are retained unnecessarily, files become bulky, occupying valuable space in cabinets, making retrieval of documents more difficult. It is therefore essential for an organisation to formulate a file retention policy taking into account the following:

- any legal requirement for the documents to be retained
- the need to retain documents for audit purposes
- the possible need for documents to be produced as evidence in a court of law
- working papers may not need to be retained once the matter has been completed satisfactorily
- if the records are duplicated elsewhere, both copies need not be retained
- whether the organisation would be at a disadvantage if the records could not be produced on a future date

The following are examples of suggested retention periods for a selection of different classes of documents, as recommended by the Institute of Chartered Secretaries and Administrators:

Retention period

Originals to be kept permanently	Board meeting minutes
	Memorandum and articles of association
	Register of directors and secretaries
	Register of members
	Major agreements of historical significance
	Patent and trade mark records
	Taxation returns and records
	Labour agreements
	Public liability insurance policies

12 years	Paid dividend and interest warrants Property lease documents (after lease has terminated) Payrolls Accident books Deeds of covenant (after final payment)
7 years	Staff personal records (after employment ceases) Employee expense accounts
6 years	Contracts with customers, suppliers and agents (after expiry) Rental and hire-purchase agreements (after expiry) Agreements with architects and builders (after completion of contract) Accounting records complying with Companies Acts (3 years if a private company) Cheques, bills of exchange etc. Bank statements Industrial training records Shipping documents (after shipment completed)
5 years	Wage records Customs and Excise returns Drivers' log books (after completion)
3 years	Insurance claims, correspondence and accident reports (after settlement)
2 years	Time cards and piece-work records Vehicle mileage and maintenance records MOT test records

Task 8.2   Mavis Brown, who deals with the filing at ALBEC Limited, complains that she is now short of space for storing current correspondence and that the files are becoming very bulky and difficult to handle, and in response to her manager's request she has drawn up the following list of the items of correspondence which she files:

1 copies of orders and invoices
2 correspondence with the Patent Office concerning patent rights
3 VAT records
4 correspondence with shipping agents
5 bank statements
6 copies of memos to employees relating to social activities
7 employees' individual pay record sheets
8 employees' record cards and correspondence
9 accident report forms

In a memo to Edwin Mark, the office manager, (1) suggest some general principles which should be followed in thinning out filed papers and (2) state how long you consider each of the above items should be retained by the firm.

Figure 42 Vertical filing cabinet

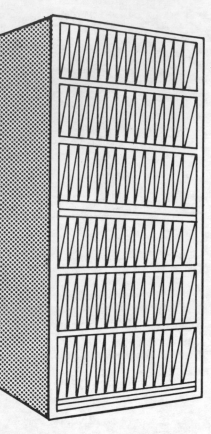

Figure 44 Lateral filing cabinet

Figure 43 Files for vertical filing

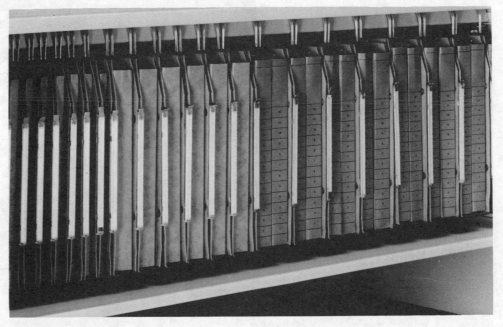

Figure 45 Lateral files

Equipment and materials

Different types of equipment are necessary for filing papers, cards, microfilm and computer discs and a selection of those currently used are given below.

Papers

Vertical filing cabinet (Fig. 42)
Papers are arranged vertically in files (Fig. 43) with title strips or labels on the top edges.

The files are suspended from metal runners fitted inside the cabinet drawers. Papers can be inserted and replaced without removing the file and the cabinets protect the contents from fire and dust.

Lateral filing cabinet (Fig. 44)
Files, as in Fig. 45, are arranged laterally with vertical title strips at the front. Space does not have to be allowed for the opening of drawers and all files can be viewed at one time.

The disadvantages are that files can become dusty because of the large opening and it can be difficult to read the file titles arranged vertically.

Rotary suspended filing unit (Fig. 46)
This system accommodates files, suspended and linked on rotating platforms, so that the filing clerk has easy and quick access to a larger number of files.

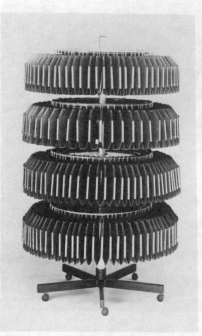

Figure 46 Rotary suspended filing unit

Figure 47 Computer printout trolley

Figure 48 Computer printout binders

Figure 49 Electronic filing system

Computer printout trolley (Fig. 47)

Binders, as illustrated in Fig. 48, are used to file computer printout and these can be housed in lateral cabinets (as illustrated in Fig. 44) or, when there is a need for the records to be portable, a trolley can be used.

Electronic filing system

This is an automatic filing system which allows files to be retrieved at the touch of a button. When a file is required, the operator keys in its index code on a push-button panel (as illustrated in Fig. 49) at the front of the filing unit and presses a retrieve button. This activates the system to locate the required file container and deliver it automatically to the operator. Once the file has been retrieved or the desired information extracted, the 'restore' button is pressed and the file container is returned to its storage location. This system can also be used for locating records kept on microfilm or computer discs.

Cards

Visible card records

Cards are fitted in flat trays in such a manner that while they overlap each other, the title of each is clearly visible (Fig. 50). Colour markers or signals may be attached to the cards to focus attention on vital facts. Transparent plastic shields can be fitted over the exposed portions of the cards to protect them from dirt and to provide a suitable carrier for signalling devices. These systems are used for records involving customers, suppliers, personnel, stock items, hire-purchase transactions etc.

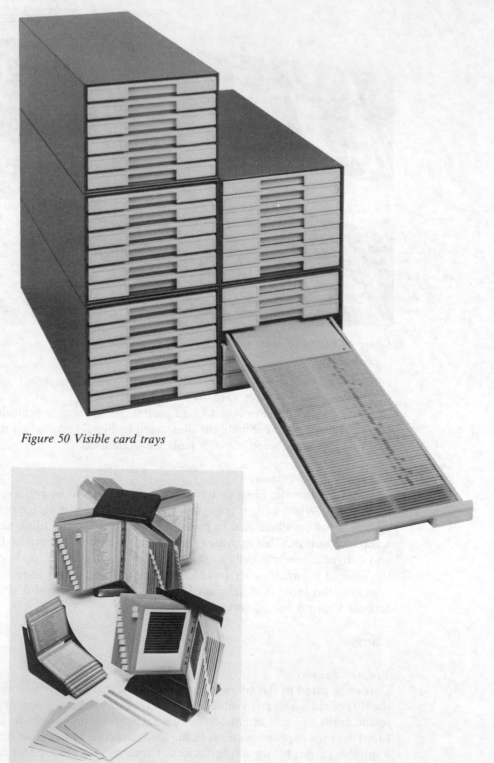

Figure 50 Visible card trays

Figure 51 Strip indexing systems

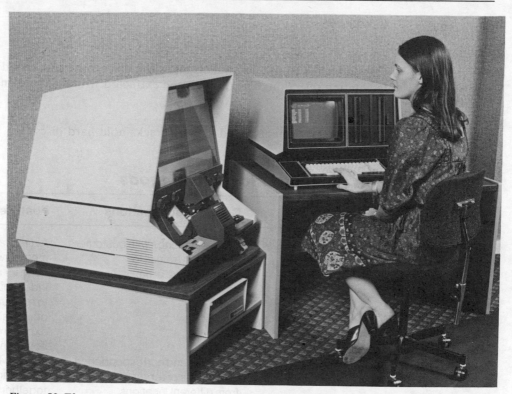

Figure 52 Electronic indexing, filing and retrieval system

Strip indexing systems (Fig. 51)

These are used for recording information on strips which are built up one above the other in containers so that all the information is visible. The strips are supplied in sheets which can be passed through a typewriter. Additions, amendments and deletions can be made without affecting the continuity of the records. The strips can be held in panels, wall fitments, books, stands, revolving units or cabinets.

Applications include mailing lists, telephone numbers, current prices of commodities and stock numbers.

Microfilm

Computer-assisted retrieval (Fig. 52)

This process is used for retrieving microfilm by computer in the following stages:

1 The original paper records are filmed by a camera and processed.
2 A VDU terminal is used to communicate directly with a computer which locates the required microfilmed document. It advances the film to the correct frame, stops it and displays it on the screen.
3 If required, a paper copy can then be reproduced by a printer.

Applications include purchase orders, invoices, stock records, personnel and customer records.

Computer

Floppy disc boxes (Fig. 53)
Clips attached to the disc wallets allow the discs to be suspended in the container facilitating selection. The discs can be extracted without removing the wallets.

Hard disc racks
Lateral metal cabinets fitted with withracks hold hard discs (Fig. 54).

File title classification methods

Method	Common applications	Features
Alphabetical by correspondent's name	Correspondence with customers or clients in a small to medium-sized organisation	A direct and quick method without the need for a separate index, but limited to small to medium-sized concerns, otherwise difficulty may be experienced in locating common names
Alphabetical by location (geographical)	Exporting and correspondence with agents or representatives from different locations	Useful where it is an advantage to group together files relating to towns, counties or countries
Alphabetical by subject	Management of an organisation, publicity, public relations	Useful where it is convenient to have all the relevant correspondence relating to one topic grouped together for easy reference
Numerical	Correspondence with a large number of clients or customers or for account records if coded and prepared by computer	File numbers can be used on letters for reference; numbered files are more easily found than alphabetical files
Numerical – decimal	Classification of books and journals in a library	Decimal numbers assist in the recall of titles

Figure 53 (top right) Floppy disc boxes

Figure 54 (right) Hard disc storage cupboards

Rules for indexing

	Examples
• The surname is placed before the Christian names and if the surnames are the same the first Christian name determines the position.	Adams, Kevin Adams, Martin
• If the Christian name and surname are contained in the name of a firm, the surname is written first followed by the Christian name and finally by the remainder of the name.	Parker, John Ltd
• If a firm has several names, the first is taken as the surname for indexing purposes.	Baker, Arnold & Weston
• The first name is taken in hyphenated names.	Ryland P Smith-Ryland B
• For impersonal names such as county councils, use the name that distinguishes it from the others for indexing purposes.	Westleigh District Council
• Names beginning with Mac, Mc or M' are treated as if they were spelt 'Mac'.	M'Bride A B McBride C D MacBride E F
• Names beginning with St are treated as if they were spelt 'Saint'	St Peter's Gallery Seaman R T
• Nothing comes before something, i.e. a name without an initial precedes a name with one.	Robert Roberts Robertson Robertson A Robertson A A
• Names which consist of initials are placed before full names.	SOS Services Ltd Sanders R P

Microfilming

Microfilming is a process for making film records of documents so that bulky originals need not be stored. They are used for recording business documents, legal documents, drawings, parts manuals, newspapers, journals and reports by reducing them in size for storage and quick retrieval.

Microfilm can be stored as follows:

- roll film – usually held in cassettes or cartridges
- a jacket can store up to 60 frames of film and can be used in situations where it is necessary to update the file periodically, such as hospital patient records
- microfiche – single sheets of film with the capacity to hold between 98 and 420 A4 documents
- computer output on microfilm (COM) – directly transferring the data from a computer on to microfilm at speeds of up to 120,000 characters per second

Microfilm can be viewed from a viewer or from a VDU on-line to a computer.
A VDU microfilm retrieval device has the ability to communicate directly with

a computer or with any other element of the electronic office, in addition to its microfilm viewing capacity. The computer records exactly where the appropriate source document is filed on microfilm and can access it very quickly, and if additional data is required from the computer this can be accessed at the same time.

A machine called a readerprinter, using either cartridges, microfiche or microfilms, simplifies searching for documents, displays them on a screen and, if required, prints copies on paper. Figure 55 illustrates this machine.

The benefits of microfilm are:

- Saving space, e.g. the total contents of a four-drawer filing cabinet can be condensed into four small rolls of microfilm and you can store up to 120,000 A4 pages on sheets of microfilm in a single A4 binder.
- Quick retrieval of documents, as it is easier to find a frame on a film than it is to search through paper files. High-speed computer-assisted retrieval (CAR) can be used to locate microfilm on a VDU.
- Film is more durable than paper and provides a more permanent record.
- Duplicates can be produced cheaply and rapidly for distribution to branches or for security purposes.
- Documents can be sent by post, especially abroad, at reduced postal rates.
- Film is tamper-proof, but for legal purposes certificates of authenticity must be filmed with the documents.

Figure 55 Microfilm readerprinter with VDU on-line to a computer

These benefits should, however, be judged against the cost of installing the necessary equipment, the time taken to film the documents and index them, and the inconvenience of having to use a viewer every time reference is made to a document.

The legal implications of microfilming

The Evidence Act 1968 allows the use of microfilmed documents as evidence in a court of law under certain conditions:

1 On any roll of film there should be, at the beginning, a 'Certificate of Intent' setting out the nature of the documents to be filmed; details from whom they were received and a statement that it is the intention to destroy the originals after the film has been inspected and found to be satisfactory.
2 At the end of the film there should be a 'Certificate of Authenticity' in which the operator declares that the microfilm is a true and correct record of the originals.

Computer data storage and retrieval

Computers are capable of storing vast quantities of data in their storage devices which consist of main storage and subsidiary storage. Main storage is used to hold the program and data for the transaction currently in hand, but once the transaction has been completed it is transferred to subsidiary storage. Data may be stored on:

- floppy discs which range from those which store about 40 pages of typed A4 data to those which accommodate about 1000 pages of A4 data
- single hard discs with capacities which range from 5 million to 75 million characters
- multiple hard discs (disc packs) used on mainframe computers with storage capacities of up to 1000 million characters

Common applications of data stored by computer include customers' and suppliers' accounts, stock control records, employee wages records, production planning, costing and budgetary control, marketing research and statistical information for management control.

Task 8.3　　Refer to the records supplied for Task 8.1 (p. 111) and suggest the filing equipment and classification methods which might be used to store them, giving the reasons for your choice in each case.

Task 8.4
1 Prepare a mailing list strip index with names and addresses in alphabetical order for all of the students in your class; and
2 Compile an alternative mailing list containing the same information but arranged geographically by students' home towns or districts.
   Note: If you have access to a computer, make a database file containing the same information.
3 Are there any advantages to be gained from using a computer database? Would the program you have used be adequate for business use? Give reasons for your comments.

Key facts

- Filing procedures

  An effective system is one which provides quick and easy reference; security; economy of space and the filed materials are easy to handle.

- Records

  Preserved on paper, film and computer discs.

- Filing administration

  Consider location; personnel; file retention policy, type of equipment; and materials and classification method.

- Filing equipment

  For papers: vertical cabinet; lateral cabinet; rotary cabinet; computer printout trolley; and electronic systems.

  For cards: visible card systems and strip indexing systems.

  For microfilm: computer-assisted retrieval systems.

  For computer: floppy disc boxes and hard disc racks.

- Classification methods

  The choice is between:

  Alphabetical: correspondent
  location
  subject

  Numerical

- Microfilming

  A process of filming documents in reduced size for quick retrieval.

- Data storage and retrieval

  The computer's 'filing cabinet' for storing vast quantities of business records.

Unit 9 *Office services*

Introduction

Office services are essential in the process of running an organisation if it is to achieve its objectives. The five stages of the functions of an office are given below together with the office services which are needed to fulfil them:

Office functions			*Office services*
1	Input	The input to an organisation – the receipt of information which is provided either by written communications (text, computer data, image) or voice.	Mailroom (incoming mail) Reception Telecommunications
2	Processing	The manipulation or conversion of information from one form to another, linking it with other data and giving it added value to the organisation.	Secretarial (typing and dictating) Reprography Stationery control Data processing
3	Storage	In different forms: paper, film and computer data.	Filing
4	Retrieval	Finding and presenting information from filed records.	
5	Output	The output from an organisation – communicating information to others.	Mailroom (outgoing mail) Telecommunications

Centralisation of services

Many firms centralise office services such as filing, typing, reprographics, mailroom, reception and switchboard. This means, for example, that instead of each department keeping its own files, there would be a central section where all paperwork is filed together; all mail would be received and despatched by one central mail section; there would be a typing centre which would supply all departments with secretarial services.

The advantages to be gained from centralisation are:

- economy of staff
- economy of equipment

127

- more even distribution of work
- more flexibility for coverage during staff absence
- better systems and equipment
- uniformity of procedures
- better control
- more effective training programmes

However, some departments have special requirements which would not lend themselves to centralisation, for example:

- personnel files are confidential and should be kept within the personnel department
- some departments need information close at hand
- some departments require constant access to a copier
- where there is a centralised typing centre, certain managers may still require their own personal secretary

Some flexibility is, therefore, essential and it is common to centralise the main services such as typing, filing, switchboard and reprographics, whilst providing limited departmental services where necessary, e.g. where there is a centralised print room, each department may have a small copier for urgent work.

Mailing procedures

Incoming mail

It is important that the incoming mail should be dealt with promptly and efficiently so that it is available for staff when they arrive at the office in the morning. The mail may be delivered to the premises by the post office or collected from the post office by one of the firm's representatives using the private bag service. If a firm requires collection to be made at other times during the day, a private box can be rented at the post office for the receipt of postal packages.

A procedure for dealing with incoming mail should make provision for:

1 careful pre-sorting of envelopes into the following categories:

	Action required
• registered mail	signed for upon receipt, opened separately and any remittances recorded
• mail marked Private, personal or confidential	delivered unopened to the persons concerned
• mail marked Urgent	opened separately and delivered immediately
• mail not addressed to the firm	reposted unopened
• all other mail addressed to the firm	opened

2 date stamping all documents
3 fastening enclosures to accompanying letters

4   checking and recording remittances received in the mail
5   copying any items of mail which have to be circulated to more than one department
6   sorting the correspondence and delivering it to a central point in each department

Outgoing mail

Outgoing mail passes through the following stages:

1   letter is checked to see that enclosures are, where necessary, attached
2   Address on the envelope is checked with the address on the letter: if there is a discrepancy, both the letter and the envelope should be returned to the typist for verification and retyping
3   letter is folded, care being taken not to fold it more than is necessary to fit into its envelope
4   letter is placed in the envelope which is sealed securely
5   envelope is weighed and stamped or franked by machine
6   first-class letters are separated from second-class letters
7   the envelopes are tied in bundles with all the addresses facing in one direction
8   special items of mail, such as registered, recorded delivery, airmail etc. which require labels or forms or have to be handed over the counter of the post office, are kept apart from the remainder of the post
9   the mailroom clerk completes the day's entries on the franking machine control card and if it is the end of the week sends it to the post office
10 the mailroom clerk arranges for the mail to be delivered to the post office, completes any necessary forms and collects the receipts; instead of the clerk having to deliver large quantities of mail, arrangements can be made for a postman to collect it from the office provided that the necessary quantities are being despatched

Machinery can be used to speed up the procedure for dealing with outgoing mail if the volume of mail justifies it. The following are examples:

- addressing machine for addressing envelopes
- collating machine for sorting and collating documents
- jogger for vibrating papers into alignment for stapling and binding
- folding machine for automatic folding of documents
- sealing machine for moistening and sealing envelope flaps
- weighing machine (see below) for weighing packets for calculation of postage
- franking machine (see below) for printing postal impressions on mail
  - machines purchased or rented from approved manufacturers
  - licence required from post office
  - credit for postage must be paid in advance
  - franking machine control cards must be completed daily and submitted to the post office at the end of each week

Electronic mailing equipment
The latest electronic franking machine has push-button controls for selecting postage values and can record the total value of postage used for individual batches

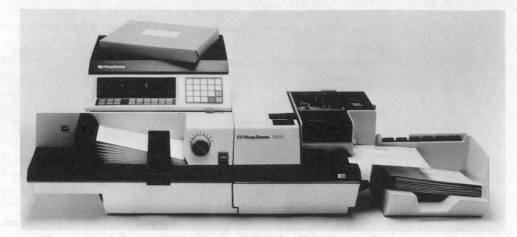

Figure 56 Combined electronic weighing and franking machine

of mail. The amounts keyed in are displayed in a digital display panel. A built-in memory can reveal how much credit is left, how much postage has been used or how many items have been franked. An electronic franking machine can also be linked to electronic scales which automatically combine the weighing, postage calculation and franking operations. The scales calculate the exact postage rate and set the correct postage value in the franking machine. These electronic machines are illustrated in Fig. 56. A remote meter resetting system using a special telephone data pad enables you to purchase additional units and reset your franking machine by telephone without having to visit the local post office.

When electronic scales are used, there is no need to refer to postal rates as these are programmed into its memory. To obtain the correct amount of postage for a packet, you place it on the scales and press the appropriate key for the service required, e.g. first class, and the rate appears instantly in a digital display panel. It can also reveal the exact weight if this is required for customs declaration forms.

Electronic mail
Electronic mail does not have to be placed in an envelope, stamped and posted in the normal way as it is transmitted electronically over telephone lines from one wordprocessor to another which may be situated in another town or country. Teletex (operated by European postal authorities) provides the necessary services for communicating text by wordprocessors at speeds of up to 3500 words per minute.

Task 9.1

1 Design a suitable layout plan for the mailroom at the Head Office of Domilux (UK) plc, taking into account principles of layout given in Unit 16. The receipt and despatch of mail is centralised at this firm, and, because of the large volume handled, modern equipment is in use.
2 Suggest how you would organise a system for dealing with the despatch of mail to the five regional sales managers and the four plants.

3 In what ways would the mailing procedures for the Jobline Personnel Agency differ from those operated by Domilux (UK) plc?

Reception

Visitors gain their first impression of an organisation at the reception desk and are greatly influenced by the manner in which they are received. The caller gains a favourable impression when:

1 The reception office is tastefully furnished and tidy. Decorative plants enhance the appearance of an office.
2 The receptionist is pleasant, polite, helpful, smart and well spoken.
3 The visitor is made welcome and well looked after, e.g.:
    (a) invite him to sit in an easy chair while waiting
    (b) supply him with an appropriate newspaper/journal to read
    (c) if there is a delay, apologise and offer a cup of coffee or tea and keep him fully informed of the position
4 A record is kept of callers expected and callers received.
5 The visitor is introduced correctly to the firm's representative by announcing his name, title and company clearly.
6 The receptionist uses the visitor's name during conversation with him. The efficient receptionist will know by name the visitors who call regularly.
7 The receptionist is tactful and helpful when a visitor (without an appointment) cannot see the person requested. In such cases, arrangements are made for the visitor to see someone else or another appointment is arranged on a mutually agreed date.
8 The receptionist has a thorough knowledge of the organisation, its activities and personnel and can supply information to visitors without having to consult others.
9 Full information is immediately available concerning the organisation as well as local hotels, train/air services, telephone numbers etc.

Telecommunications

See Unit 7.

Secretarial services

Typewriting, audio-typewriting and wordprocessing functions are carried out by secretarial staff working either in individual offices or in a centralised typing centre. Typing centres are usually more economical where there is a large amount of routine typing, whereas dispersed individual office facilities are more effective for serving the needs of executives requiring a personal service and where the nature of the work is confidential. An increasing number of offices are now being equipped with electronic typewriters, but there are still many manual and electric typewriters in use.

Basic electronic typewriters

These have automatic electronically controlled margin settings; paper feed; pitch selection (i.e. width of characters); tabulation stops; carriage return; and repeat keys. They also have automatic correction facilities, including a small memory of approximately 132 characters. Errors are corrected by backspacing and overtyping.

Memory typewriters

Memory or 'intelligent' typewriters have a larger correction memory (approximately 500 characters) than the basic electronic typewriters. Some have a visual display window which makes correction easier and allows the typist to correct errors as they are made and before the print is committed to paper. Other features include formatting storage, i.e. retaining tabulation settings in the memory; automatic centring and additional print and pitch selection, including emboldening, i.e. printing characters in bold type.

Text editing and text processing machines

These have larger memories which are capable of storing 8, 16 or 32 kilobytes (abbreviated K). A byte is the amount of memory required to store one character and a kilobyte represents 1024 bytes (or characters). A machine with a capacity of 8 K has a memory capable of storing up to 8192 characters and is, therefore, able to store several pages of text. The larger machines have a working memory for editing text at the point of typing and also a backing store in which floppy discs are normally used. They also have a visual display screen to aid the typist in editing and processing text. When a piece of work has been typed in its final form, it can either be automatically printed on paper and cleared from the memory or transferred to a floppy disc for permanent storage.

Wordprocessors

Wordprocessors are screen-based systems, i.e. the operator's key actions are displayed on a screen. The amount displayed varies between full page, half page and single line according to the type used. The text can be stored on hard discs, floppy discs, magnetic tape or magnetic cards for subsequent amendment or printing. Wordprocessors are normally capable of:

- editing text on the screen by inserting new material and deleting unwanted material
- adding or deleting paragraphs
- moving words, sentences, paragraphs and columns to other parts of the page
- automatic numbering of pages
- justifying margins, i.e. providing equal and perfectly straight left- and right-hand margins
- scrolling text vertically and horizontally on the screen, i.e. moving the cursor through text from one position to another

- holding data in a buffer store for later use
- allowing documents to be merged or a mailing list to be merged with a circular letter
- printing one page of a document whilst the operator is typing the next page
- allowing a number of documents to queue for printing in turn
- underscoring, centring and indexing automatically
- verifying the spelling of words

Key factors when considering the purchase of a wordprocessing system

1 Analyse the work to be undertaken and estimate the memory capacity required, bearing in mind both current and future needs. This will normally be incorporated in a feasibility study.
2 Decide which configuration is required, such as:

(a) stand-alone (a single self-contained wordprocessor)
(b) shared resource (two or more workstations sharing the same printer and possibly storage devices)
(c) shared logic (several workstations having access to the same processor, storage devices and printer)
(d) local area network (for connecting wordprocessors, computers and telecommunications in one network)

3 Decide whether to have a dedicated wordprocessor or a microcomputer with a wordprocessing package. A dedicated wordprocessor is one which has been specially designed solely for wordprocessing.
4 Consider the need for compatibility with equipment already in use.
5 Bear in mind the costs involved:

(a) hardware (the physical parts of the wordprocessor)
(b) software (the programs and operating manuals)
(c) furniture
(d) accommodation
(e) materials (stationery, discs, ribbons etc.)
(f) training of users and authors and redeployment of staff
(g) maintenance of equipment and software packages

6 Arrange for demonstrations of various makes and seek advice from other users of the equipment.
7 Consider the changes in office procedures which must be made.
8 Consult and keep staff informed of your proposals.
9 Consider the advantages and disadvantages of purchasing equipment outright, leasing and rental schemes – bearing in mind obsolescence and the rapid changes in technology.

Common applications for wordprocessors include:

- automatic typing of standard or form letters merged with a mailing list to provide top copies of letters to selected names and addresses
- updating price lists, telephone directories, mailing lists, parts lists where amendments can be inserted without retyping all of the matter
- typing the drafts of reports, minutes, articles etc. Once the draft has been typed,

the typist can make amendments and the machine automatically reformats the pages without any further retyping and checking

Dictation equipment

There are three main categories of dictation equipment:

1 central dictation network systems used by large organisations which are either connected to a telephone system or to a separately wired circuit
2 desk-top machines
3 portable hand-held (pocket-size) recorders

Remote dictation systems

A remote dictation system consists of a recording machine or, as is usually the case, several recording machines which are operated remotely from several dictating units allocated throughout the offices. This system is particularly useful in a large office where it is not economically practicable to provide individual dictating machines for all who require facilities. Each dictator has access to a microphone, or some other form of recorder, from which the dictation is immediately transmitted to the point of transcription (the typists' room).

The dictation system can be linked either to a PABX or PBX telephone network or a separately wired circuit, and contact is made to a central bank of recording units by dialling a special number on the telephone.

A more even flow of dictation can normally be expected from a remote dictation system and this makes the even distribution of the typing easier.

Centralised dictating equipment falls into three main categories:

1 **Bank**   A bank of recorders is located in the typing centre linked by telephone to dictation points throughout the organisation. Dictation is received and controlled at the bank and allocated by a supervisor to the audio-typists who have transcription machines on their desks. Communication between the dictators and the typists is, therefore, via a supervisor and there is no direct communication.
2 **Tandem**   The audio-typist is equipped at her desk with a 'tandem' installation containing dual controls in which recording can take place on one machine while she transcribes dictation from the other. Dictation points are linked by telephone to the tandem installations and in this system direct communication is possible between the dictators and typists.
3 **Direct link**   Dictation material is relayed from remote-controlled dictation points direct to the typist with the facility of personal contact. The recording and transcribing unit can be sited anywhere on the premises and not necessarily in the typing centre. Dictation and transcription can be made simultaneously and independently of each other, e.g. the typist can begin transcribing 8 seconds after dictation by the executive.

Centralised direct-link dictation systems employ the latest technique of computer logic. When someone picks up a telephone to dictate, the system electronically compares each typist's outstanding work with her known typing speed and routes the caller to record directly on the unit of the typist able to do his work earliest.

Typing turnround time is kept to a minimum with no break in work flow between author and typist.

On the system's control panel, dials show daily work input, output and current backlog for each typist's recorder unit and the turnround time that backlog represents. This information is augmented by a continuous graph showing overall workloads. If a priority item is dictated, the typist can scan quickly forward to it and transcribe it out of sequence, while it is still being dictated if necessary. When the priority item has been typed, a digital counter guides the typist exactly to the point at which she interrupted her normal work. To clear a unit's work in an emergency, perhaps if a typist is ill, two typists can plug into one unit and simultaneously transcribe different items of work from the same tape.

A guide for the recording of dictation

At the beginning of a whole dictation:

1 Announce your name and department.
2 Indicate any special reference to be used for your correspondence.
3 Say if you wish any item to be given priority.

At the beginning of each passage:

4 Assemble your facts before you start dictating.
5 Indicate the document required and whether it is for internal or external use.
6 Mark the index or scale to show the starting point of each passage.
7 Say how many copies you require with any instructions concerning distribution.
8 Quote the reference number/file number.
9 Dictate names and addresses of correspondents or refer to their names in correspondence which will accompany the recording.
10 Say if you require a variation from the normal layout of correspondence.
11 Dictate the salutation.

During the course of dictation:

12 Indicate paragraphing and capital letters *before* the text to which the instruction refers.
13 It is advisable to dictate the full stops, question marks, colons, semi-colons, dashes, exclamation marks, brackets and quotation marks. You are not expected to dictate every comma, but you can assist the typist by the inflections of your voice. It is also helpful if you can give special instructions, i.e. 'open brackets . . . close brackets', in a slightly different tone from your normal voice, so that they can be recognised as instructions and not typed by mistake.
14 Spell out foreign and unusual words, using the phonetic alphabet (if necessary) and pronounce difficult words slowly and clearly.
15 Keep the volume of your voice as low as practicable.
16 Hold the microphone fairly close to the mouth and speak directly into it.
17 Do not speak too quickly or in jerks, but speak into the microphone at the speed which is used for dictating to a shorthand-typist.
18 Avoid clipping words using the 'on-off' switch.

At the conclusion of each passage:

19 Dictate the complimentary close.
20 If there are enclosures, state the size of envelope required.
21 If a correction has to be made, refer to it on the index slip.
22 Mark the index or slip to show the end of the passage.

At the conclusion of the whole dictation:

23 Indicate that you are signing off.

Task 9.2   Using a dictating machine, record a memo to Edwin Monk, Office Manager of ALBEC Limited, recommending the purchase of a wordprocessor for Pam Brown's use. Explain how it could be used in the firm and what steps should be taken to select a suitable machine.

Longhand drafts

Drafts written in longhand should be easy to read as otherwise they will cause difficulties for the typist and other people who may have to read them. Some typing centres actually refuse to accept badly-written work from executives as it is unproductive for the typist to spend time trying to decipher it.

Proof-reading and editing

Proof-reading
When checking work of which you were the author, remember that typing mistakes may have occurred because you made a mistake when dictating, used clumsy sentences or simply confused the typist with the instructions given. It is particularly important to check figures and spellings before reading a passage through for the general sense.

Editing
If the draft needs amending, e.g. for deletions, insertions, changes, re-sequencing etc., make sure all instructions are clear to the typist. Some of the commonly-used correction signs are given in Fig. 57.

Task 9.3   1 Read the longhand draft in Fig. 58.
2 Proof-read the typed version in Fig. 59.
3 Edit the typewritten version carefully.
4 Suggest reasons for the mistakes made in the typewritten version.

Reprography

The process of making copies or duplicates of documents for circulation is known as reprography. It is normally a centralised service as this enables the equipment and materials to be used more economically, adequate storage space can be made

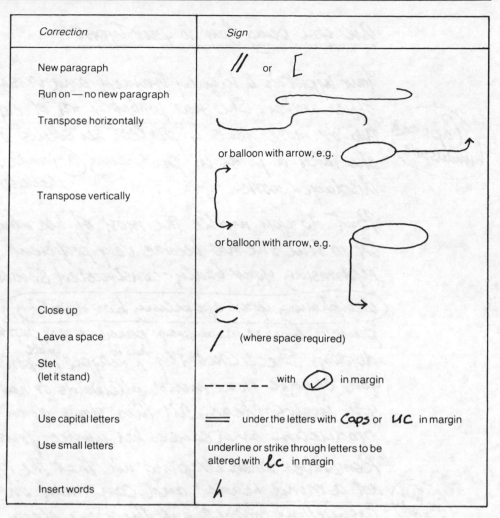

Correction	Sign
New paragraph	// or [
Run on — no new paragraph	
Transpose horizontally	
	or balloon with arrow, e.g.
Transpose vertically	
	or balloon with arrow, e.g.
Close up	
Leave a space	/ (where space required)
Stet (let it stand)	– – – – – – with ✓ in margin
Use capital letters	══ under the letters with *Caps* or *UC* in margin
Use small letters	underline or strike through letters to be altered with *lc* in margin
Insert words	⋏

Figure 57 Commonly-used correction signs

available for them and specially trained staff can be employed in providing a good-quality service for all departments.

The principal methods of reproduction are:

- carbon paper and carbon-free paper (NCR)
- duplicators
- copiers
- wordprocessors and computers

Duplicators

Although there are still a few spirit and stencil duplicators in use today, most organisations use an offset-litho duplicator. In this process the litho image on the plate is offset in negative form on to a rubber blanket and then transferred from the blanket into positive form on copy paper. The litho image on the plate accepts ink but repels the water.

Are you being fair to your typist?

Your typist is a highly trained and versatile office worker. She has probably att'd college for two or more years to perfect her skills & she takes a pride in producing accurate, well-displayed work.

Caps and underscore.

check sp.

But do you make the most of her abilities? It is true she has become very proficient at rephrasing your badly-constructed sentences, deciphering your appalling handwriting, inserting punctuation re-arranging paras & improving your display. She frequently has to retypes whole reports because you change your mind afterwards or have not made your instrs clear. All this slows down her rate of production and causes her unnec. frustration.

"Remember when drafting wk that the typist is not a mind reader and can only interpret instructions correctly & if they are clear. & Proper names shd be written in cap. letters, technical words & numbers shd be easy to read and instrs shd be written clearly in the margin || If there is prev corresp. this sh be attached so she can look up info such as addresses, names etc.

in the first place

✓ Pl. type in ~~single~~ ~~double~~ line spacing.

Figure 58 Badly written manuscript

Are you being fair to your typist?

Your Typist is a highly trained and vursatile office worker. She has

probably attend college for two or more years to prefect her skills

and she takes a pride in producing, accurate, well-displayed work.

But do you make most of her abilities? It is true she has become very

profisient at rephrasing your badly-constructed sentences, desiphering

your apalling handwriting, inserting punctuation, re-arranging paras

and improving your display. She frequently has to retype repotrs

because you change your mind afterwards or have not made your

instructions clean. All this slows down her rate of production and

causes her unneccesary frustration. Remember when draughting work

that the typist is not a mind reader and can onyl interpret in the

first place instructions correctly if they are clean.

Proper names should be written in caps, technical words & numbers

should be easy-to-read and instructors should be written clearly in

the margin.

If there is previous correspondance this shall be attached so she can

look up infomation such as addrresses, names etc.

Figure 59 Typewritten version of Fig. 58

Special features of the offset-litho duplicator include:

- very good quality reproduction and copy paper
- capable of reproducing large quantities, i.e. up to 50,000 copies from metal plates and 2000 copies from paper/plastic plates
- suitable for reproducing office forms

Copiers

Electrostatic copiers

An image of the document is projected on to a light-sensitive surface, a selenium-coated drum or plate, which is electronically charged. Where the original image area is dark there is a charge and where it is light there is no charge. Powdered ink is attracted to the charged 'dark' areas. Plain 'bond-type' paper is brought into contact with the drum or plate and an electrical charge beneath the paper attracts the powder from drum or plate to paper, forming a positive image. The powder is fused to the paper by heat to form a permanent copy.

The more advanced machines have a central microprocessor unit which controls and monitors all the copier's functions. It ensures that the toner supply is automatically regulated to give the best possible quality reproduction and avoid unnecessary waste. The microprocessor identifies any faults which may occur and warning lights draw the operator's attention when, for example, the paper or toner is running out, or the paper is misfeeding. Up to 30 originals can be automatically fed into the machine without the need for separate insertions by the operator. The copies can be reduced in size or enlarged and printed on different sizes of copy paper. By loading cassettes with different sizes of paper, the operator can switch from one size to the other at the press of a button. Multi-station collating devices are fitted to copiers for rapid collating and stapling of documents, a facility which enables the copier to be used for reproducing larger quantities.

Colour copiers (electrostatic)
These copiers use several different coloured toning powders to build up coloured copies of charts, diagrams, drawings, designs, sales leaflets etc. The quality of reproduction is excellent but, as it is an expensive process, it is only suitable for short runs and would only be viable for large organisations or for copy centres.

Laser 'intelligent' copiers
These are advanced copiers capable of volume copying and accepting information directly from computers and wordprocessors. The image of the original is converted into a digital electrical signal as the intermediate process instead of using a drum. This signal turns the laser on and off to reproduce the image which can be processed, transmitted to other locations or stored for later recall. The machine is in two parts: a reader and a print unit which work separately from one another, allowing one reader to be interfaced with up to three printers to produce 135 copies a minute. The printer units can be remote from the reader unit to meet the departmental copying needs of a company. Long-life toner is used which produces up to 20,000 copies at one filling.

Special features include:

- printing part of an original
- relocating parts of an original in the finished copy
- reversing out graphics or text, i.e. white on black instead of black on white
- variable reduction and enlargement

An illustration of a laser copier is shown in Fig. 60.

Laminating

Machines are available for laminating papers or cards for protection against moisture, dirt, grease and tampering. The document is placed in a machine with a heat process which seals it between layers of transparent film. It is used for noticeboard notices, valuable documents, sales literature, book or record dust jackets, menus and any papers which require protection against wear and tear.

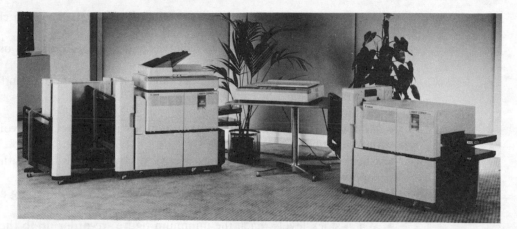

Figure 60 Laser copier

Task 9.4   What considerations should influence a firm's choice of reprographic equipment?

Task 9.5   Say with reasons which method of reprography and any ancilliary equipment you would use in each of the following tasks:

1 Six copies of a page of a trade journal has to be reproduced for internal distribution by the Director of Housing for Westleigh District Council.
2 The Personnel Manager of Westleigh District Council wishes you to reproduce a staff handbook which will be issued to all staff employed by the council. It must give a favourable impression and be easy to handle. Photographs and drawings will be included. Reprints and updated editions will be required from time to time.
3 Wendy Jones, the Sales Supervisor of the Jobline Personnel Agency, wishes you to reproduce a circular which will be sent to 100 employers advertising the agency's office services.
4 The Marketing Director of Domilux (UK) plc has asked you to reproduce 5000 copies of a two-page sales catalogue.
5 The reproduction of a file copy of a letter to be typed by Pam Brown of ALBEC Limited.

Control of stationery

It is important to utilise stationery economically and to control its use so that adequate stocks are always available.

The following are key factors for the efficient organisation of a stationery stockroom:

- Appoint one person to be in charge of issuing and ordering stationery.
- Allocate a central store room for housing stationery supplies.
- Allocate regular times for the issue and collection of supplies.

- Arrange the stationery neatly in cupboards or on shelves with clear labels at the front.
- Place heavy items on the lower shelves and arrange the items used frequently in the most accessible positions.
- Store any highly inflammable materials in sealed containers and preferably in a metal cupboard or cabinet.
- Prohibit smoking in the storeroom.
- Adopt a FIFO (first in first out) system for issuing stock to avoid deterioration.
- Check that every issue of stock is covered by a requisition, authorised by a supervisor.
- Enter every issue and receipt on a stock control card, keeping a watchful eye on stock levels.
- When stock levels reach the minimum figure, re-order up to the maximum level.

Filing

See Unit 8, Records management.

Task 9.6   What factors might management consider in reducing costs for:

1 the production of business letters
2 the use of stationery
3 the use of a telephone?

Key facts   Office services consist of:

	Mailing procedures for incoming and outgoing mail
	Reception for receiving visitors
	Telecommunications for switchboard, telex and facsimile telegraphy
	Secretarial services for typewriting, audio-typewriting and wordprocessing
	Internal printing/reprography for copying and duplicating
	Control of stationery for office supplies
	Filing for records on paper, film and computer
Centralisation	it is generally more convenient and less costly to organise office services centrally, although provision has to be made for some services to

Unit 10 *Data systems*

Most information received by an office needs processing. An employee's gross pay must be converted to net pay by working out income tax and national insurance deductions; completion of a customer's order involves informing production or stores, arranging delivery and preparing the account.

The procedures, documentation, methods and equipment used to process information all form part of a data system. Many activities are fundamental to all businesses, e.g. buying, selling and payment of wages. For these activities, the basic procedures and documentation used by different firms are usually similar, although computerisation may affect form design and reduce the need for paperwork.

An efficient data system may incorporate the following:

- controls to avoid fraud, inaccuracies and delays
- standardisation of format, e.g. external data such as customer orders may need to be converted to a standard form before being processed
- standardisation of procedures throughout the firm, e.g. for purchasing
- use of multi-form sets to save time and to avoid errors in transferring data from one document to another (see page 37)
- good form design
- use of modern technology to increase accuracy and output

Buying and selling

Figure 61 illustrates the documents which flow between a buyer and a seller in a credit transaction and the departments involved in the process.

Task 10.1

You are employed in the purchasing department of Domilux plc. The purchase requisition in Fig. 62 has been sent to you by the storekeepr.

1 Complete an order (Fig. 63), using the price list in Fig. 64. You need the panels in 10 days.
2 Referring to the document flow chart in Fig. 61, say which departments would receive a copy of the order and for what purpose.
3 A letter of inquiry is shown in Fig. 65. In what circumstances would this be sent?

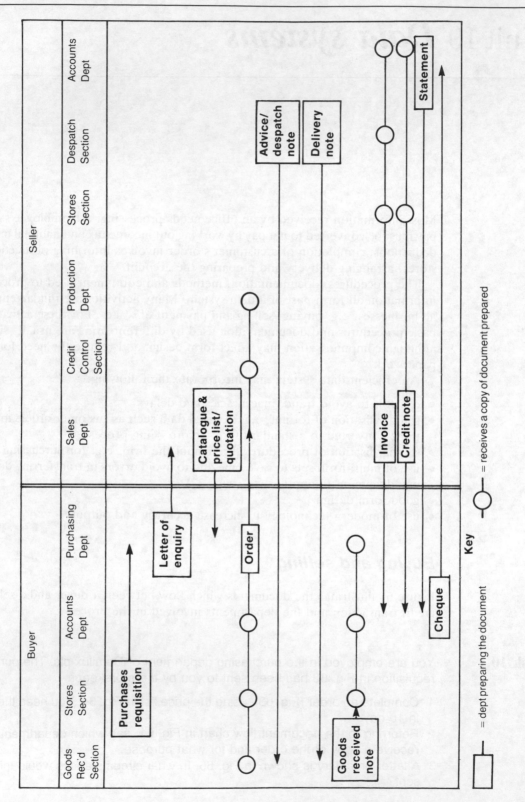

Figure 61 Document flow chart

```
                    PURCHASES REQUISITION

             No .........  651  ........................................

             Date .....  4 - 12 -8-  ...............................
```

Quantity	Description	Supplier's Cat No	Purchase Order No	Supplier
60	Control panels for automatic washing machine	HC 120	689	ALBEC

```
 Signed .........  P. Trout          Approved ......................................
                                                              Buyer
 Authorised ......  S. Sims
```

Figure 62

Task 10.2

You are working as a trainee at ALBEC Ltd in the administration section.

Reply to the letter of inquiry from Domilux (Fig. 65) using the costing information supplied below.

You will need to quote the price per unit, taking into account cost of materials and overheads and allowing for 50% net profit.

Terms and delivery 2 months; 1 month net cash; minimum order 500; 6 months' notice of cancellation of contract.

Costing information:
Pump No P1074

Qty	Items	*Bought-out components* Part No.	*Estimated price per 1000* £
1	Pump body	11095	3120.00
1	Bearing	3024	1040.00
1	Bearing	3025	1040.00
2 off	Seal	1034	370.00
1	Impeller	1060	1600.00
6 off	Screw	2048	300.40
1	Shaft	8314	2170.88
6 off	Washer	2049	209.35

Less scrap allowance 1%

Total materials cost per 1000

Overheads

Direct labour	39 hrs @ £2.96		
Fixed overheads			491.00
Carriage			60.00

Overheads cost per 1000

Date		No 689

ORDER

DOMILUX (UK) PLC
128 Hannington Lane, Westleigh, Midlandshire WM5 4AX

Telephone 225945   Telex 594928

To:		Cost code					
		Location					
		Requisition					
		VAT Reg No					

Reference	Qty	Description	Unit price	Price £	p

Special instructions	Total £	

Signed:

Figure 63

Task 10.3   You are working in the purchasing department at Domilux. In reply to the letter of inquiry sent by the Purchasing Manager of Domilux plc (see Fig. 65) the following quotations have been received:

- ALBEC Ltd (an existing supplier) can supply the pumps at £   each (see Task 10.2 for price), minimum order 500; 2 months' delivery; 1 month net cash.

- Eastham Electronics (a reputable supplier not used before) can supply them at £25 each less 17½% discount; any number; 1 month delivery; 5% cash discount one month.

- P G Philip & Co (an unknown supplier) can supply the pumps at £19 each for orders over 1000, £22.50 each for orders 500–1000; 4 months' delivery; 1 month net cash.

1 Select the most suitable supplier and draft a letter accepting the terms subject to a favourable trial period. Say that initially you will place an order for 800 pumps, to be delivered at 200 per week commencing in 10 weeks' time. If these prove satisfactory, you will sign a long-term contract for regular supplies.
2 Complete an official order for the first 800 pumps, including delivery instructions.

Task 10.4   In order to reduce the amount of typing while still retaining the personal touch, the Purchasing Manager has asked you to draft a standard letter of inquiry which could be used on the wordprocessor and to which variables can be added as required. The letter should allow for insertion of suppliers' names and addresses as well as all the details normally required on a quotation.

Receiving goods

1 When goods are delivered to the loading bay, the receiving clerk checks them against the purchase order.
2 If goods appear to be correct, the clerk signs the delivery note and sends the goods for technical inspection by Quality Control.
3 The clerk then prepares a goods received note in triplicate and sends this with goods to stores.
4 If goods are found to be damaged or short, a damage/short report is prepared for the supplier.

Distribution of copies of goods received notes and damage/shortage reports
1 Accounts (Purchase Ledger Section) to await arrival of invoice.
2 Storekeeper to enter receipt of goods on stock card.
3 Buyer to attach his copy to the order.

ALBEC
ALL BRITISH ELECTRICAL
COMPONENTS LIMITED

Telephone Westleigh 28195

Telex 281942

Registered Office: Unit 5 Boyatt Wood
Industrial Estate
WESTLEIGH
Midlandshire
WM3 2PD

Registered England No 181000

Your Ref: TM/JH

Our Ref: DP/SB

PRICE LIST

Product Code	Description	Price
		£
01135	Programmer XAC3	29.00
01136	Programmer XAC4	31.20
04205	Thermostat PO42	25.40
04207	Thermostat PO43	29.20
04209	Filter T902	0.75
03905	Filter T804	0.87
01126	Motorised Valve N931	6.80
01127	Motorised Valve N932	6.25
01129	Control panel HC 120	65.10
01130	Control panel HM 129	68.50
01135	Water pump W852	22.50
01137	Water pump W853	21.90

Directors: B Jones (MD) A Baxter C White E Monk L Symonds K Adams
D Parkes

Figure 64

DOMILUX (UK)
—— plc ——

Registration No: 103874

Registered Office: 128 Hannington Lane WESTLEIGH Midlandshire WM5 4AX

Telephone: Westleigh 225945 Telex: 594928 Cables: DOMILUX WESTLEIGH 4AX

Our Ref:

Your Ref:

Dear

Pump for Automatic Washing Machine DL/200

We are shortly launching a new type of washing machine for which we require a pump design as in the attached specification.

We expect sales to reach in excess of 20,000 over the next two years and are looking for a reliable supplier.

If you are interested, will you please let me have a quotation for supplying approximately 800 pumps per month.

Yours faithfully

DOMILUX (UK) PLC

Chief Buyer

Enc

Distribution: Prospective suppliers

                Buyer - for file

                User dept - for information

Directors: Sir Harry Paton MD B Collins A Miller G de Ville P Harmer

Figure 65 Letter of inquiry asking for a quotation

Purchase control

Most firms buy goods on credit, paying suppliers the following month after the goods have been received.

1 When the supplier's invoice is received it is checked against the goods received note and purchase order for quantities, prices, and calculations. A rubber-stamped impression is used to confirm the checking has been done.

   The purpose of this is to authorise payment and to ensure that the expenditure is posted to the correct accounts.
   If there were any discrepancies, damaged or missing goods, credit notes should have been received from the supplier and checked in the same ways as invoices.

2 If cash discount is given for prompt payment, a cheque will be sent immediately. Otherwise, the invoice is credited to the supplier's account in the purchase ledger and filed to await receipt of the monthly statement of account.

3 When the supplier's statement arrives, it is checked against outstanding invoices and credit notes before payment is authorised.

4 Once payment has been made, the supplier's account is updated and the statement filed.

Selling goods

When an order is received from a prospective customer – whether by telephone, telex, letter or in person – the following procedures and documentation are involved.

1 An order form may be received or raised containing name and address of customer, date of order, description of items, terms, delivery address, date(s) required.

Distribution:	production/stores	– works order
	accounts	– to await supplier's invoice
	sales	– to file copy

2 The customer's credit limit is checked (existing customer) or his credit-worthiness is checked (new customer).

3 An acknowledgement/confirmation of the order may be sent if there is likely to be a delay.

   | *Distribution:* | customer | – top copy |
   | | sales | – file copy |

4 An advice note may be sent to inform customer that the goods have been despatched so that arrangements can be made to receive them.

   | *Distribution:* | customer | – top copy |

5 A delivery note is sent with the goods. Prices are masked off this copy.

Distribution:	despatch (2 copies)	– 1 for customer to keep
		1 for customer to sign and return via the lorry driver
	stores	– to enter on stock record

6 The invoice (see Fig. 66) indicates the cost of the goods, VAT and terms. It is normally sent with the goods or soon after they have been despatched.

ALBEC   All British Electrical Components Ltd

Registered Office:

Unit 5
Boyatt Wood Industrial Estate
WESTLEIGH
Midlandshire
WM3 2PD

INVOICE

Telephone: Westleigh 28195

Telex: 281942

VAT Registration No. 4018592 81

INVOICE TO:

Domilux (UK) Plc
128 Hannington Lane
WESTLEIGH
Midlandshire
WM5 4AX

DELIVER TO:

Domilux (UK) PLC
128 Hannington Lane
WESTLEIGH
Midlandshire
WM5 4AX

ACCOUNT NO. 012549	CUSTOMER REFERENCE D/129	ORDER DATE 20/11/	DESPATCH DATE 2/12/	INVOICE NUMBER 3291	INVOICE DATE/ TAX POINT 2/12/	SHEET 1

PRODUCT CODE	DESCRIPTION	INVOICE QUANTITY	UNIT PRICE	PRICE PER	NET VALUE	VAT RATE %	VAT AMOUNT
01136	Programmer XAC4	16	31.20	1	499.20		
	Less 12½% discount				62.40		
				Total	436.80	15%	65.52
				VAT	65.52		
				Net Total £	502.32		65.52

Figure 66 Example of invoice

151

Distribution:	customer	– top copy
	sales	– file copy
	accounts	– to enter in sales ledger
	stores	– to enter on stock record
	despatch section	– for delivery of goods

7 A credit note may be issued for goods returned or damaged or for a downward adjustment in price.

Distribution:	customer	– top copy
	sales	– file copy
	accounts	– for sales ledger
	stores	– to enter on stock record

8 A statement of account is sent to the customer at the end of the accounting period listing all transactions during the month and any previous balances unpaid.

Distribution:	customer	– top copy
	accounts	– file copy

9 A remittance advice is usually sent by the customer with his cheque.

10 An aged debtors' list is produced periodically so that reminders of overdue accounts can be sent as necessary.

Credit control

Most customers are allowed 30 days in which to pay. The credit control function is to ensure that debts are paid on time. This involves

- checking new customers for credit-worthiness by taking up references (bank/trade/credit card company/status enquiry agent)
- setting a credit limit for each customer
- keeping an up-to-date record of each customer's purchases and payments
- chasing debts as soon as they become overdue

Task 10.5 You are employed in the accounts department of ALBEC Ltd.

1 Complete an invoice – No 3482 – to Domilux (UK) plc for the goods delivered as per your delivery note 6549 in Fig. 67; date it for 10 December 198... The price of the control panels is in the price list in Fig. 64.
Note: terms are 12½% trade discount.

2 Complete a credit note No. C210 for 5 of the control panels sent on 10 December as they were damaged and returned.

3 Complete a statement (Fig. 68) for December from the following details:

1/12 bal b/f £5692.10	(£3200.23 relates to month ending 31 October)
2/12 Invoice 3291	£500.10
10/12 Invoice 3482	see above
12/12 Credit note C210	see above
15/12 Invoice 3834	£200.00
19/12 Cheque for £3200.23	
23/12 Credit note C310	£40.50
28/12 Returned crates – credit note C315	£15.00
30/12 Cheque for £1000 received	

Delivery Note Nº   6549

ALBEC (All British Electrical Components Limited)
Unit 5, Boyatt Wood Industrial Estate, Westleigh, Midlandshire WM3 2PD

Telephone: Westleigh 28195

Telex: 281942

Customer delivery address

⌐
    Domilux (UK) plc
    128 Hannington Lane
    WESTLEIGH
    Midlandshire
    WM5 4AX
    ⌐   ⌐

Your order number	Quantity ordered	Document number
112364	60	1
Carriage details		Date despatched
Our van		6.12.8-

Quantity despatched	Balance outstanding	Description	Cat. number	Unit of issue
60	—	Control Panels	HC 120	6

WHITE COPY – Customer's delivery note   PINK COPY – Consignment note   BLUE COPY – Accounts   GREEN COPY – Stores

Figure 67

153

ALBEC LIMITED
Unit 5, Boyatt Wood Industrial Estate
Westleigh
Midlandshire
WM3 2PD

Telephone: Westleigh 28195

Telex: 281942

STATEMENT TO

⌐   ¬

STATEMENT

Page	Account No.	Date
1	0695	

⌐   ¬

		BALANCE
	B/FWD. ▶	

DATE	REFERENCE	DEBIT	CREDIT	

DETAILS OF ACCOUNT RENDERED				▲ THE LAST AMOUNT IN THIS COLUMN IS THE SUM DUE
Over 90 days	60 Days	30 Days	Current	

Figure 68

Task 10.6   You are working at Domilux Head Office and have received a monthly statement from ALBEC (see Task 10.5). There appears to be a discrepancy and you have been asked to sort it out by referring to the documents completed in Task 10.5 and the information below.

1 Invoice 3291 (see Fig. 66) was wrongly calculated.
2 You returned 4 of the programmers sent on invoice 3291 because they were faulty.

Recalculate the statement and draft a covering letter to ALBEC pointing out the discrepancies.

Computerised procedures for buying and selling

1 A wordprocessor can be used to prepare letters of inquiry or any standard letters using texts stored on a disc. Also the suppliers' names and addresses can be merged from a mailing list file to a text file to provide automatic typing in one operation of both letters and address.
2 All forms used in buying and selling can be completed on a wordprocessor, the machine tabulating to the correct positions on the forms and automatically reproducing any standard data.
3 Suppliers' and customers' records can be filed on a computer disc providing a rapid means of locating and printing details from them.
4 To order goods by computer:
  (a) the operator keys in catalogue/part numbers to reveal on the terminal screen:
   • a description of the item
   • the preferred supplier and any other suitable suppliers
   • the current price
   • discounts allowable
   • carriage charges
   • normal delivery time
  (b) the operator keys in details of the order placed to:
   • record it in the purchase record file
   • print the order at the end of the day
   • sort the orders for one supplier to be printed on the same form
5 To prepare invoices and statements by computer:
  (a) the operator keys in the code number of the customer to print out the customer's name and address on the invoice form.
  (b) the operator keys in the product code number and the quantity for each item ordered to print out the type and quantity of goods with their unit and total prices
  (c) when the last item has been entered the computer calculates and prints the gross total price of goods ordered, discounts, VAT and the net invoice price
  (d) when all of the invoices for a day have been completed, the computer can be instructed to print out:
   • the daily total of sales and if necessary the total sales for each country, region or division

- the totals of each product sold
- the totals of each product remaining in stock after the day's sales

(e) at the end of the month the statements are printed automatically from the data entered into the sales record file when the invoices and credit notes are prepared

6 If terminals are 'on-line' to a computer the following tasks are carried out automatically:

(a) when the order clerk keys in details of an order, the computer stores it on the purchase record file

(b) when the goods received clerk keys in the details of goods received, the computer checks whether these agree with the data supplied in (a) on the purchase record file

(c) when the accounts clerk keys in details from the supplier's invoice the computer checks these with the data supplied in (a) and (b) on the purchase record file and then enters the result in the supplier's account

Export procedures

The procedures required for exporting goods overseas are specialised and vary from one country to another. Whilst it is worth a large organisation such as Domilux having its own export department employing specialist staff, ALBEC uses an export agency to deal with all the formalities.

The formalities likely to be required are

- obtaining export licence
- preparing documentation for overseas importer
- preparing shipping documents
- preparing documentation for customs clearance
- certification of documents by overseas embassy and/or chamber of commerce
- distribution of documents to bank, customer, agent, carrier

The documentation which may be involved includes the following:

- Bill of lading which gives details of the vessel and ports of loading and discharge. It is required by the bank/agent as evidence that the goods have been despatched and for customs clearance in the country of destination.
- Certificate of insurance which gives details of items insured and their values.
- Certificate of origin which is signed by the local chamber of commerce to say that goods are of UK origin.
- Shipping note which usually includes name and address of exporter, importer and shipping agent, details of consignment, information about payment and delivery of documents etc.
- Movement certificate which is required for movement of goods in EEC countries.

Details of export documentation can be obtained from the Banks' Export Departments or from the Simplification of International Trade Procedures Board.

Production control

The purpose of production control is to:

- meet delivery dates required by customers
- maintain quality and quantity of output
- ensure a smooth flow of work
- keep machines and equipment in good working order
- prevent holdups and bottlenecks
- utilise resources efficiently (i.e. labour, machines and materials)

This involves

- drawing up production schedules indicating what is to be produced and when
- allocating machines and personnel
- ordering materials and components in sufficient time to meet production schedules
- supervision of production lines
- progressing of work to avoid bottlenecks and delays
- being capable of switching production to another product without delay if the situation demands it (e.g. machine breakdown or urgent customer requirement)

Documentation

- Materials schedule – provides a list of materials for any particular product.
- Operations schedule – details labour, machines and tools required.
- Cost summary – prepared from materials and operations schedules.
- Works order – gives details of quantity required and delivery date.
- Stores requisition – to book materials and tools from store as required.
- Purchase requisition – for requesting items not kept in stock.
- Job ticket – issued to operators to detail their part of the job – passed to wages section to calculate bonus payments.
- Inspection report – completed by quality control as jobs or assemblies are completed.

Stock control

The large quantities of stock kept by Domilux plc represent tied-up capital. Strict controls are necessary to ensure:

- materials are available when required for production
- stock is safeguarded against loss through theft, deterioration or damage
- overstocking does not occur
- accurate records are available for accounting purposes

Storage

All items of stock are coded for easy identification and stored in code order. Incoming goods are normally stored behind existing stock and the oldest stock is issued first to guard against deterioration, i.e. first-in first-out (FIFO). Small items such as nuts and bolts are kept in bins, whilst large items such as washing machines are stored on pallets ready for transporting to customers. Other items are stored on shelves or in large bays. Access to the stores is restricted to storemen only and there are separate counters for goods inwards and goods outwards.

Stock levels

Minimum level – the minimum stock held is enough for current production, usually 4 weeks. Stock should never fall below this level.

Maximum level – the maximum stock held for each item is calculated by maximum usage per week × maximum delivery time plus re-order level.

Re-order level – is calculated by average delivery time × average usage plus minimum level. See Fig. 69.

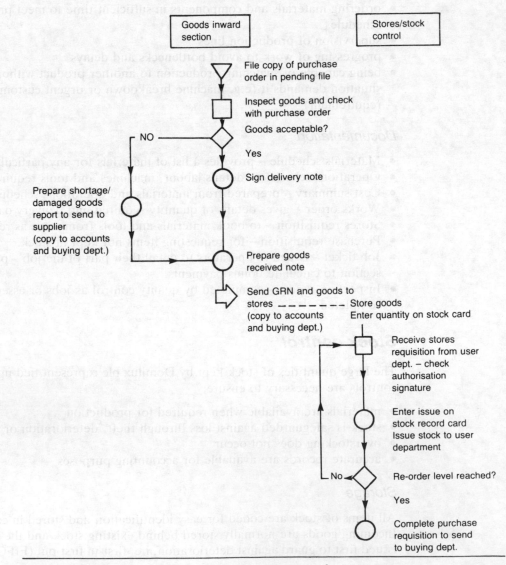

Figure 69 Process flowchart for receiving and issuing stock

Task 10.7   Work out minimum, maximum and re-order levels for washing machine motors code: 68492.

Average usage	200 per week
Maximum usage	300 per week
Minimum usage	150 per week
Maximum delivery time	8 weeks
Minimum delivery time	2 weeks

Task 10.8   **(for part-time students)**

Describe the purchasing and stock control system which operates in your own organisation.

Are there any ways in which it could be improved? You should consider such aspects as organisation, documentation, control and convenience.

Task 10.9   At your college the resources for office administration are probably kept in a central location so that students and staff may have easy access.

In order to improve the service for users, you are to carry out a review of all resources and to suggest improvements to the present system. It is suggested you work in groups of 3/4 for this exercise, each person in the group dealing with a particular category of stock, for example:

    textbooks
    leaflets
    reference books
    class exercises/assignments/computer software
    forms

1 Complete a stock inventory.
2 Devise a new or improved stock system (either manual or computerised) which will satisfy the following criteria:
    (a) a stock record is made for each stock item
    (b) information can be accessed easily
    (c) issues and receipts can be recorded
    (d) the name of the supplier is recorded
    (e) minimum, maximum and re-order levels can be shown.
3 Suggest any improvements which should be made regarding content, location or method of storage of stock.

Methods of payment

1 Cheques are the most common method of payment used by businesses.
2 Credit transfer is often used to pay wages and may also be used to pay suppliers if they request it.
3 Standing orders may be used for regular fixed payments, e.g. for lease of vehicles, rent of premises etc.

4 Direct debit is sometimes used to pay variable regular payments such as insurance or rates.

5 Cash is only normally used to pay for small items and travelling expenses. A float of money is kept by the petty cashier for these transactions.

6 Credit cards may be issued to executives such as the buyers and sales representatives so that they do not have to pay travelling, entertainment and subsistence expenses out of their own pockets. The credit card company renders an account to the firm at the end of every month.

7 When goods are bought from suppliers overseas, payment is normally made through a bank by one of the following methods:

(a) mail transfer – the purchaser instructs the bank to transfer a stated sum of money to the supplier's bank account overseas. This may be arranged by airmail, telex or computer links (electronic funds transfer);

(b) bill of exchange – this is similar to a cheque but is usually post-dated so that the purchaser does not actually pay for the goods until he receives them;

(c) documentary credit – the money is transferred to the supplier's bank before the goods are shipped but can only be credited to the supplier's bank account when he produces the bill of lading (see page 156) as evidence that the goods are on their way.

Task 10.10

1 Each director at ALBEC Ltd is issued with a credit card for business use and the accounts are paid to the credit card company by ALBEC Ltd every month. The directors use the credit cards to purchase petrol, take clients or suppliers out to lunch, pay for overnight hotel expenses etc.

The accountant has asked you to design a form which could be used to analyse the expenditure so that the appropriate expense accounts can be debited and tax allowances claimed where appropriate. The directors will be requested to complete the form when the credit card statements arrive.

The form should provide for the director's name, credit card account number, date of purchase and name of payee. The expenditure analysis should include entertaining, travel and subsistence, business petrol, private petrol, car expenses, gifts and other expenses. The form should request that any private expenditure is shown clearly and that a remittance to cover this amount must be given to the cashier as this will not be paid by the firm.

2 Some of your retail customers pay by credit card. Explain what procedures would be adopted by your firm to obtain money for such sales.

Petty cash

Small items such as office stationery, taxi fares and postage are usually paid for from petty cash. The petty cashier is responsible for a float of money from which expenses can be reimbursed on production of a petty cash voucher authorising the expenditure. The petty cash account is broken down into analysis columns to show how the money has been spent.

At the end of the period, the columns are totalled and the book balanced. The total from each column is then debited to the appropriate expense account in the nominal ledger – see Fig. 70.

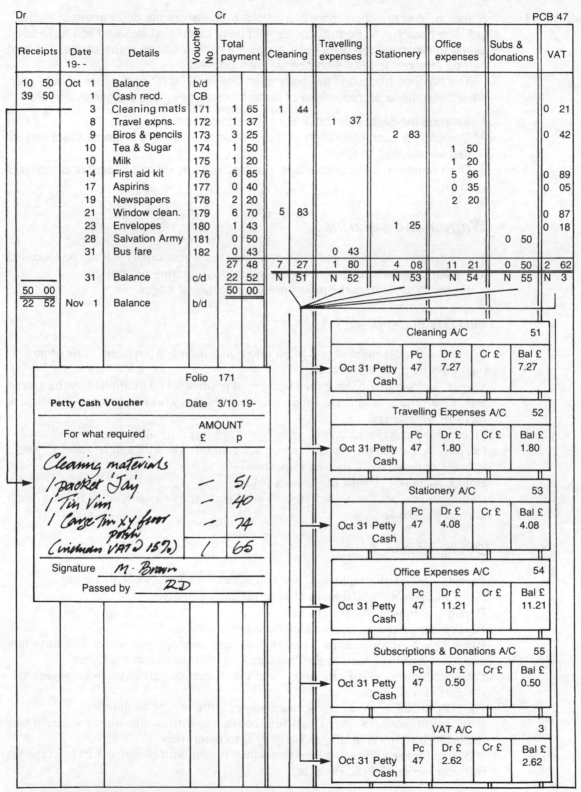

Dr				Cr							PCB 47
Receipts	Date 19- -	Details	Voucher No	Total payment	Cleaning	Travelling expenses	Stationery	Office expenses	Subs & donations	VAT
10 50	Oct 1	Balance	b/d							
39 50	1	Cash recd.	CB							
	3	Cleaning matls	171	1 65	1 44					0 21
	8	Travel expns.	172	1 37		1 37				
	9	Biros & pencils	173	3 25			2 83			0 42
	10	Tea & Sugar	174	1 50				1 50		
	10	Milk	175	1 20				1 20		
	14	First aid kit	176	6 85				5 96		0 89
	17	Aspirins	177	0 40				0 35		0 05
	19	Newspapers	178	2 20				2 20		
	21	Window clean.	179	6 70	5 83					0 87
	23	Envelopes	180	1 43			1 25			0 18
	28	Salvation Army	181	0 50					0 50	
	31	Bus fare	182	0 43		0 43				
				27 48	7 27	1 80	4 08	11 21	0 50	2 62
	31	Balance	c/d	22 52	N 51	N 52	N 53	N 54	N 55	N 3
50 00				50 00						
22 52	Nov 1	Balance	b/d							

	Folio 171
Petty Cash Voucher	Date 3/10 19-

For what required	AMOUNT £	p
Cleaning materials		
1 packet 'Jay	—	51
1 Tin Vim	—	40
1 Large Tin x y floor polish	—	74
(inclusive VAT @ 15%)	1	65
Signature	M. Brown	
Passed by	RD	

Cleaning A/C				51
	Pc	Dr £	Cr £	Bal £
Oct 31 Petty Cash	47	7.27		7.27

Travelling Expenses A/C				52
	Pc	Dr £	Cr £	Bal £
Oct 31 Petty Cash	47	1.80		1.80

Stationery A/C				53
	Pc	Dr £	Cr £	Bal £
Oct 31 Petty Cash	47	4.08		4.08

Office Expenses A/C				54
	Pc	Dr £	Cr £	Bal £
Oct 31 Petty Cash	47	11.21		11.21

Subscriptions & Donations A/C				55
	Pc	Dr £	Cr £	Bal £
Oct 31 Petty Cash	47	0.50		0.50

VAT A/C				3
	Pc	Dr £	Cr £	Bal £
Oct 31 Petty Cash	47	2.62		2.62

Figure 70 Petty cash documents

Task 10.11

Situation: You are spending a few weeks in the accounts department of ALBEC Ltd. The person who normally deals with petty cash is off sick and you have been asked to reconcile the petty cash account for the previous week so that the float can be restored to £500 (the normal balance held).

The balance of cash in the petty cash box is £200.62 and issues should only have been made on production of an authorised petty cash voucher.

1 Balance the petty cash book from the information given (Fig. 71).
2 Complete a cash requisition to the cashier requesting the amount required to restore the float to £500.
3 Draft a memo to the accountant, pointing out any discrepancies or errors you found.

Wages and salaries

The calculation of wages and salaries is one area where errors will not be tolerated and great care must therefore be taken when computing net pay.

Figure 72 illustrates the procedure for calculating wages.

Methods of remuneration

Salary – a fixed annual sum divided into equal monthly payments. Overtime is only paid by prior agreement.

Wages – calculated on the agreed number of hours worked multiplied by the agreed rate. Overtime is usually paid at a higher rate. Hours worked are recorded on clock cards or timesheets.

Piecework – calculated according to items produced or operations completed. Output is recorded on job cards which are countersigned by a supervisor. Payment is made only for work passing inspection.

Bonus systems – reward the faster worker.

Commission – paid as an incentive to sales staff and is usually in addition to their normal basic wage.

Documentation

Payroll – list of all employees' pay and deductions for a week or month

P11 – individual deduction sheet kept for each employee

Payslip – itemised pay statement

P2 – notice of coding sent to employee by tax office

P45 – 3-part form issued by an employer when an employee leaves to inform new employer and tax office of tax deducted so far in the current tax year.

P60 – employer's certificate of pay and tax deductions given to an employee at the end of a tax year

P46 – notification to tax office of employee without a code number

P30 – remittance card sent to tax office each month with cheque for tax and insurance deducted less any statutory sick pay paid to employees

P35 – employer's annual declaration which is sent with completed P11s to the tax office at the end of the tax year

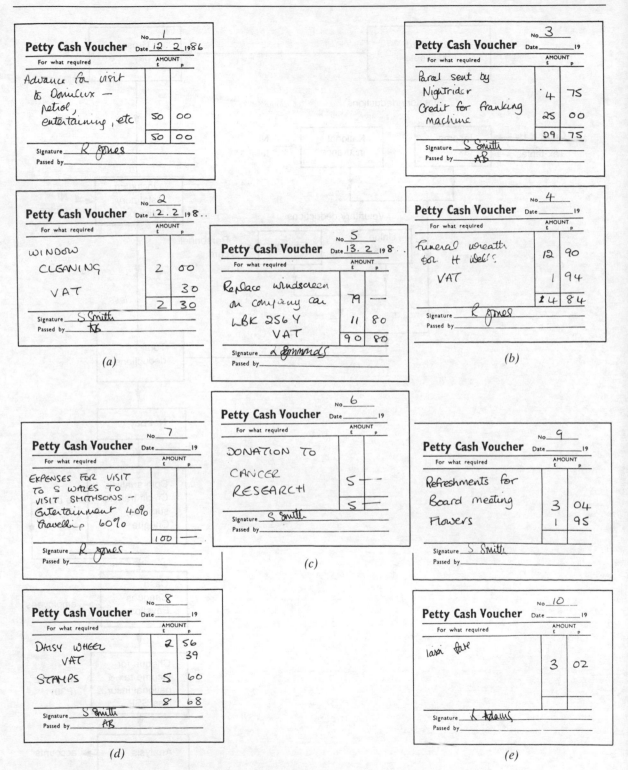

Figure 71 Petty cash vouchers for Task 10.11

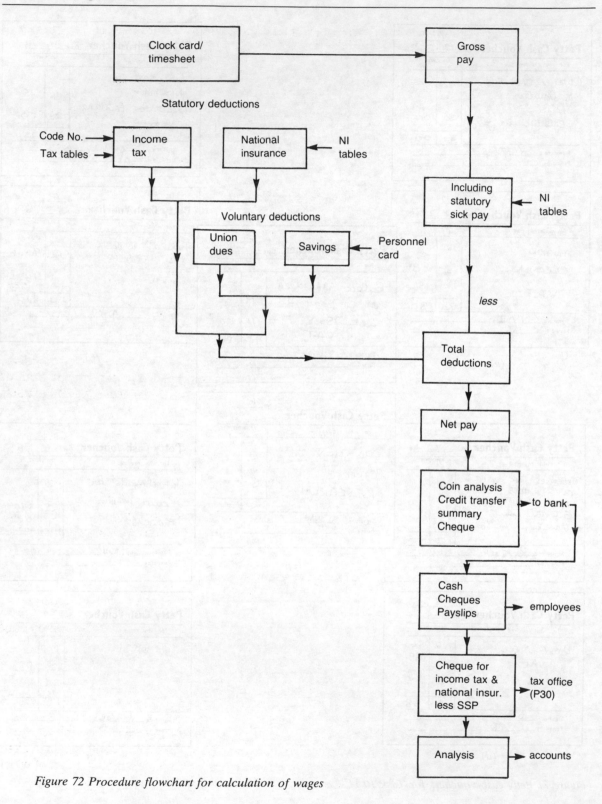

Figure 72 Procedure flowchart for calculation of wages

Tax Tables – Free Pay Tables A and Taxable Pay Tables B to D
National Insurance Tables which includes a section on statutory sick pay

Statutory sick pay

Statutory sick pay (SSP) is a scheme for most employees to receive a basic amount of pay from their employer when they are off sick for more than 3 days at a time. The employer claims back any money paid out from the Collector of Taxes, Board of Inland Revenue (see DHSS leaflet N1227 for details).

Computerised wages

When a computer is used to calculate and prepare wages, the employees' pay record sheets are stored on disc and updated each week or month. The income tax deductions and national insurance contributions are extracted from the computer 'memory' and the payroll and pay advice slips printed together with a cash analysis to indicate the number of notes and coins required from the bank. The input to the computer can be keyed in on a terminal or provided automatically by a time recording system.

Task 10.12   You are working in the accounts department at ALBEC Ltd. A new clerical trainee has just been taken on and is to spend a few weeks in your department. You will need to refer to the clock cards (Fig. 73), P45 extracts (Fig. 74) and the P11 extracts (Fig. 75).

1 Provide the trainee with the following:
    (a) a list of procedures to follow based on the flow chart in Fig. 72.
    (b) the current rate of income tax and national insurance
    (c) a brief explanation of the cash benefits covered by national insurance
    (d) an explanation of how statutory sick pay works
2 To start the trainee off, show her how to calculate the net pay for week 3 for the two employees shown below, using current tax and national insurance tables or a computer program.
    Note: Other deductions:
        Voluntary deductions – Social fund 75p – all
                            SAYE – Green £2.50
                                Smith £2.00
3 A new employee has just started. From the P45 and clock card shown on page 166, enter the details and calculate his net pay for week 3.
4 Complete a coining analysis showing coins and notes needed for pay packets.
5 Complete the employees' payslips (Fig. 76).

Task 10.13   You are working in the accounts department at ALBEC Ltd.
        The total weekly payroll amounts to over £6000 of which £4500 is paid in cash. In addition, you have a monthly payroll of £9500 for salaried staff, most of which is paid by credit transfer.

CLOCK CARD				
No 97			Name: D Moseley	
Week ending: 26 April 198-			Week No 3	

Day	In	Out	In	Out	TOTAL HOURS
M	0801	1301	1401	1701	
Tu	0759	1300	1400	1700	
W	0756	1300	1401	1700	
Th	0800	1259	1359	1601	
F	0801	1300	1400	1600	
TOTAL					

Ordinary time .... hrs @ £2.60 (up to 38 hours)	£
Overtime .... hrs @ £3.90	
TOTAL GROSS WAGES	

CLOCK CARD				
No 96			Name: S Green	
Week ending: 26 April 198-			Week No 3	

Day	In	Out	In	Out	TOTAL HOURS
M	0800	1301	1400	1700	
Tu	0756	1300	1358	1656	
W	0759	1301	1400	1701	
Th	0800	1302	1401	1804	
F	0801	1300	1400	1701	
TOTAL					

Ordinary time .... hrs @ £2.80 (up to 38 hours)	£
Overtime .... hrs @ £4.20	
TOTAL GROSS WAGES	

CLOCK CARD				
No 95			Name: R Smith	
Week ending: 26 April 198-			Week No 3	

Day	In	Out	In	Out	TOTAL HOURS
M	0801	1202	1300	1700	
Tu	0759	1200	1300	1702	
W	0802	1202	1301	1659	
Th	0801	1203	1258	1700	
F	0800	1201	1300	1602	
TOTAL					

Ordinary time .... hrs @ £2.00 (up to 38 hours)	£
Overtime .... hrs @ £3.00	
TOTAL GROSS WAGES	

Figure 73

National Insurance number:	KB 25 09 31
Name:	DAVID MOSELEY
Date of leaving:	10.10.8–
Code at date of leaving	278 H
Last entries on deduction card:	
Week No.	2
Total pay to date	£201.70
Total tax to date	£28.20

Figure 74 Extract from P45 – employee leaving – copy of employer's certificate

Employee's name:	ROBERT SMITH		SARAH GREEN	
Employer's name:	ALBEC		ALBEC	
National Insurance number:	ZT 15 86 21 A		KA 34 58 19 A	
Date of birth:	10.10.67		23.06.63	
Works No:	95		96	
Tax code:	145L		125L	
National Insurance contributions:	*Week 1*	*Week 2*	*Week 1*	*Week 2*
	£	£	£	£
Total of employee's and employer's contributions payable	14.83	14.83	20.77	21.44
Employee's contributions payable	6.86	6.86	9.61	9.92
Pay in the week including SSP:	76.00	76.00	106.40	110.60
Total pay to date:	76.00	152.00	106.40	217.00
Total free pay to date as shown by Table A:	28.06	56.12	24.22	48.44
Total taxable pay to date:	47.94	95.88	82.18	168.56
Total tax due to date as shown by Taxable Pay Tables:	14.10	28.50	24.60	50.40
Tax deducted in the week:	14.10	14.40	24.60	25.80

Figure 75 Extract from P11 – deductions working sheet

Name	Date	Works No.	Basic pay £	Over-time £	Gross pay £	Deductions				NET PAY £
						NI £	Income tax £	Other deductions £	Total deductions £	

Figure 76 Payslip

It is Monday morning and you are calculating the weekly payroll for last week ready to be paid out on Friday.

The following queries arise during the morning. State what action you would take in each case either to solve the problem or to prevent it happening again.

1 A new employee has started but has lost his P45.
2 An employee says he was £1 short in his pay packet on Friday.
3 An employee previously paid by cheque requests to be paid in cash.
4 You are unable to find an employee's individual deductions working sheet (P11).
5 An employee has been off sick five times in the last 3 months and was off sick again last week for 4 days. You suspect he is taking advantage of the SSP system.
6 The financial director has asked you for suggestions to improve security against fraud and theft.

Equipment

Just as the use of forms assists in the organisation and communication of data, so the use of equipment and machines can help to speed up the task of analysing and classifying it. Although there is now a wide variety of machines and equipment available to suit every type of data processing, unless the volume of work warrants the purchase of sophisticated technology the expense cannot be justified. Even with the current trend towards automation, there are still many organisations which rely on relatively simple methods and equipment for their clerical operations.

Some of the systems currently available are described below.

Electronic calculators

A wide variety of models is now available ranging in size from those as small as credit cards to desk-top models with a printout facility. Choice will depend on the functions required but for office use it is sensible to buy one which has a store and recall memory and which can calculate mark-ups, discounts and VAT automatically by keying in a pre-set percentage.

Manifold registers

These machines are frequently used in shops to provide a receipt or invoice for the customer. Continuous stationery is inserted in the machine and pulled across the writing surface. After the document has been written, the crank handle is operated to release the top copy for the customer whilst a carbon copy is retained inside the machine for filing.

Imprinting machines

These are used in shops where payment is made by credit card. The embossed card is inserted in a machine with the carbonised document and when pressure is exerted an imprint of the account number and customer's name and address appears on the form.

Cash registers

Most cash registers print an itemised receipt for customers and retain a copy inside on which details of all the machine's operations are printed, serving as a check against the cash takings. Some automatically record the information on to magnetic tape for computer input. Others are linked directly to the computer so that when stock codes are entered at point-of-sale the stock records are automatically updated.

Cheque-writing machines

Large organisations use cheque-writing machines for paying suppliers and employees. It is very difficult to alter the cheques and therefore provides security against fraud.

Computers

The use of computers is discussed in Unit 11.

Methods of document preparation

Handwritten

Many documents are still handwritten. Where identical information needs to be entered on more than one document, time can be saved by superimposing one on top of the other using carbons or carbon-impregnated forms. The documents can be masked or shaded where information is not required.

Typewritten

The illustration of an invoice set out on page 37 is produced on receipt of an order from a customer. The copies may be used for the advice note, despatch note, works/ stores order, accounts copy etc. These documents can be typed simultaneously using carbons or carbon-impregnated paper. The paper is usually very flimsy and copies are shaded in areas where information is not required. Each copy is a different colour to aid identification.

Master document

Where a large number of documents are required for a transaction, e.g. for export purposes, a master document is prepared which contains all details concerning the transaction. Before copies are made, any information not required for a particular document is masked off.

Computer printout

Nowadays much data processing is computerised. Integrated systems enable several documents to be generated from one input, e.g. when an order is received the details are entered into the computer which automatically creates or updates the customer's account; prints out an invoice, despatch note, works order and accounts copy; prints out a list of materials/components required to make the product if necessary; updates the stock records and generates a new order if the minimum level is reached; and prints out a monthly statement of account for the customer when required.

Whilst automated data processing is cost-effective in terms of time and labour, great care must be taken when entering the original data as any mistakes made at this stage may prove very costly if they result in the customer's requirements not being satisfied or wrong prices being charged.

Batch processing

It is usually more efficient to process documents in 'batches' rather than individually as they enter the system, e.g. the preparation of invoices can be done once a day; the processing of wages can be done once a week.

Cycle billing

Many organisations spread out the sending of statements to customers instead of leaving them all until the end of the month. This could mean customers A–G receiving statements in week 1 every month, customers H–M in week 2 and so on. This system not only evens out the workload but helps to improve the cash flow.

The main criteria to apply when considering what system to adopt for data processing are:

- will it speed up the work?
- will it save manpower costs?
- will it improve accuracy?
- will any equipment purchased be fully utilised?
- will presentation be improved?
- are changes in procedures and methods necessary?

Task 10.14   If you are in employment:

1 Review the information received, provided or processed by your section and state how it is used, processed, filed, indexed etc. You may present this information in any form. Attach as many examples as possible of forms and documents used.
2 Redesign one of the forms you use which you think needs improving and explain why (see page 263 for guidelines).
3 For this form, draw a chart to illustrate distribution of copies and their purpose (see page 257 for guidelines).
4 In the process of your work, you find that some forms become obsolescent and wastage occurs because stocks are still kept. Suggest some sensible rules for control of forms to avoid wastage and duplication whilst still retaining adequate stocks.

Task 10.15   This task relates to the business you set up in Task 1.7 (p. 28).

Now that the business has been in operation for some time, there is clearly a need for more efficient documentation systems. With your partners, discuss the documentation and systems needed and

1 Design a logo to be used on all company letters and documents.
2 Design a set of forms which you need to use in your particular enterprise, stating their purpose and distribution – see guidelines for form design on page 263.
3 Design a poster publicising your firm's services/products ready for a special trade exhibition for local firms being sponsored by the Chamber of Commerce in the near future.
4 Suggest any equipment which would increase efficiency, bearing in mind cost-effectiveness.

Key facts   *Data systems include*

Procedures	– list of routines to be followed to process information
Method	– how procedures should be carried out
Sequence	– order in which procedures should be carried out
Documentation	– forms required to record, distribute and control data
Machines and equipment	– used to improve accuracy, productivity and presentation.

Unit 11 *Information technology*

Introduction

As you will have discovered in preceding units, the processing of all types of information is being increasingly affected by computer technology.

During the last decade, wordprocessing and data processing have been encouraged to merge, making it possible for files to be accessed by more than one program. Later in this unit you will see examples of how various electronic devices can be linked together to form an integrated network of communications.

The boom in microcomputers has been instrumental in speeding up the developments in information processing as these desk-top systems, as illustrated in Fig. 77, are relatively cheap, easy to operate and very flexible in the range of applications for which they can be used. There is a wide range of software available and programs can be adapted or specially written to fit particular needs.

Portable battery-powered personal models, as illustrated in Fig. 78, now provide the opportunity for computers to be used outside the office, at home or at any place where the speedy access or inputting of data is crucial. This notebook-sized portable computer weighs less than 10 pounds, measures $13 \times 10 \times 3$ in and has a full 25-line by 80 characters LCD screen.

What is a computer system?

A computer is defined in British Standard 3527:1962 as 'any device capable of automatically accepting data, applying a sequence of processes to the data and supplying the results of these processes'.

A computer system is made up of hardware (the equipment needed to input information, process it and produce output) and software (the programs which tell the machinery what to do).

Computer configuration

An example is illustrated in Fig. 79.

Figure 77 Desk-top computer system

Figure 78 Battery-powered portable computer

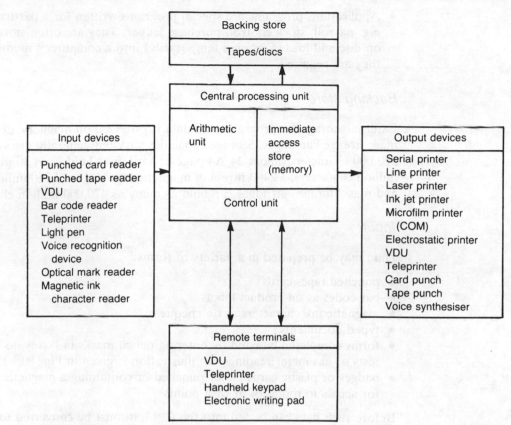

Figure 79 Computer configuration

Central processing unit (CPU)

The CPU consists of the following:

Control unit – controls the input and output devices and the order in which operations are carried out.

Arithmetic unit – performs all calculations at a very high speed in binary arithmetic.

Immediate access store (memory) – contains resident programs which control the computer and provides temporary storage for applications programs and data currently being processed. The memory's capacity is limited by the number of characters (bytes) it can hold, e.g. 16K, 32K, 256K. K represents 1024, therefore a 16K computer can hold $16 \times 1024 = 16,384$ characters. Large computers can store as many as 32 megabytes = 32 million characters.

Programs

A computer can only operate from a set of instructions which tells it what to do.

- Resident programs contain operating instructions for routine procedures such as storing files, diagnosing errors, faults etc.

- Applications programs are special programs written for a particular function, e.g. payroll, stock control, purchase ledger. They are often stored externally on disc and loaded (copied temporarily) into a computer's memory each time they are required.

Backing store

External storage for programs and data is provided on magnetic discs, tapes or mass storage cartridges. Storage capacities vary but generally discs hold about 300,000 characters (about 24 A4 pages); hard discs hold from 30 million to 300 million characters; a 2400 ft reel of magnetic tape can hold 160 million characters; and mass storage cartridges can hold as many as 470,000 million characters.

Input

Data may be prepared in a variety of forms:

- punched tapes/cards
- bar codes as on product labels
- magnetic ink characters as on cheques
- typed documents
- forms completed by hand by entering pencil marks in boxes, as in objective tests or gas meter readings; an illustration is given in Fig. 80.
- badges or plastic cards either punched or containing a magnetic strip as used for access to rooms or at cash points

Before such data can be fed into the CPU, it must be converted to a form which is intelligible to the machine, i.e. to binary characters. This involves the use of interface equipment such as the readers, sensors or scanners listed in Fig. 79 (input devices), but some methods of input do not require separate interface equipment to interpret the data. For example, the CPU can automatically convert information which is input directly via VDUs, teleprinters and light pens and process it immediately or transmit it on to tape or disc for processing later.

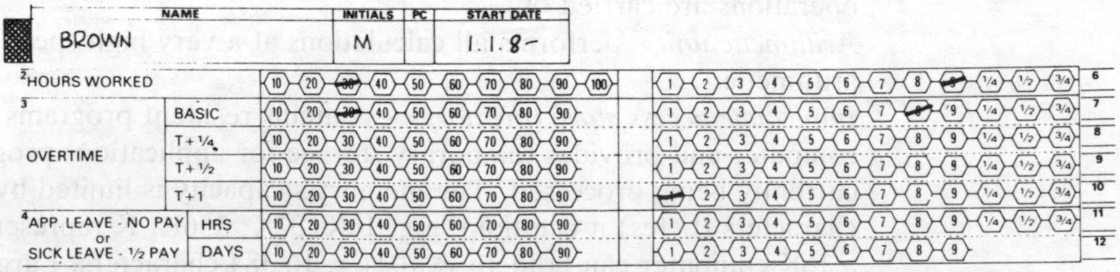

Figure 80 Mark recording document

Task 11.1　Investigate various methods of inputting information into a computer and give examples of when they are used. Comment on the suitability of each method for the example given.

Output

Information which has been processed will automatically be transferred to the storage medium, e.g. tape or disc. If the output is required as input data for another operation it may be produced in the form of punched cards or in a similar machine-readable form. Human-readable output may be produced on VDU terminals, printers or microfilm.

VDU terminals

VDUs display information keyed in or requested where no written record is required.

Factors affecting the choice of VDUs include:

- screen colour combination, e.g. black on white, orange on black, green on black etc.
- adjustable contrast control
- adjustable screen, i.e. tilting vertically and horizontally
- number of characters to a line
- anti-glare, flicker-free screen
- highlighting capacity
- reverse video effect
- amount displayed (varies from one line to full page of A4)
- scrolling capacity
- accessibility of control switches
- keyboard facilities, e.g. function keys, noise control switch, independence from VDU etc.

Printers

These provide output on forms, single sheets of paper or continuous stationery. Printers may be impact, i.e. the print head comes into contact with the paper, or non-impact and some are bidirectional, i.e. they print backwards as well as forwards.

A comparison of the various printers in use is given below:

	Printer	Print method	Approx. speed per min.
Impact	Serial (1 character at a time)	Daisywheel	3 A4 pages
	Serial (1 character at a time)	Dot matrix (draft quality)	Slightly faster than above
	Line	Drum or chain	15 A4 pages
Non-impact	Page	Laser	36 A4 pages
	Page	Ink-jet	Faster than laser
	Page	Electrostatic	120 A4 pages

Impact printers are the most commonly used as they are reasonably priced, provide very good quality output and are suitable for use with carbon sets of documents. Daisywheels are available in a variety of type styles and pitches and the printers can handle a variety of stationery.

Non-impact printers are extremely costly and are therefore only suitable for large-scale operations. They have the advantages of being fast, quiet and making no impression on copies underneath. They are, however, unsuitable for use where multi-copies are required as they can only make one copy at a time.

Factors affecting choice of printers include:

- ability to operate independently of VDU and keyboard
- facility to allow pause button to stop printing when required
- availability of acoustic hood
- quality of print
- ability to change type style and pitch

Computer systems available

1 Stand-alone systems which are totally self-contained, having their own CPU and printer.
2 Shared resource systems which have the facility of sharing printers, storage etc.
3 Shared logic systems which consist of several terminals connected to the same CPU (a minicomputer or mainframe computer) and share resources such as printers, OCRs etc. The terminals are 'dumb', i.e. they cannot operate independently of the central computer, which may slow down response time in busy periods.
4 Distributed logic systems which consist of several 'intelligent' terminals connected to the same CPU. Each terminal has its own disc drive and its own computing power enabling it to operate independently of the main computer.
5 Local area networks (LANs) consist of single coaxial cable routed round the office into which a variety of equipment may be linked via interfaces and plugs, allowing data to be transmitted from one workstation to another. The data is transferred in packets of digital signals which travel round the network until they arrive at the terminal to which they are 'addressed'. LANs can be linked to any other LAN or computer, using modems and the public telephone network (see Fig. 81).

Different levels of computerisation

See Fig. 82.

Do computers make mistakes?

Apart from problems caused by faulty electrical connections, most mistakes occur because of human error in programming or inputting information.

Program faults may occur if the programmer has based the program on wrong information. However, as with any system, a computer program should initially be run on a trial basis so that any snags can be rectified before it is put into general use.

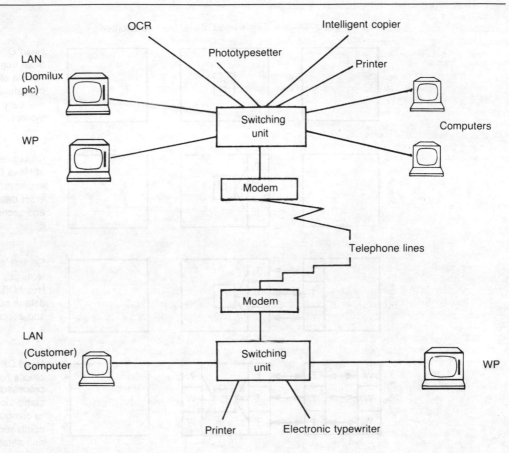

Figure 81

Input errors can be avoided by verifying data, as in the following examples:

1 Control totals – each batch of source documents can be totalled on a calculator before being put into the computer, and this total is compared with the total printed by the computer after input.
2 Machine verification – each batch of documents can be input by two different operators. Any disparities are highlighted by the computer and the second operator checks to see where the fault has occurred.

Computer applications

The major uses of computers in commerce and industry are for:

- management information
- communications
- clerical routines
- control systems
- research and design

177

Firm's remote offices	Firm's head office	Customer's office

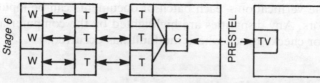

Stage 1 — Head Office has computer. Input from departments, remote offices and customers are carried manually using a batch system.

Stage 2 — Departmental terminals at Head Office linked to computer on-line to enter data in computer and access data from it.

Stage 3 — Remote offices have terminals on-line to Head Office to enter data in computer and access data from it.

Stage 4 — Head Office and remote offices have word processors which can be stand-alone or connected to computer to provide combined use of text and databases.

Stage 5 — A 'paperless office' situation in which electronic mail is conveyed direct between the firm and its customers.

Consumer's home

Stage 6 — With the aid of a 'home deck' console and TV set the consumer communicates 'on screen' to the firm from his own home to place orders, transfer money, etc. The communication is made by telephone to the British Telecom Prestel Computer Network.

Note: This is a representative selection of the various stages in technological development in offices. It does not, however, take account of micro and minicomputers which may be used in the departments and at remote offices.

Figure 82

Management information

The computer enables a wide range of up-to-date, accurate information to be available to management for fast decision-making. Sales forecasting, marketing, manpower planning, production planning, costing and budgetary control are all made easier by the computer's ability to analyse trends, compare the likely outcomes of employing various strategies and solve problems by using operational research techniques.

Databases can be set up to provide management with all kinds of information, e.g. a directory of personnel; electronic diaries; statistical information; costing information; training courses; travel information, customer mailing lists, and so on.

Communications

As you will have noted in Unit 7, the biggest leap forward in technology has been in the field of communications. Applications include:

- electronic switchboards, page 95
- telex, page 101
- electronic mailing, page 104, 130
- facsimile telegraphy, page 101
- telephone writers, page 102
- datel, page 103
- teletex, page 104
- viewdata, page 104
- wordprocessing, page 132
- intelligent copiers, page 140
- teleconferencing page 99

Further developments in communications are as follows:

- talking terminals which enable order enquiries to be keyed in remotely via a keypad linked to telephone lines; the computer gives a pre-recorded spoken answer indicating if the stock is available before the purchaser places an order
- banking – money can be transferred overseas directly by computer links (electronic funds transfer), see also page 160
- computerised typesetting in which text is automatically formatted into columns for newspapers, magazines and books; various type styles and pitches can be used for display purposes; the output is produced on positive film or bromide paper from which printing plates can be made

Clerical routines

Applications include:

- payroll, page 165
- buying and selling, page 155
- stock control, page 157
- filing, page 117, 123, 124
- accounting, page 35

Control systems

- access – entry to security areas is controlled by means of coded badges/cards or voice recognition devices
- production – many factory production operations are now performed by computerised machines, e.g. car assembly
- monitoring – dangerous processes involving fire or explosion risks and critically ill patients in hospital can be monitored by computers which alert staff to danger by emitting a 'bleep' or siren
- logging – telephone calls, use of copiers etc. can be logged to show usage by people/departments

Research and design

CAD/CAM systems are commonly used to design products, parts, architectural drawings, office and factory layouts, road systems, electrical and electronic networks. Diagrams can be projected three-dimensionally on the screen and enlarged at the press of a button.

Task 11.2   Give your views on the types of new technology which are currently being used or could eventually replace the existing conventional office systems listed below.

Conventional office	Electronic office
1 Document preparation:	
shorthand, longhand drafts	optical character recognition
dictation	
typing: cut and paste	
retyping	
error correction	
photocopy	
typesetting	
2 Message distribution:	
desk telephone	
answering machine	
telex	
courier, Post Office mail services	
meetings	
3 Personal information:	
paper-based files	
index cards	
in/out trays	
desk diary	
planning boards	
4 Information access:	
written and telephone enquiries	
mail ordering	
catalogues and timetables	
the media	
directories	

The automated office

The idea of a paperless, electronic office is not new, and there are several strong reasons why the move towards automation is accelerating:

* technology is becoming cheaper
* office overheads are becoming more expensive, i.e. staff, office space, running costs
* the mail service is declining
* equipment is becoming more compatible
* systems are more 'user friendly'
* organisations need fast, reliable communication in order to be competitive
* there is now a move towards working at home

The office of the future will be more closely integrated, i.e. the various items of equipment such as wordprocessors, copiers and telex terminals will be linked to each other and to a central computer database, providing a quicker exchange of information without the need for paperwork. Office workers will have a terminal with a screen which can communicate with terminals of other employees, customers, suppliers, banks etc. Messages will pass from one terminal to another and be held in memory banks for the storage and retrieval of records and correspondence, and electronic mail could make the mailroom, as we know it today, obsolete. The integrated network system within an organisation will also be linked to the national and international public telecommunications networks, as shown in Fig. 83, to provide instant communication between the computers and wordprocessors of different organisations. These communications can be in the form of voice, text, data and image. An electronic office is illustrated in Fig. 84.

The effects of office automation on systems and people

System changes

1 *Feasibility study.* Whenever automation is to be introduced, a feasibility study should be carried out by a team consisting of representatives from user departments, an O & M specialist (or the equivalent) and a computer systems analyst. At the end of the study, a feasibility report will be produced.

   The feasibility report should include terms of reference; details of the current system; details of the flow of information between departments; an outline of the proposed system; costs involved including hardware, software, running costs and staff; estimated savings in terms of money, time and staff; benefits to be gained in terms of efficiency, accuracy, control etc.

2 *Implementation.* This involves:

   * redesign of forms for input and output
   * coding and editing data for input
   * job redesign
   * training of staff
   * consulting user departments for feedback
   * monitoring the new system and correcting faults
   * running the new system parallel with the old system during the trial period

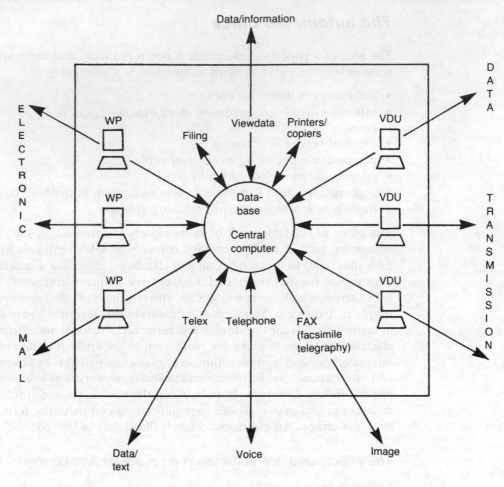

Figure 83

Environmental aspects

Although a modern computer does not need a controlled environment, as it can operate effectively between 10 and 30°C, consideration needs to be given to lighting, humidity, ventilation, temperature and noise levels. Other aspects to be considered are the design of workstations and seating, the provision of adequate power points and the flow of work.

Physical aspects

Potential health problems may arise from:

- stress caused by boredom, slow computer response time, poor environmental conditions and worry about responsibility: this can be relieved by job rotation and job redesign
- posture where workstations are poorly designed: this can be relieved by installing adjustable seating, desks of the right height and allowing regular breaks
- radiation risks are minimal, but some people think it unwise for pregnant mothers to work on VDUs.

Figure 84 An electronic office with display terminal, storage input/output units, processor, tape units and line printer

- eyestrain may be caused by glare, reflections and lack of contrast: VDU work should be carried out in shady conditions rather than in brightly-lit work areas; it is wise for operators to have eye tests periodically
- screen flicker may affect epileptics, but this can usually be avoided by adjusting VDU controls

Work changes
You will be able to appreciate the changes which computerisation makes if you compare the preparation of wages manually with a computerised system (see pages 163–5). In fact, a payroll of 200 people would take two clerks two days to complete manually, whereas one clerk would take only half a day to do the same work using a computer.

Changes in jobs may entail:

- less boring, routine calculations and transferring of information
- a greater workload compared with the manual system
- more time sitting at the desk
- coding and editing input data into numerical form
- storage and retrieval of information on computer discs or printout rather than from conventional files
- use of passwords and codes to access files instead of using keys to open cabinets

- routines for deleting, updating and copying files and logging faults
- working from home instead of in the office

Job design
The benefits of computerisation to an organisation have already been outlined, but what about the effects on people?

One of the white-collar unions, APEX, has carried out a study of the effects of automated systems on content and job satisfaction. One interesting contrast was between the jobs of production control and telesales. Whereas automation has effectively degraded the job of a production control clerk by reducing the need for making decisions and exercising skills of communication and diplomacy, the quality of work of the telesales clerk has been greatly improved by the availability of on-line information on stock, purchasing, prices and discounts.

This study points to the fact that automation is not necessarily desirable as the unmotivated production clerks are unlikely to perform as enthusiastically, efficiently or flexibly as the telesales clerks.

Care must therefore be taken to redesign jobs, with people as well as machines in mind.

This is considered more fully in Units 18 and 20.

Task 11.3   Choose any office procedure and explain how it has changed following computerisation.

Task 11.4   1 Investigate the ways in which your organisation uses computer technology. If you are not employed, suggest the ways in which computer technology could be used by one of the organisations in the case studies.

2 Working in groups of 3/4, discuss the advantages and disadvantages of these applications in terms of:

(a) efficiency
(b) accuracy
(c) cost
(d) suitability for purpose
(e) provision of information
(f) job satisfaction

3 Produce a summary of your conclusions in the form of a chart and describe the kind of organisation for which the applications would be suitable or unsuitable.

Task 11.5   Situation: On the advice of a firm of management consultants and their own office manager, the board of directors of ALBEC have decided it would be sound business practice to install a computer to deal with various administrative tasks which are at present carried out manually.
Either individually, prepare a feasibility report to the office manager;

or in groups of 3/4, prepare an oral/visual presentation to the board of directors giving details of:

1 your views for or against the proposal
2 possible areas of application
3 staffing
4 equipment required
5 costs
6 accommodation and space requirements
7 changes in systems and procedures necessary
8 any other factors and procedures necessary
   Note: See page 70–4 for guidelines on the preparation of formal reports. See page 190 for guidelines on giving oral presentations.

Privacy of information

It is becoming increasingly easy for people to access vast databanks of information both in the office and the home at the touch of a key. To protect individuals whose personal details may be recorded on various computer files, e.g. police, medical, tax, insurance records etc., the Data Protection Act was passed in 1984. This Act regulates the use of automatically processed information relating to individuals and the provision of services in respect of such information, but it does not cover the processing of personal data by manual methods.

The data protection principles include:

1 Personal data shall be processed fairly and lawfully.
2 Personal data held for any purpose shall not be used or disclosed in any manner incompatible with that purpose.
3 Personal data shall be accurate and, where appropriate, kept up-to-date.
4 Appropriate security measures shall be taken against unauthorised access to, or alteration, disclosure or destruction of, and against accidental loss or destruction of, personal data.
5 An individual shall be entitled:

   (a) at reasonable intervals and without undue delay or expense:
      • to be informed by any data user whether he holds personal data of which that individual is the subject; and
      • to access any such data held by a data user; and
   (b) where appropriate, to have such data corrected or erased.

   Individuals may also be entitled to claim compensation in certain circumstances if the data is inaccurate or appropriate security measures have not been taken.

Task 11.6

Integrated Assignment
During your second year at college, you are to chair a seminar on any relevant topic which you have either enjoyed studying on the course or which you would like to research further.

1 Prepare a paper of no more than 1000 words.
2 Read this to the class and chair a discussion.

Note: remember to read the guidelines for controlling discussions given on page 219.
Suggested time for seminar: 30 minutes.

Key facts

Office automation includes computerisation of:

communications
management information
control systems
clerical routines
research and design

Integration of systems is made possible by:

local area networks
interface equipment
telecommunications networks
programs

Installation of computers involves:

study of existing system
assessing applications
devising new system (including forms and procedures)
assessing costs (staff, equipment, overheads)
estimating savings to be made
assessing benefits to be gained
training staff
installing system
monitoring and reviewing new system
making modifications as necessary

Unit 12 *Interpersonal relationships*

Introduction

An employee is required to build and maintain relationships with individuals and groups both within and outside the organisation, the types of contact depending on his status and the nature of his job.

Figure 85 illustrates the range of relationships which might be encountered by a manager, supervisor or secretary.

The way in which people communicate will be very much influenced by these relationships and the circumstances in which communications are made.

Communications often fail when the receiver considers the manner, style or tone of the communication is inappropriate.

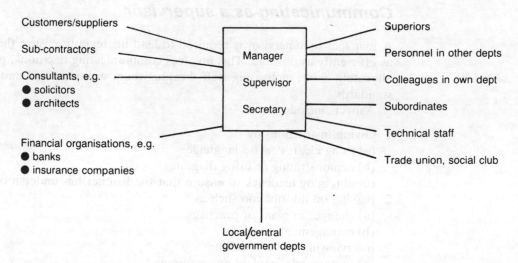

Figure 85 Relationships at work

Task 12.1

Consider the following communications:

1 Manager to secretary late on Friday afternoon: 'Can you get this letter and report typed up – they must go tonight.'
2 Supervisor to subordinate in an open-plan office: 'Why didn't you check this properly – I'm fed up with sorting out other people's mistakes.'

3 Personnel officer to office junior at teabreak in the canteen: 'You'd better make an appointment to see me about your college report.'

4 O & M officer to manager at meeting: 'I'm not very impressed with the way stock is recorded. I've come up with a much better method.'

5 Secretary to expected visitor: 'Mr Jones isn't here. He must have forgotten you were coming.'

6 Telephonist to irate caller: 'It's no use getting shirty with me – I didn't sell you the vacuum cleaner.'

7 Training officer to trainee: 'Management takes a dim view of people who make mistakes.'

8 Accounts clerk to supplier: 'We're in a bit of financial trouble at the moment, but we'll pay as soon as we can.'

9 Subordinate to manager: 'You're wrong. It works much better the way I suggested.'

10 Salesman to production department: 'If you don't get this delivered by the 10th, we shall lose the order.'

After reading the above verbal communications:

(a) Criticise them from the point of view of manner, tone and style.

(b) Suggest the reactions they are likely to produce.

(c) Suggest how they might be better worded.

Communicating as a supervisor

A manager or supervisor is required to lead his team to ensure the job is done as efficiently as possible. This involves communicating decisions, planning and allocating work, motivating staff, keeping them well-informed and maintaining standards.

Aspects include:

1 Giving instructions by
   (a) using clear, concise language
   (b) demonstrating or using diagrams
   (c) obtaining feedback to ensure that the listener has understood

2 passing on information such as
   (a) changes in plans or practices
   (b) management decisions

3 interviewing and counselling
   (a) to persuade, explain or encourage
   (b) to assist or give advice
   (c) to discipline
   (d) to reassure
   (e) to appraise performance
   (f) to deal with a complaint

Interviewing and counselling

An interview is a face-to-face conversation with a definite purpose. It therefore needs to be carefully planned to achieve its objective.

Points to consider are the

1 purpose – why it is necessary
2 content – what will be discussed in what order
3 place – where it will be held
4 timing – when and how long it will last
5 personality of subordinate:
   (a) how best to approach the individual
   (b) the degree of formality
   (c) the tone and style to be adopted

At the interview:

1 open the interview by explaining the purpose and setting the tone
2 listen carefully (see page 192)
3 be flexible by adapting style according to how interview proceeds
4 ask open-ended questions to encourage response
5 use body language to convey approval, interest etc. (see page 193)
6 close the interview by explaining what has been achieved or what is expected of the employee

After the interview, there should be a follow-up to ensure any action agreed has been carried out.

Communicating as a subordinate

The role of a subordinate is to assist the superior by carrying out instructions willingly and precisely; being loyal and supportive; anticipating the superior's requirements; being resourceful and showing initiative. This will involve

• accepting requests courteously and without arguing
• listening properly and giving feedback to show understanding
• anticipating likely questions and having answers ready
• offering suggestions or help
• making constructive criticisms of current or proposed work systems

Communicating with a group

The types of group encountered at work are

• work groups, e.g. sections, project teams
• social groups, e.g. friends, social clubs
• committees, set up for particular purposes

Groups usually have certain characteristics which sometimes make it difficult for an outsider to be accepted, including

- a recognisable identity
- a common purpose or goal
- a hierarchy which usually includes a leader
- a code of behaviour or attitude
- control over who should be included/excluded from membership
- a united 'front' to outsiders even when there is disagreement internally

Task 12.2

1 Relate the characteristics described above to
  (a) a work group
  (b) a social group
  (c) a committee
      with which you are familiar and give examples of how they apply.
2 Give an example of an occasion when you have either been excluded from a group or excluded someone else from your group. Explain why this happened.
3 What difficulties might you encounter in communicating with a group?

Task 12.3

Communicating with a group at work may be as part of a team (see page 283), as a participant at a meeting (see page 220) or to present information to a large or small audience.

Most people at work will have loyalties to several groups and individuals.

1 Identify what these groups might be.
2 Give examples of situations when these loyalties might conflict.

Addressing a large audience

Examples of when verbal presentations may be required are:

- to launch a new product
- to deliver a financial report to the board, to the shareholders, to financial backers
- to instruct trainees on an induction course
- to present information to a committee
- to address a mass meeting of the workforce
- to make an after-dinner speech

Planning is the keynote for success and will include:

- the purpose of the speech – what you are trying to get across
- the content – facts to be included and in what order; how you are going to start and finish
- visual aids – whether you need to use OHPs, videos or slides (see page 233)
- accommodation and equipment – check availability
- notes – prepare main points of your talk on cards, just headings and 'trigger' words are sufficient

Delivery

Do	*Don't*
Start with purpose of talk, e.g. a quotation or a provocative question	Start with clichés or apologies
Use brief notes for reference	Read your speech
Speak clearly	Mumble
Keep to the time allocated	Rush
Use visual aids for complicated information	Rely on words for involved explanation
Use non-verbal signals, e.g. eye contact, facial expressions	Worry about pauses – they break the talk up
Vary your pitch of voice	Speak in a monotone
End with a summary, an appeal for action or a quotation	End by 'trailing off'

Communicating with people in other departments/ organisations

It is often necessary to liaise with people in other departments/organisations who may be of a higher or lower status. Tact and diplomacy will be needed when making requests, giving reminders or explaining reasons for delays. Although loyalty to your own department is necessary, you must always remember that the objectives of the organisation come before those of individual departments.

Interviewing buyers/salesmen

When interviewing buyers or salesmen, skills needed include the ability to

- think very quickly
- interpret facts and figures quickly
- make quick decisions
- say 'no' firmly and politely
- negotiate
- present information clearly and concisely
- recognise personality traits and utilise them to your advantage
- remain calm under pressure

Interpersonal skills

Most of a manager's time is spent in communication of one kind or another: 30% of this time is spent in talking and 50% in listening. It is surprising that relatively few managers have learnt how to listen well.

Task 12.4
1 Try to think of three people at work or college who you feel are bad listeners. In each case, list the reasons why you feel this way.
   You will probably have thought of things like

- interrupts while I'm still speaking
- is always too busy
- misunderstands what I say
- makes assumptions
- never lets me finish
- only hears what he wants to hear
- doesn't seem interested
- looks at his watch
- fidgets
- doesn't look me in the eye

2 Now assess yourself as a listener using the list you have just made.

Listening for success

The main reasons for listening are

- to obtain information for later recall – most people forget what they hear very quickly
- to understand how a person feels

You will find it beneficial to form better listening habits by

- actively concentrating
- ensuring there are no interruptions, e.g. telephone calls
- avoiding distractions such as noise, poor seating, doodling
- making eye contact and using body language (see page 193)
- asking open-ended questions like 'Tell me about . . .'
- asking for facts
- probing for more information, e.g. 'In what way do you feel . . .'; 'Could you give me an example?'
- giving encouragement by interjecting with verbal and non-verbal messages, e.g. 'I see', 'I understand', nods, smiles, leaning forward
- repeating back what the speaker has said to show you are trying to understand and that you are interested
- summarising to condense the information
- taking only very brief notes as this can impair your listening

Benefits of good listening include
- finding out information
- learning about people and how their minds 'tick'
- improving relationships and morale
- obtaining new ideas and suggestions
- discovering why employees are not performing well
- help with solving problems

Speaking skills

Speaking skills involve

- thinking before you speak
- structuring what you have to say logically
- good use of vocabulary
- good timing
- good pronunciation and articulation
- avoiding annoying mannerisms

Non-verbal communication

Non-verbal communication is the use of 'body language' to replace or reinforce the spoken word. The ability to interpret non-verbal signals is of great importance in relating to how people feel. For example, a shrug may indicate extreme dissatisfaction; raised eyebrows may indicate that the words 'Yes, I'll get it to you by 4 o'clock' really mean 'You're a bit optimistic.'

Some common examples of body language are listed below.

Expressions, gestures and movements

- narrow/widening eyes
- looking at/looking away
- frowns
- wrinkling/dilating nose
- pursing/smiling/grimacing mouth
- head movements
- pointing/drumming/clenching fingers
- tapping feet

Physical contact

- slap on back
- shaking hands

Posture

- leaning back/forwards in chair
- hunched up
- arms folded

Task 12.5   List examples of body language you have observed and describe what they convey to the listener in different situations.

Barriers to communication

Certain psychological and physical barriers between people may distort the communication process and cause misunderstandings and confusion.

1 Status – communications between superiors and subordinates tend to be rather cautious, the superior wishing to maintain authority and the subordinate protecting himself from criticism. A formal and rigid 'line' relationship may funnel the process of communication too narrowly, restricting the dissemination of information.

2 Educational/social background – differences sometimes cause feelings of inferiority/superiority.

3 Age, sex, culture – natural differences may affect outlook and perception.

4 Language – misunderstanding and incorrect interpretation may result from the use of inappropriate or ambiguous language, i.e. vocabulary or sentence construction may be too difficult or too simple. This is particularly the case where specialist or technical jargon is used.

5 Background knowledge – lack of expertise or knowledge of a subject may impair understanding.

6 Manner/tone – tone, gestures, facial expressions and mannerisms may convey disapproval, disbelief, aggression etc.

7 Preconceived judgement – either party may have already made up his mind about the outcome and therefore be unreceptive or only hear what he wants to hear.

8 Rivalry/jealousy – personality clashes or guarding of one's own area of work may affect objectivity and the degree of co-operation given.

9 Perception – sometimes people view situations in a completely different light, e.g. what may appear as initiative to one person may be seen as high-handedness by someone else.

10 Poor listening – inattention results in lack of knowledge and misconceptions.

11 Lack of time – executives may always be 'too busy' to talk except by appointment, engendering a feeling of remoteness and lack of involvement.

12 Physical surroundings – lack of privacy, visual/oral distractions or badly-arranged furniture may inhibit discussion.

13 Distance – where offices are spread out, it is often impracticable to communicate verbally except by telephone. Closed doors also inhibit would-be communicators.

14 Self-esteem – people may be afraid to speak their mind in case they expose a weakness.

If these barriers are recognised, many of the problems can be fully or partially overcome. For example, a room can be booked for confidential discussions; avoidance of technical jargon will put a person at ease; allowance can be made for someone who may be at a psychological disadvantage. Many executives adopt an 'open-door' policy, encouraging staff access to discuss routine or urgent matters whenever convenient without waiting for an appointment. In the long run this often results in saving rather than wasting time – particularly if staff discipline themselves by keeping to the point – and it certainly pays dividends in terms of promoting good staff relationships.

Task 12.6   You are working as a personnel assistant at Westleigh District Council Offices. During the course of your work you are required to communicate with staff at all levels.

Part A
For each of the following situations explain

(a) what form of communication you would use;
(b) the barriers you might encounter and the techniques you would use to overcome them.

Situations
1 Inform a trainee that his work has received an adverse report from a departmental manager.
2 Inform a departmental manager that his expenses appear to be unreasonably high.
3 Indicate to a junior employee that her progress is satisfactory but that her manner of dress is not really suitable.
4 Inform an employee aged 45 that his application for promotion has been rejected.
5 Notify a trade union representative that cutbacks will be required and 10% of the staff in his section are to be made redundant.
6 Invite internal candidates for promotion interviews.
7 Introduce details of a staff appraisal scheme.
8 Persuade a rather formal executive to comply with management policy by adopting the use of Christian names with all staff.
9 Inform an employee that he worked insufficient hours last month on the flexitime system and must make it up this month or have pay deducted.
10 Placate your superior who has accused you of going over his head by putting forward a suggestion for a seminar to *his* superior instead of routing it through your direct superior.

Part B
In pairs, carry out the interviews required for 1 and 10, adopting appropriate roles.

Task 12.7   Give a short talk to your group on one of the following topics:

● addressing a large audience
● interviewing and counselling
● telephone techniques
● chairing a meeting
● interviewing salesmen
● giving instructions

People in Organisations

Key facts

Interpersonal relationships are influenced by

- the status of the sender and receiver of a message
- the circumstances in which the message is communicated

Conflict may occur when an employee

- has more than one boss
- has loyalties to opposing sides as in, for example, a trade union dispute
- has personal relationships with business colleagues outside work

Barriers to communication include

- status
- sex/age
- poor listening
- language, tone and style
- perception
- distractions
- personality clash

Interpersonal communication can be improved by

- developing good speaking and listening skills
- taking into account line relationships, possible barriers to communication, the context of the communication

Unit 13 *Work planning*

Introduction

You will by now have realised that your studies become easier to manage if you organise and plan your workload to make maximum use of your time. In the same way, when you are at work, you will be a much more efficient employee and achieve greater productivity if you

- have a work routine for recurring activities
- establish priorities
- meet deadlines
- co-ordinate tasks to meet overall objectives

By planning routine or expected tasks in advance you will not only get more work done but you will also find time to fit in unexpected tasks in the confidence that nothing has been overlooked.

Types of planning

Work plans are normally

- long-term, e.g. policy planning by board of directors for next 5 years
- medium-term, e.g. departmental plans to implement policies made by board
- short-term, e.g. day-to-day planning of activities required to fulfill objectives

Whereas long-term plans are of a very general nature, medium-term plans will be more detailed and include budgeting and staffing considerations. Short-term plans are made by individuals to enable them to organise and plan their own activities to meet the general objectives. All plans should be reviewed periodically.

Methodical working

Inefficiency

- costs money: jobs take longer or are done badly
- loses business: slow response to enquiries; incorrect information or goods sent; promises not kept

- loses respect: for employer by his seniors; for employee by his employer and colleagues

Efficiency is

- more impressive
- more economic
- conducive to: promotion; pay increase; job satisfaction; greater responsibilities; better working relationships

Planning ahead allows

- smoother working
- better control
- freedom from the stress of trying to remember everything

It is therefore important to look at routines and planning more closely.

How to plan

1 Make a list of any routine activities that occur periodically and note them in your diary.
2 Always plan ahead, e.g. next day's jobs the day before, next week's jobs the previous Thursday/Friday.
3 Write everydown down – make general notes first, then add more detail as time gets closer.
4 Use aids such as diaries, bring-forward systems, charts.
5 When planning your day:
   (a) assess priorities by deciding what must, should or could be done
   (b) do priority jobs first
   (c) do difficult jobs in the morning.
6 Look ahead to ancitipate future requirements.

Task 13.1   Situation: You are working in the Head Office of Domilux plc and are spending a month in the sales office with Tom, Matthew, Ann and Richard. You noticed that while the supervisor was away, several problems occurred:

1 Telephone enquirers seemed to be kept waiting a long time while clerks searched through files on their desks or papers in their trays.
2 Matthew seemed to be working on several queries at a time and was constantly being chased.
3 Ann kept running out of items of stationery.
4 You received a telephone call from an irate customer who said that the sales clerk had promised to ring back. When you finally discovered that Tom had taken the original call, he said he had no record but vaguely remembered the query.
5 Ann had been requested to prepare a very difficult quotation, but kept putting it off in order to complete smaller tasks.

6 Richard was off sick for 2 days and work was delayed because no-one was quite sure of the procedures to follow.

7 A letter of complaint was received from a customer asking why no reply had been received to her previous letter. On checking the file, you found a memo had been sent to the production department 3 weeks ago asking for information regarding her complaint, but no reply had so far been received.

As you wish to avoid making the same mistakes yourself, prepare a list of general guidelines which would help you to be well-organised and methodical in your work, e.g. keep a tidy, well-organised desk.

Task 13.2

1 identify any typical activities which the secretary to the sales director of Domilux plc might encounter in her work (routine and non-routine).

2 How often must these activities be done (e.g. daily, weekly, monthly, quarterly, yearly)?

3 Make a list of daily activities and assess their priorities, i.e. jobs which *must* be done; jobs which *should* be done; jobs which *could* be done.

Co-ordination and control

At any level in an organisation, work must be co-ordinated to meet overall objectives. This involves control, communication, co-operation and flexibility.

Control

Someone must have overall responsibility for the work and have the authority to make decisions.

Communication

Aspects include:

- ensuring that each individual knows exactly what he has to do, where and how it is to be done, and when it is required
- making sure that there is a proper reporting procedure so that the person in overall charge is kept up-to-date with developments
- keeping people informed of progress, changes in plans, etc. by meetings, memos etc.
- consulting people for advice and ideas

Co-operation

This entails

- keeping to deadlines so that other people's activities are not delayed
- respecting the priorities of other people/departments and being aware of other people's problems
- working as a team

Flexibility

This involves

- adjusting plans to meet changing circumstances
- being prepared to fit in urgent tasks and catch up on non-urgent or routine work later

Methods of planning work

Checklists

These can be used in almost any situation, e.g. to plan an event or conference; to itemise stocks to be re-ordered; to list the day's or week's activities.

Activity scheduling

The items written down in the checklist are sorted into the order in which they are to be carried out. Key items are highlighted, i.e. those items on which others depend. For example, it is no use getting tickets printed for the annual dinner until a restaurant has been booked.

Time scheduling

The time required to perform each activity is added to the activity schedule. The individual times are added up to determine the total time, bearing in mind that some items will be carried out simultaneously. This enables a deadline to be set.

For example, the main activities involved in producing a company handbook are:

Preparation of illustrations	3 weeks
Preparation of drafts	4 weeks
Editing drafts	1 week
Reproduction on wordprocessor	1 week
Proof-reading	1 day
Amending	1 day
Printing, collating, binding	1 week

Action sheet

This determines the number of days/weeks/months before an event that each activity must be undertaken (see Fig. 86). It is compiled from the time schedule.

Bar charts

These present the same information as an action sheet in a pictorial manner. It is easy to see at a glance how activities relate to each other and whether deadlines are being met.

Activity	Latest time for completion	Started	Completed
1 Preparation of illustrations	2 weeks	6/4	
2 Preparation of drafts	5 weeks		
3 Editing drafts	4 weeks		
4 Reproduction on wordprocessor	3 weeks		
5 Proof-reading	2½ weeks		
6 Text editing	2 weeks		
7 Printing/collating/binding	1 week		
8 Distribution	same day		

Figure 86

Activity	Weeks beginning								
	6/4	13/4	20/4	27/4	4/5	11/5	18/5	25/5	2/6
Preparation of illustrations									
Preparation of drafts									
Editing drafts									
Reproduction on wp									
Proof-reading									
Text editing									
Printing/collating/binding									
Distribution									

Figure 87

Gantt charts are often used in production control (see Fig. 87).

Diaries

It is essential to keep a diary to remind you of appointments, jobs, deadlines, telephone calls etc. They range from pocket-book size to large desk diaries providing a page for each day. Many people keep both a pocket and a desk diary; it is important to check both and to make sure information is transferred from one to the other regularly.

Entries in diaries should be concise and easy to read, for example:

1100	J Watts (Domilux)	re Water Pumps in Board Room
1200–1400	J Watts (Domilux)	Lunch at Red Lion Hotel
1430–1700	Board Meeting	(tea required at 1530)

Planners

These are monthly or yearly diaries in the form of a chart so that the information is easy to read for planning purposes. See also page 234, Unit 15.

Electronic diaries

See page 36.

Bring-forward systems

Any item which needs action at a later date should be noted in a follow-up or bring-forward system. Systems in use are:

- diaries
- bring-forward files in which letters or reminders are filed in pockets (each pocket representing a day of the month)
- card index system where reminders are filed in date order

Follow-up systems should, of course, be checked daily and appropriate action taken to see the job through.

Pending files

These are useful for keeping papers currently being worked on so that they are tidy and accessible. They should be checked regularly and if action is not to be taken within the next day or two, it is better to file the documents and make a note in the bring-forward system to remind you to take action at the appropriate time.

Plan charts/boards

The wide range available includes magnetic boards on which symbols, strips and letters can be arranged; whiteboards on which information can be written with wipe-off pens; pegboards; charts for holiday rotas; year-planners etc. More information is given in Unit 15.

Work requisition forms

Where work is sent for typing, copying or printing, or where machines are sent for repair, it is useful to have a standard document for completing details of work required including date, number of copies required, single or back-to-back, stapled etc.

Task 13.3   Situation: Westleigh District Council is installing a new centralised print room. Any printing/copying will only be undertaken if it is accompanied by an authorised requisition.

Design a form which can be attached to work, giving clear unambiguous instructions to the print room staff.

Making appointments

If you are making an appointment to visit a person in another organisation, you will need to know

- the person's name, status, extension/room number
- the name, address and telephone number of the organisation and how to get there
- the time, date, duration and location of the meeting
- parking, security and reception arrangements

Planning meetings

See Unit 14.

Task 13.4

In groups of 2/3, you are required to plan an event. Your planning should include:

1 a checklist
2 a time schedule
3 an action sheet or bar chart indicating deadlines
4 draft memos, letters, programmes, invitation cards, agendas, publicity leaflets, tickets etc. required in connection with the event.

Suggestions for events:

a fund-raising event
an induction course
a business trip abroad
an office party
an open day at college or your place of work
a conference
an exchange visit with students in another part of the country (this should include a programme of events for the week when students visit your own college)

Task 13.5

Situation: You have arranged for a guest speaker, Mr K Andrews, to visit your college next Thursday morning to talk about industrial relations. He is travelling from a town 45 miles away and will be staying for lunch.

Draft a letter to Mr Andrews, including all the information he needs for the day and enclosing a plan giving directions on where the college is situated.

Task 13.6

For this activity you should use your full-time or part-time employment.

Situation: You are being seconded for 6 months to another department to cover for an employee who is taking maternity leave. In order that nothing is overlooked while you are away, you are required to prepare notes for a trainee who is to take over your existing job until you return. Your notes should include the following:

1 brief details of any routines which should be undertaken daily, weekly or periodically;
2 a full set of instructions for one of the regular tasks you are required to do.

You should present this information in the most suitable form.

Key facts

Work planning is necessary to ensure:

deadlines are met
the workload is spread
priorities are established

Principles of work planning are to:

develop methodical working habits
use standard routines for recurring activities
base planning on longest unit of time applicable to the job
divide jobs into 'must do', 'should do' and 'could do'
review work plans periodically
co-ordinate activities needed for fulfilment of task
see the job through

Aids to work planning are:

checklists
time schedules
activity schedules
bar charts
diaries
reminder systems
work requisition forms
wall charts and boards

Unit 14 *Meetings*

Introduction

It is estimated that managers spend up to 50% of their time in meetings of one kind or another. This implies that a meeting must be one of the most effective forms of communication.

Yet is it? Most people seem to have the impression that meetings are just a waste of time – there are too many and they go on for too long. Perhaps you have attended meetings which have been badly run and you were annoyed or frustrated because they seemed unproductive. Can you think of any examples where this was so? What were the reasons?

Why, then, have meetings at all? The truth is, when they are organised and run efficiently, they make an extremely useful contribution to communication, decision-making and consultative processes. The opportunity which a meeting affords to exchange ideas and opinions, to modify views or simply to impart information cannot be substituted by any other medium, either written or electronic.

Functions of meeting

Meetings may be held for any one or a combination of the following reasons:

- to consult, exchange views and discuss matters of common interest
- to negotiate, e.g. a wage award
- to inform staff about new work procedures or update them on other current developments
- to make decisions by democratic means
- to solve problems by pooling expertise
- to plan or monitor progress, e.g. production
- to investigate occurrences, e.g. accidents
- to make recommendations to a parent committee or an executive

Types of meetings

The term 'meeting' ranges over a wide spectrum from the informal exchange of ideas between 2 or 3 people to the very formal 'statutory' meeting governed by

MOST FORMAL	
Royal Commissions	Local government council/committee
Tribunals	Public enquiries
Statutory company	Management/TU disputes
Creditors	Shareholders
Departmental	Executive committee
	Advisory committee
Social committee	Ad hoc (set up to discuss one-off issues)
Working party	Progress meeting
Problem-solving	Seminars
(brain storming)	
LEAST FORMAL	

Figure 88

rules and procedures, such as those laid down in a Company's Memorandum and Articles of Association. The range of formality in meetings is illustrated in Fig. 88.

Although informal meetings are held more often than formal meetings, there are no set procedures laid down for running them and they are therefore harder to plan and control. Guidance on techniques for controlling meetings is given on page 217.

Differences between formal and informal meetings

Informal	*Formal*
No formal procedures are laid down in a constitution or standing orders	Formal procedures are specified in rules contained in a written constitution or standing orders
Informal recording	Formal documentation
Meeting called by memo or telephone	Meeting convened by notice and agenda
Informal notes may be taken and circulated and decisions taken by consensus or by person running the meeting after considering the views of the participants	Decisions are reached by voting after motions are proposed and seconded and recorded in minutes
No formal rules which enable the person running the meeting to decide on the procedure	Conducted according to the procedures and rules laid down in constitution, statute, standing orders, by-laws etc.
No formal protocol or meeting terms used	Formal protocol and meeting terms used
Person calling the meeting acts as chairperson or group leader, conducting it as circumstances demand	Meeting conducted by officials which usually include chairperson, vice-chairperson, secretary

Organisation of formal meetings

Legal requirements

Companies and local authorities are required by law to hold certain meetings on a regular basis. These meetings are governed by set procedures laid down in a constitutional document, viz.

Companies: The Memorandum and Articles of Association contain rules regarding meetings of shareholders, their voting rights and proxies (a proxy is a person authorised to act on behalf of someone else).
Local authorities: Acts of Parliament and standing orders govern meetings of various committees and sub-committees.

Other types of organisation such as clubs and voluntary bodies are usually governed by a written constitution drawn up by founder members.

Documentation for meetings

Notice

Before a formal meeting can be held, sufficient notice (as specified in the written constitution) must be given to those entitled to attend (see Fig. 89).

Sometimes the notice will be in the form of a personal letter or memorandum from the secretary to members. It is quite usual for it to be accompanied by an agenda which states the business to be transacted.

```
                   NOTICE OF MEETING OF

         ALBEC SPORTS AND SOCIAL CLUB COMMITTEE

         The next monthly meeting of the Committee will be held in the

         Works Canteen on Friday 13 March 19.. at 1415 hours.

         Items for inclusion on the Agenda should reach me by 27

         February 19..
                                Signed:  Ernest Clark

                                         Hon Secretary
```

Figure 89 Example of notice of meeting

AGENDA

ALBEC SPORTS AND SOCIAL CLUB COMMITTEE MEETING

to be held on Friday 13 March 19.. at 1415 hours in the Works Canteen

1 Apologies for absence

2 Minutes of last meeting

3 Matters arising

4 Correspondence

5 Treasurer's financial report

6 Consider Mr D Webb's proposals for the annual dinner   Paper 1

7 Consider proposals to be made to the company for financial

   assistance towards the purchase of a mini-bus   Paper 2

8 Any other business

9 Date of next meeting

                                        E Clark

                                        Hon Secretary

Figure 90 Example of agenda

Agenda

An agenda is a programme of the subjects to be discussed at a meeting in the order in which they will be taken (see Fig. 90). It is usually sent to members 7–14 days in advance to give them the opportunity to consider the items in detail.

The agenda is prepared by the secretary in consultation with the chairperson, and the items of business dealt with at the previous meetings are taken into consideration. Members of the club, committee or board may be invited to submit items for inclusion before it is typed and circulated.

The customary order of the business should be observed: if, for example, a chairperson is to be elected, this would be the first business of the meeting and would be carried out under the supervision of a temporary chairperson.

Chairperson's agenda

A special version of the agenda is prepared by the secretary for the chairperson during the last few days before the meeting. The secretary prepares more information than is given in the ordinary agenda and spaces are provided on the right-hand side of the paper for the chairperson to add written remarks as the meeting proceeds. Documents needed for reference during the meeting are attached to this agenda by the secretary.

Task 14.1

Situation: You have just been appointed secretary of the Health and Safety Committee at Domilux plc and have been told that the committee meets on the last Friday of each month.

Prepare an agenda for the next meeting which is held in the works canteen. Include the usual items, as well as the following:

1 provision of handrails on the stairs to the canteen
2 running of first-aid courses

Minutes

Minutes are a record of the proceedings of a meeting and are kept to preserve a brief, accurate and clear record of the business transacted. They should be written up as soon as possible after the meeting and should be wholly in the third person and in the past tense.

Types of minutes	Advantages
Resolution minutes – record decisions reached with only brief details of preceding debate	Conceal arguments and conflicts from outsiders who may read the minutes at a later date
	Concise
Narrative minutes – include details of the discussion as well as decisions	Encourage responsible attitudes amongst members
	Provide psychological boost to named individuals
	Give useful information to members unable to attend
Action minutes – include a column specifying who is to take action on any decisions made	Ensure follow-up action is taken
	Clear delegation of work

Whichever format is used, it is only necessary for the secretary to summarise the main points of the discussion as a verbatim record is not required.

However, the wording of resolutions must be exactly in the form in which they were passed and the names of proposers and seconders noted. The order of items is the same as they appeared on the agenda. Examples of the various formats of minutes are illustrated in Figs. 91–93.

Before the minutes are typed, the secretary agrees the draft with the chairperson. The final version is then circulated to members before the next meeting.

At the meeting, the chairperson will call upon the secretary to read the minutes of the last meeting. If they have previously been circulated they may be taken as read if this is agreed by members. Any mistakes must be altered before the minutes are signed as correct by the chairperson because once signed they are unalterable.

DOMILUX PLC

MINUTES OF MEETING

A meeting of the Health and Safety Committee was held in the Works Canteen on Friday, 30 March 198- at 1400 hrs.

Present

Mr R C Brown (Chairperson)
Mr J L Hubert
Ms C Jones
Mr J Painter
Mrs L R Sampson
Mr A B Smith
Miss R Williamson
Mr P W Adams (Secretary)

In attendance: Mr J Porter (Safety Officer)
Mr R T Symes (Maintenance Engineer)

1 Apologies

Apologies were received from Miss R Allen and Mr T Hodgson-Briggs.

2 Minutes

The minutes of the last meeting, which had been circulated, were taken as read, approved and signed by the Chairperson.

3 Matters Arising

The Safety Officer reported that the new 'no parking' signs had been erected in the road leading to the main staff car park.

4 Canteen Stairs

Miss Williamson drew attention to the hazardous condition of the stairs leading to the canteen. The queues waiting at the servery at peak meal times often extended to the stairs and, as a result, minor accidents had been reported during the past few months.

Mr Smith agreed that the canteen stairs were a hazard and, on behalf of the members of his Trade Union, he asked if action could be taken as soon as possible to make the stairs safer.

The Safety Officer thought that the provision of handrails would improve the situation.

After further discussion it was agreed to ask the Maintenance Engineer to advise on the most suitable type of handrail and to seek approval from management for the work to be put in hand as soon as possible.

Figure 91 Narrative minutes

5 First-Aid Courses

Ms Jones expressed concern that very few employees were capable of administering first-aid and when the Works Nurse was not available in the Medical Centre in an emergency it was difficult to locate someone who could attend to it. She asked if some first-aid courses could be organised to train members of staff in basic first-aid skills.

Mrs Sampson suggested that, in order to encourage a good response from the staff, the courses should take place during business hours.

It was agreed that the Safety Officer should seek the approval of the Personnel Manager to hold first-aid courses during business hours and that the Safety Representatives should be asked to ascertain the names of volunteers to attend the courses from their departments.

6 Any Other Business

Mr Painter asked if, in view of the increased use of VDUs in both factory and offices, the committee was satisfied that there were no health risks associated with their use, especially for staff who were required to read from screens for lengthy periods.

The Safety Officer stated that all known precautions were being taken, but if the committee so desired he would report further on this matter at the next meeting and it was agreed to ask him to undertake this task.

7 Date and Time of Next Meeting

It was decided to hold the next meeting of the committee on Friday 28 April 198- at 1400 hrs.

Chairperson

28 April 198-

4 Canteen Stairs	It was generally agreed that the canteen stairs were hazardous and that the provision of handrails would make them safer.
	RESOLVED: That the Maintenance Engineer be asked to advise on the most suitable type of handrail to be fitted to the stairs leading to the canteen and to seek approval from management for the work to be put in hand as soon as possible.

Figure 92 Extract from the narrative minutes in Fig. 91 using resolutions

		Action
5 First-Aid Courses	Ms Jones expressed concern that very few employees were capable of administering first-aid and when the Works Nurse was not available in the Medical Centre in an emergency it was difficult to locate someone who could attend to it. She asked if some first-aid courses could be organised to train members of staff in basic first-aid skills.	
	Mrs Sampson suggested that, in order to encourage a good response from the staff, the courses should take place during business hours.	
	It was agreed:	
	1 That the Safety Officer should seek the approval of the Personnel Manager to hold first-aid courses during business hours.	Safety Officer
	2 That the Safety Representatives should be asked to ascertain the names of volunteers to attend the courses from their departments.	Safety Representatives

Figure 93 Extract from the narrative minutes in Fig. 91 using an action column

It is useful to keep minutes in a loose-leaf book as this enables them to be typed. If this method is used, very great care must be taken in ensuring their safety as papers can easily be lost or misplaced. Minutes should be kept locked away when not in use as they provide a permanent record of the proceedings at a meeting and can be referred to at a later date when the business discussed is being reviewed. They can also be consulted to discover why certain decisions were taken.

Guidelines for taking notes at meetings

Informal meetings

Normally only brief notes are required, detailing suggestions or action required. After the meeting, memos are sent to the people concerned, reminding them of tasks they are to undertake.

Formal meetings

If you are required to act as secretary at a formal meeting, the following guidelines will help to ensure that your minutes are concise, accurate and complete and that they comply with the procedures laid down in the constitution.

Before the meeting

1 Check the layout and style required by looking at previous minutes or consulting the chairperson.
2 Write down the date, time and venue of the meeting.

During the meeting

3 Make a list of the names of people present.
4 Make a note of absences, with reasons (this is required for Apologies for absence).
5 For each item on the agenda write down:
  (a) a heading and a reference number
  (b) a brief summary of the main points of discussion
  (c) exact details of decisions taken
  (d) number of votes for and against
  (e) action required, when and by whom.
6 Whilst making notes:
  (a) take in more than you take down
  (b) ask about points you do not understand or ask members to repeat items which you have not been able to record
  (c) only record facts, not opinions
7 Note date, time and place of next meeting.

After the meeting

8 Draft the minutes as soon as possible while the meeting is fresh in your mind.
9 Submit the draft to the chairperson for approval.
10 Check the minutes for accuracy and layout.
11 Have the minutes typed in correct format and check carefully
12 Circulate the minutes to members, including those absent from the meeting, as well as other people affected.
13 File the minutes in sequence.

Task 14.2

1 Write the following in the form of a minute for inclusion in the minutes of the Health and Safety Committee:

I suggest that a light should be provided over the door into the car park as there is a steep step down from the works exit which is a hazard when it is dark. Several people have already tripped and there will be a serious accident soon if nothing is done. I hurt my ankle there last week and I had to go to the doctor with it.

This suggestion, agreed by the committee, was made by Catherine Jones.

2 In your own words, explain the main points to observe when taking minutes.

Terminology

The following list contains some of the most commonly used technical terms connected with meetings.

AGM	annual general meeting to which all members are usually invited.
Ad hoc	meaning 'arranged for this purpose', e.g. when a committee is set up to make arrangements for a business exhibition.
Addressing the chair	all remarks must be addressed to the chairperson, and members must not discuss matters between themselves.
Adjourn	to hold a meeting over until a later date.
Advisory	giving advice or making recommendations, but not taking decisions.
Amendment	an addition or deletion to a motion which must be proposed and seconded in the normal way.
Casting vote	a second vote usually allowed to the chairperson (except in the case of a company meeting) when there is an equal number of votes 'for' and 'against' a motion.
Committee	a group of people elected for a fixed term of office to represent an organisation and make certain decisions on its behalf.
Consensus	agreement by general consent, no vote being taken.
Co-option	the power given to a committee to allow others to serve on it.
Ex officio	given powers or rights by virtue of office, e.g. a safety officer may be an *ex officio* member of the works committee.
Honorary	unpaid post, e.g. hon secretary.
Motion	a proposal being discussed at a meeting.
Mover	one who proposes and puts forward a motion.
Nem con (nemine contradicente)	no one voting against.
Opposer	one who speaks against a motion.
Point of order	the drawing of attention to a particular rule of procedure.
Postponement	to defer a meeting to a later date.
Proxy	a person acting on behalf of another.
Quorum	the minimum number of persons who must be in attendance to constitute a meeting – the number is laid down in the written constitution.
Recommendation	suggestion made by an advisory commitee to a parent committee.
Resolution	a formal decision carried at a meeting. It cannot be rescinded at the meeting at which it was adopted.
Rider	an additional clause or sentence added to a resolution after it has been passed.

Right of reply	given to the proposer of a resolution to speak once after it has been discussed and before the motion is put to the meeting.
Seconder	one who supports the proposer of a motion.
Sine die	meeting without an appointed day, or indefinitely.
Standing commmittee	a committee which has an indefinite term of office.
Sub-committee	a small committee appointed by a parent committee to deal with some aspects of its work. The sub-committee must report back to the committee periodically.
Ultra vires	beyond the legal power or authority of the body or organisation.
Unanimous	all being in favour.

Task 14.3   Answer the following questions briefly and as quickly as possible.

1 What happens if a quorum is not reached?
2 Who (a) signs, (b) prepares and (c) agrees the minutes of a meeting?
3 Who is entitled to a proxy vote?
4 (a) What documents are used for committee meetings? (b) Why are they used? (c) In what ways do they differ when used for annual general meetings?
5 Under what circumstances would an extraordinary meeting be held?
6 Explain the differences between a motion and a resolution and say how each can be changed.
7 What happens if a member says there is an error in the minutes?
8 Explain the differences between *ex-officio* members and co-opted members.
9 What is meant by the term 'honorary'?
10 Why is it a good idea for an organisation to draw up a constitution for itself?
11 Why is the secretary the hardest-working member of a committee?
12 What does it mean if (a) a casting vote is taken; (b) a motion is carried *nem con*; and (c) a motion is carried unanimously?

Official roles and responsibilities

Chairperson

The role of the chairperson has been defined as:

to preserve order, take care that the proceedings are conducted in a proper manner and that the sense of the meeting is properly ascertained . . . (*National Dwellings* v. *Sykes*, 1894)

This will involve the following duties:

1 preparing properly for the meeting by familiarising himself with the items under discussion
2 ensuring that the meeting is valid, i.e. adequate notice given and quorum present

3 keeping order
4 dealing with items in the order of the agenda and keeping discussion within limits, allowing all points of view to be expressed
5 dealing with points of order
6 taking a vote, declaring the result or taking a poll (written vote)
7 signing minutes
8 closing, adjourning or postponing meetings
9 agreeing with the secretary the content of the agenda and minutes

Secretary

The secretary makes most of the arrangements, carries out the bulk of the administrative work and liaises with committee members; works very closely with the chairperson, ensuring that he is kept fully informed of developments and has all the information required for the meeting.

The secretary's duties include

- preparing and circulating all the documentation required for the meeting
- booking the room, organising refreshments and seating arrangements etc.
- dealing with all correspondence
- keeping records and minutes

The secretary's job is perhaps the most demanding and time-consuming of any of the officials. It requires great organisational skill and the ability to anticipate requirements; also the ability to extract the relevant and important points from a discussion and present them in an impersonal and accurate written form.

As an administrator, you will be assumed to possess these necessary skills and will quite likely be asked to undertake this role at some stage.

Treasurer

It is only necessary to appoint a treasurer if the committee controls funds, e.g. subscriptions or contributions.

The treasurer's duties will be

- collecting, recording and banking income
- recording and making payments
- presenting financial reports to members and advising on financial matters
- ensuring the organisation is able to pay its debts
- presenting audited accounts at the annual general meeting

Seating arrangements

It usually falls to the secretary to plan the seating arrangements for a meeting. If a large number of people is expected, then it is probably best to set the chairs out in rows. For smaller meetings, any of the layouts illustrated in Fig. 94 could be used.

Whichever arrangement is used, the chairperson should be in full view of all

Meetings involving chairperson and secretary:

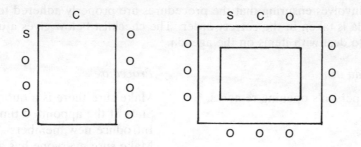

Meetings involving chairperson, secretary and other officials:

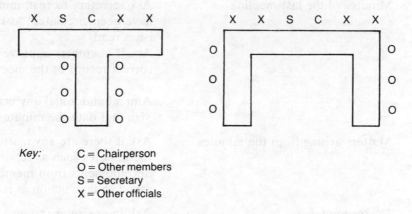

Key: C = Chairperson
            O = Other members
            S = Secretary
            X = Other officials

Figure 94 Seating arrangements for meetings

the participants and the secretary should be seated to his right to give assistance or provide files when required.

Normally, the secretary will arrange for members to have a supply of writing paper and see that water and ashtrays are provided. The secretary will also ensure that spare copies of agendas, reports etc. are available in case they are needed.

Chairing a meeting

So far we have concentrated mainly on the organisational and administrative aspects of meetings as these are extremely important. However, as you will have discovered at the beginning of this Unit, many meetings are unproductive because they are inefficiently run.

Two aspects should be considered:

1 conducting the meeting according to the rules
2 keeping order

Conducting the business according to the rules

This involves ensuring that the procedures are properly adhered to and that the agenda is taken in the correct order. The checklist below gives a useful guide on how to deal with items on the agenda.

Agenda item	*Procedure*
Chairperson's opening remarks	Make sure there is a quorum Start at the appointed time Introduce new members Make sure everyone has an agenda
Apologies for absence	Ask secretary to give apologies
Minutes of the last meeting	Ask secretary to read minutes (if they have been circulated, assume they have been read) Ask if 'members approve them as a correct record of the meeting held on . . .' Amend and initial any errors Sign and date the minutes
Matters arising from the minutes	Ask if there are any matters arising from the minutes such as reports on developments from members who were asked to take action at the last meeting
Correspondence	Ask the secretary to give details of any correspondence received since the last meeting Deal with matters arising from correspondence
Reports	Reports circulated can be assumed as read Ask author to speak briefly about the report Call for a motion to adopt the report Chair the discussion of the motion Call for a vote
Motions and resolutions	Check that a motion is concise and unambiguous (one sentence only is preferable) Call for a proposer and seconder Do not alter a resolution once it has been passed
Any other business	Restrict this to non-controversial issues Limit discussion to a minimum – where

more detailed discussion is necessary, it
will normally be referred back to the next
meeting as an agenda item

Date, time and place of next meeting | Agree these and announce the decision
clearly
Close the meeting

Task 14.4

Situation: You are the secretary of the Students' Union at your college and amongst
your duties is organising and running the monthly meetings of the executive
committee which are held on the first Monday of each month.

Draw a flowchart illustrating the main activities you will have to carry out each
month before, during and after the meeting.

Keeping order

One of the keys to keeping order and thereby avoiding time-wasting is an
understanding of how groups work. If you have attended meetings you will have
encountered at least some of the personality types identified below. In fact, most
people have a combination of these characteristics and may change their role during
the meeting as circumstances change. The successful chairperson is one who is
able to recognise the strengths and weaknesses of the participants, utilise the positive
aspects of people's personalities and know how to deal with potential problems.

Hints on dealing with different personality types

Personality type	Effect on others	Possible action
1 Over-talkative	disrupts; wastes time; discourages others; bores; breaks the ice	interrupt tactfully; let group deal with him; take one of his points and ask for someone else's comments; limit his time
2 Argumentative	wastes time; gives both sides of the case; takes things personally	avoid conflict; let group deal with him; keep calm
3 Positive	motivates others; supports	use him to carry meeting forward
4 Shy	makes no contribution; may appear bored	ask questions at suitable times; compliment him for his contributions
5 Inarticulate	difficult to understand	interpret what he says tactfully
6 Know-all	stifles other people's views; overbearing; misleads	use his expertise

| 7 | Mediator | afraid to cause offence; pours oil on troubled waters; takes heat out of argument; can stifle constructive argument | use him for support |
| 8 | 'Ideas' man | volunteers original suggestions; sometimes impractical; stimulates others | encourage new ideas; throw ideas open to meeting |

These are just a few of the personality types you may encounter. Perhaps you would like to add some more of your own.

Task 14.5 As chairperson of a committee, in what circumstances might you use the following sentences?

1 'Could we consider that point in more detail later?'
2 'We would be interested to hear your opinion.'
3 'Let me repeat that.'
4 'Could I take your first point and ask for other opinions?'
5 'Perhaps you have had some experience of the matter.'
6 'I would prefer to hear other members' opinions first.'
7 'I appear to have misled you.'
8 'I wonder if others agree?'
9 'Your point is very interesting, but as we are pushed for time, can I speak to you later about it?'

Note: It will help if you refer to the hints on dealing with different personality types listed above.

Leading informal meetings

Controlling informal meetings can sometimes prove difficult for someone who is inexperienced as there are no set rules or vested authority to rely on. However, you will find it easier if you

- in the absence of an agenda, make a list of topics you wish to discuss
- outline your objectives to the participants and make sure they (and you!) stick to them
- employ strategies such as those suggested on page 219 to deal with the various personality types
- summarise the discussion at appropriate points
- make brief notes of suggestions or decisions made and action to be taken
- thank people for their contributions
- inform people afterwards by letter or memo of any action they are requested to take

How to get your point across

At most of the meetings you attend, you will be a participant rather than an official. Whether you are attending a formal departmental meeting or an informal meeting with colleagues, you will be a more effective contributor if you employ a few basic skills and professional techniques, such as

- making sure you are properly informed by doing background research before the meeting
- being ready for opposition by anticipating likely questions
- being aware of personality types of other participants and adapting your approach to win them over to your point of view
- listening to what others have to say in order to assess the general feeling before speaking yourself
- being as concise as possible, otherwise people may lose interest in your contribution
- being tactful if you are trying to prove someone else is wrong as no-one likes to 'lose face' in front of others
- being courteous at all times

Task 14.6   If you do not obey the rules of courtesy at meetings, you may be labelled as arrogant, rude or a bore. Make a list of bad habits which might cause other people to regard you in this way.

Task 14.7   Divide the class into three groups:

1 Discuss the qualities needed by one of the following officials of a fund-raising committee (each group to select a different official): chairperson; secretary; treasurer.
2 Make a list of these qualities on the chalkboard or OHP for the rest of the class to see.

Task 14.8   If you are a full-time student:

1 Arrange to attend a meeting of your local council and write up the minutes afterwards.
2 Compare the procedures used at this meeting with any other meeting you have attended.

If you are a part-time student:

1 Arrange to attend a meeting at your place of employment and write up the minutes afterwards.
2 Compare this meeting with meetings attended by other students in your class in terms of procedures, officials, documentation etc.

Task 14.9   For this activity, divide the class into two groups. Each group will in turn:

1 Organise a meeting, drawing up an agenda, arranging seating and providing the necessary documentation.
2 Elect the officials required.
3 Participate in the meeting.
4 Produce a set of minutes in an appropriate form.

Each group will in turn:

1 Observe the other group's meeting.
2 After the meeting, comment on
   (a) conduct of the meeting
   (b) control aspects
   (c) seating arrangements
   (d) documentation

Some suggested topics for discussion at the meetings:

1 Canteen facilities at the college.
2 Arrangements for a residential course.
3 The organisation of a fund-raising activity.
4 An exchange visit with another college in a different part of the country.
5 The effects of a paperless office on future office workers.
6 The setting up of a college employment agency for students.

As an observer, you should consider the following points:

1 Was the meeting conducted properly?	Order of items followed?
	Motions clearly put?
2 Was a framework for discussion given by the chairperson?	Were the objectives stated?
	Was a background given?
3 Was the discussion controlled?	Was it relevant?
	Was it logical?
	Did everyone understand the points made?
	Was the chairperson tactful, impartial, firm?
4 Was everyone fully utilised?	Did everyone participate?
	Did chairperson guide members?
	Did chairperson make suitable summaries?
5 How did members interact?	Give details of personality types and effects of attitudes
6 Seating arrangements	Were they suitable?
	Did they aid discussion?
7 Documentation	Were they appropriate, well-prepared and accurate?

Key facts to consider when organising and running meetings:

- planning – time, date, venue, whom to invite
- documentation – records to be kept
- procedures – rules laid down by constitution
- official roles of participants and their duties
- how to be an effective speaker
- how people interact in groups
- follow-up procedures – to ensure action is taken on decisions

Unit 15 *Presentation of graphical and statistical information*

Introduction

Communication of data in a form that is easy to absorb and interpret is an essential skill for the administrator. It is true that 'one picture is worth a thousand words' and an illustration can often save lengthy verbal or written explanations. Statistical information, in particular, is usually much easier to grasp when presented on a graph, chart or planboard rather than orally or in typewritten form. Directions are made clearer if accompanied by a map or diagram. The use of colour and emboldening of text can be very effective in highlighting facts which the communicator wishes to emphasise.

Visual control systems enable progress and situations to be monitored and controlled systematically and efficiently, and can indicate trends or future requirements. The increasing use of computer packages to produce spreadsheets, graphs, charts and diagrams both on the screen and in printed form saves time, but skill is needed in interpreting and analysing them.

Statistical tables

Where it is important to give a precise breakdown of figures, it is usual to present them in the form of a table or tabulation, as shown in Fig. 95.

It is quite common for tables such as this to be produced automatically as part of a computerised sales program. Totals of product sales or comparative figures for different periods can be extracted at the press of a button. The disadvantage with this method of presentation is that it is not easy to pick out information at a glance. For example, if you wished to know which was the best-selling item or which product made the largest percentage increase over the year, you would have to study the figures carefully and carry out a number of calculations first. In other words, you cannot obtain a quick visual impression of trends or how product sales compare with each other.

Task 15.1

1 Using a calculator, calculate and complete the totals of all appliances in Fig. 95 and cross-check vertically and horizontally.
2 Which product had the largest total sales value for the year?

DOMILUX PLC
Summary of Sales for Year ended 31 December 198–

Appliance	Home Sales = H / Export Sales = E	Jan–Mar £	Apr–Jun £	Jul–Sep £	Oct–Dec £	Totals £
Washing machine	H	4920	3010	5030	6420	
	E	2340	6821	3159	3971	
Refrigerator	H	1980	2590	4360	1500	
	E	2480	3970	7820	5400	
Spindryer	H	1500	1600	1200	1920	
	E	1600	1800	1952	3210	
Tumbledryer	H	2950	1820	1590	4060	
	E	2824	4218	3700	1963	
Freezer	H	1890	8580	4640	2820	
	E	7298	1624	5948	1972	
Kettle	H	3920	4200	7896	6259	
	E	1684	6400	8201	5495	
Vacuum cleaner	H	2358	4821	6549	3120	
	E	1321	1965	1064	1029	
Steam iron	H	3336	3140	4120	6824	
	E	3421	3978	5241	8172	
Totals						

Figure 95

3 Which product showed the largest percentage increase of sales in the second half of the year compared with the first half?

4 Can you identify and account for any seasonal fluctuations in sales?

5 Why is a table the most suitable way of displaying this type of information?

Charts and graphs

Various types of graphs and charts may be used to interpret statistical information in a form that is easy to understand.

Line graphs

Line graphs may be single-line or multi-line and are useful for showing comparisons, trends or changes, e.g. sales, purchases, imports, exports, absenteeism, labour turnover etc.

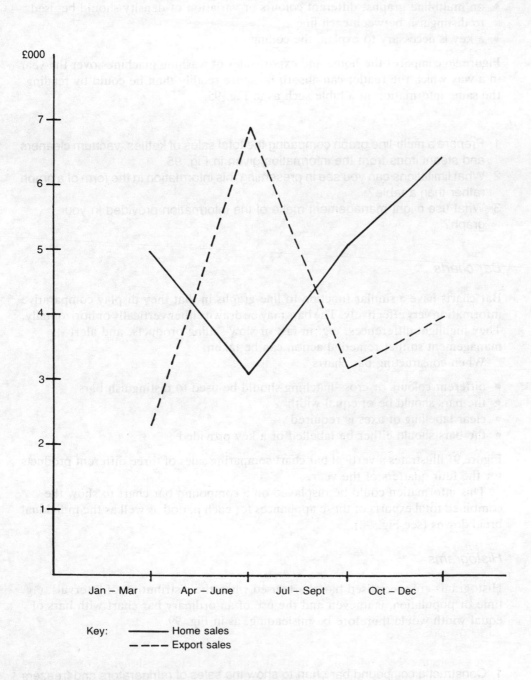

DOMILUX PLC

Comparison of Home and Export Sales of Washing Machines for year
ended 31 December 198-

Figure 96 Line graph

Important points to remember when constructing a line chart are:

- the graph must have a title
- both the vertical and horizontal axes must be labelled
- the scale should be suitable
- on multi-line graphs, different colours or variation of density should be used to distinguish between each line
- a key is necessary to explain the coding

Figure 96 compares the home and export sales of washing machines over the year in a way which the reader can absorb far more readily than he could by reading the same information in a table such as in Fig. 95.

Task 15.2

1 Prepare a multi-line graph comparing the total sales of kettles, vacuum cleaners and steam irons from the information given in Fig. 95.
2 What limitations can you see in presenting this information in the form of a graph rather than a table?
3 What use might management make of the information provided in your graph?

Bar charts

Bar charts have a similar function to line graphs in that they display comparative information very effectively. The bars may be drawn either vertically or horizontally. They highlight differences, e.g. in fast or slow-selling products, and alert management so that remedial action can be taken.

When constructing bar charts

- different colours or cross-hatching should be used to distinguish bars
- the bars should be of equal width
- clear labelling of axes is required
- the bars should either be labelled or a key provided

Figure 97 illustrates a vertical bar chart comparing sales of three different products for the four quarters of the year.

This information could be displayed on a compound bar chart to show the combined total exports of these appliances for each period as well as the individual breakdowns (see Fig. 98).

Histograms

Histograms are specialised bar charts used when the distribution of intervals, e.g. time or population, is uneven and the use of an ordinary bar chart with bars of equal width would therefore be misleading, as in Fig. 99.

Task 15.3

1 Construct a compound bar chart to show the sales of refrigerators and freezers for the four quarters from the information given in Fig. 95.

DOMILUX PLC

Exports of Washing Machines, Spindryers and Tumbledryers for year ended 31 December 198-

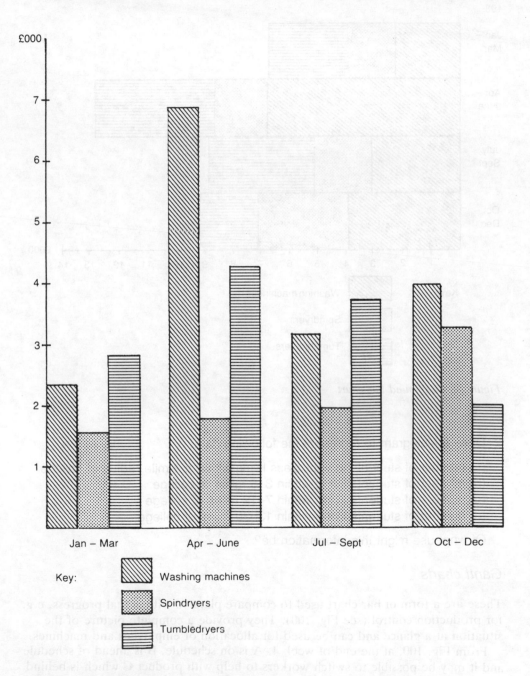

Figure 97 Bar chart

DOMILUX PLC

Exports of Washing Machines, Spindryers and Tumbledryers for year
ended 31 December 198-

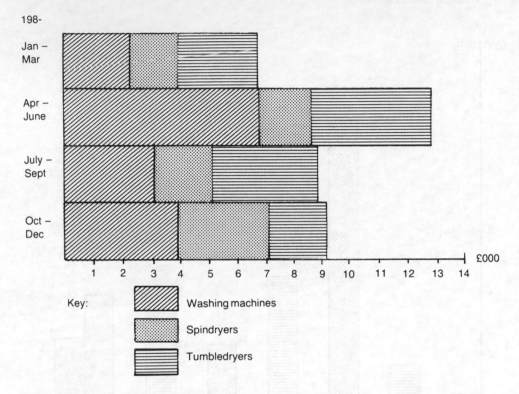

Figure 98 Compound bar chart

2 Draw a histogram to represent the following data:

   (a) number of students in your class living within a 2-mile radius of college
   (b) number of students living within 3–6 miles of college
   (c) number of students living within 7–12 miles of college
   (d) number of students living within 13–20 miles of college

   Of what use might this information be?

Gantt charts

These are a form of bar chart used to compare planned with actual progress, e.g.
for production control (see Fig. 100). They provide a complete picture of the
situation at a glance and can be used for allocation of employees and machines.

From Fig. 100, at the end of week 4, A is on schedule, B is ahead of schedule
and it may be possible to switch workers to help with product C which is behind
schedule.

Westleigh District Council

Number of people using Leisure Centre facilities during the year 198-

Age Group	Numbers
0–15	6500
16–25	8000
26–40	4800
41–75	2900

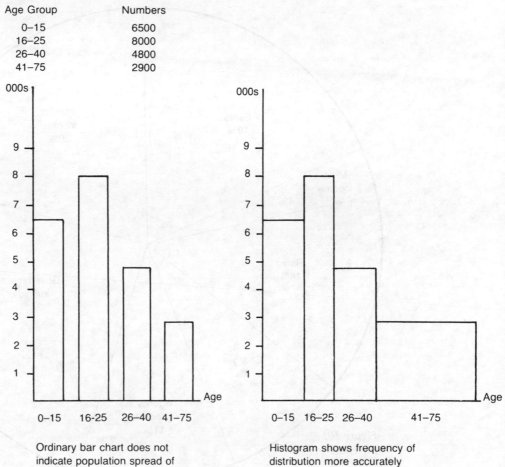

Ordinary bar chart does not indicate population spread of each group

Histogram shows frequency of distribution more accurately

Figure 99

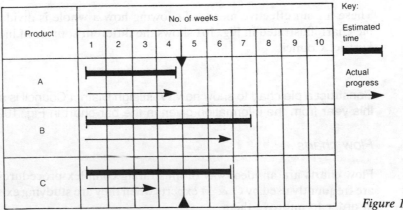

Figure 100 Gantt chart

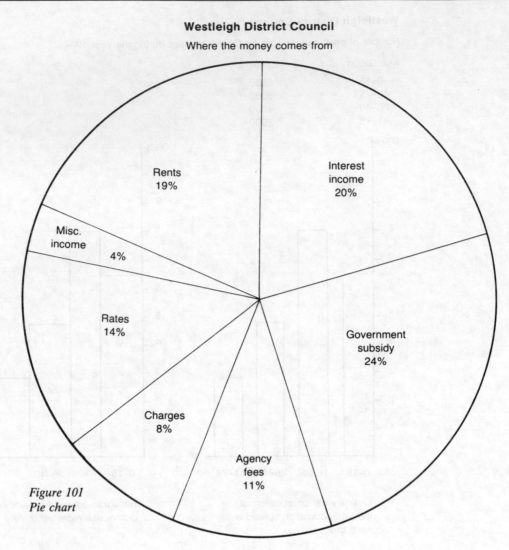

Westleigh District Council

Where the money comes from

Figure 101
Pie chart

Pie charts

These are an effective means of showing how a whole is divided into shares. The pie chart illustrated in Fig. 101 shows the different sources of income for Westleigh District Council.

Task 15.4   Construct a pie chart to show how Westleigh District Council is spending its money this year from the information given in the bar chart in Fig. 102.

Flow charts

Flow charts are an ideal way of illustrating complex procedures or systems and are frequently used by O & M experts when they are studying existing office systems in order to improve them.

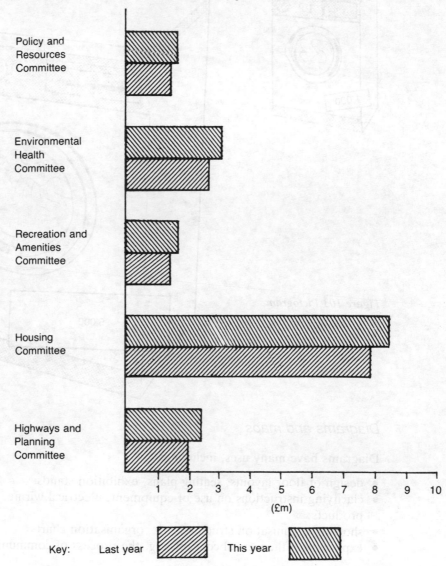

Westleigh District Council

Where the money goes

Policy and
Resources
Committee

Environmental
Health
Committee

Recreation and
Amenities
Committee

Housing
Committee

Highways and
Planning
Committee

1 2 3 4 5 6 7 8 9 10

(£m)

Key: Last year   This year

Figure 102 Horizontal bar chart

Examples of procedure flow charts are given in Figs. 72 and 116.

Pictograms

Pictograms give a pictorial illustration of statistics, making them more meaningful to the reader. An appropriate symbol or picture is used to represent a particular amount, as shown in Fig. 103.

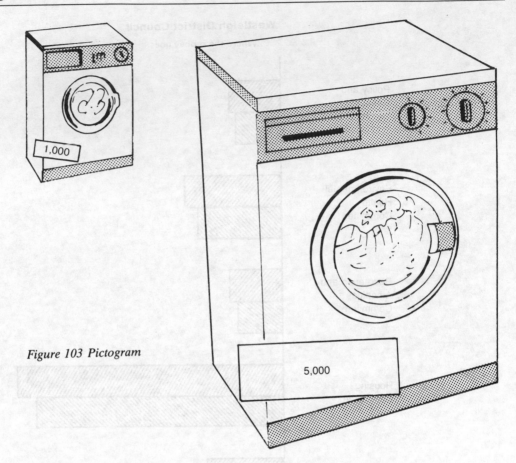

Figure 103 Pictogram

Diagrams and maps

Diagrams have many uses, including:

- design of floor layouts, seating plans, exhibition stands
- clarifying instructions on use of equipment, electrical wiring, assembly of products
- showing organisation structures, viz. organisation charts
- explaining a theoretical concept, e.g. the process of communication

To be effective, diagrams should:

- incorporate clear and accurate labelling
- use colour or emboldening to emphasise key facts
- be drawn to an appropriate scale

Maps range from simple diagrams sent to delegates attending meetings and conferences to the detailed Ordnance Survey maps and road maps supplied in travel books.

Care should be taken when giving directions in the form of a map that all details are accurate and up-to-date as the time factor is important when people are travelling and any confusion could mean being late for an appointment.

Task 15.5   Prepare a route plan with accompanying instructions to explain how to reach your college from your local railway station or bus station (as appropriate).

Overhead projector transparencies

Overhead projectors provide a cheap and effective back-up for lectures or presentations. Transparencies are easy to prepare by hand, using permanent or non-permanent pens, or they can be produced on copying machines from a good original.

Transparencies are particularly useful for showing diagrams, graphs and charts and for emphasising key points.

When preparing transparencies:

- text should be clear and large enough for the audience to read easily (typewritten material is too small)
- the minimum of information should be included, such as a summary of the main points
- colour should be used to provide emphasis
- a heading is required
- diagrams should be as simple as possible

When using the projector:

- make sure it is in focus
- switch off in between use as the glare can be distracting for the audience
- it is often useful to reveal limited information by masking the remainder until it is required

Advantages of using this method of presentation are:

- cheapness and ease of preparation
- its visual impact aids retention and creates greater interest in the subject matter
- the speaker is able to face the audience and continue speaking while using the projector

If the transparencies are to be used again, they should be mounted in cardboard frames and indexed before being stored in upright boxes.

Slides, films and videos

Slides, films and videos give impact to lectures and presentations by showing real examples of the situation. However, unless they are professionally prepared and up-to-date, the audience may quickly lose interest.

Slides are particularly suitable to show new products, processes, plant or buildings and have the advantage of being cheap and easy to prepare. It is also possible to prepare a taped commentary which can be synchronised with the slide sequence and set up to run automatically.

Films and videos can be used in almost any situation, e.g. to demonstrate operation and applications of new technology, interviewing and counselling techniques, and in any kind of training situation.

Many marketing presentations incorporate the use of slides, films or videos.

Visual control boards

Situations, progress and current trends can be monitored and controlled by visual control boards which are versatile and adaptable to show changes as they occur. A situation requiring adjustment once a month need not be displayed on an elaborate control board, and the graphs and charts described earlier in this Unit may be all that is required; but where the situation changes at more frequent intervals, a quicker and more highly mechanised arrangement is needed. As with graphs and charts, different colours are used in most visual control boards to distinguish and contrast the situations.

Visual control boards are not only employed in controlling production, sales, progress, stores, parts available for assembly, stock control, shop loading, despatch work and statistics, but they can also be used to indicate trends in expenditure, the allocation of personnel and many other purposes. Several kinds are manufactured and brief descriptions are given of the principal ones:

1 Dyna board in which plastic signals are clipped on round bar sections. The plastic signals can be written on and moved along the board either horizontally or vertically. An illustration of this board is given in Fig. 104.

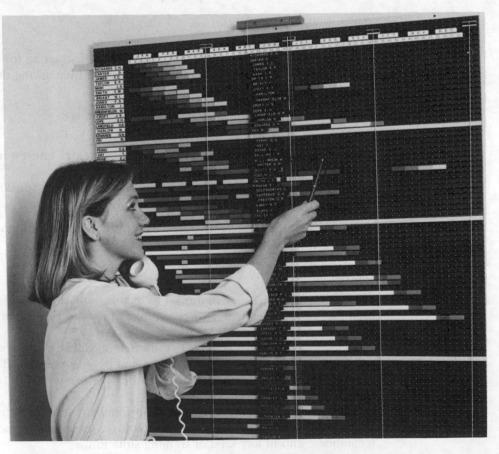

Figure 104 Dyna board

Figure 105 Card rack for work planning

2 Channel-type planboard which consists of cards, work tickets, job cards or plastic strips which are fitted into channels. This is simple to operate and economical to maintain because pieces of plain card on which the details are hand or typewritten are normally all that is necessary (see Fig. 105).

3 Perforated panels and pegboards consist of a flat panel perforated to give a regular pattern of slots or holes. Signalling devices in the form of studs, clips, pegs or flat discs are fitted into the slots or holes to indicate the pattern of the situation depicted in the chart.

4 A magnetic system employs individual name strips which are magnetically fitted to a board. The strips can be moved easily, and this system is particularly good whenever rapid re-allocation of information has to be made. It can be used for allocation of personnel in departments, reservation of hospital beds, hotel bookings etc.

5 Plastic self-adhesive boards have a smooth transparent skin of plastic. The markers are pieces of plastic made in various shapes, sizes and colours which contain a small quantity of static electricity. They are lightly pressed on to the board and fixed securely. Information can be written on the markers, which makes them suitable for a wide range of applications including machine loading, stock control, sales records etc.

Task 15.6   Refer to the report on absenteeism of production staff on page 72.
Redraft the report, presenting the statistical information in a more appropriate way to give visual impact.

Task 15.7	**Integrated Assignment**

Situation:

Full-time students – assume that you are an administrative trainee in either the organisation where you gain your work experience *or* in one of the organisations represented in the case studies at the beginning of this book.

Day-release students – assume that you are an administrative trainee in your own organisation.

Your organisation has ten YTS clerical trainees who spend 4 days a week on-the-job and 1 day a week at the local college of further education to study for business qualifications. Most of their training involves learning how to carry out various clerical tasks, but 2 hours a week are devoted to general instruction on the role and services provided by your organisation. This instruction is given by different people, according to the topic being covered. One of the topics is to be 'Sources and Use of Financial Resources'.

Prepare an oral presentation, supported by handouts, charts and/or OHP transparencies, showing in simple terms:

1 how your organisation is financed
2 how your section is funded
3 the purpose for which funds are used within your section
4 procedures which apply within your section regarding planning, allocation and control of expenditure, relating these to budgeting and accounting principles

Your presentation should last about 15 minutes.

Key facts

Visual aids in the office include:

- tables
- graphs and charts
- diagrams and maps
- OHP transparencies
- slides, videos and films
- visual control boards

Factors affecting choice include:

- cost
- ease of preparation
- suitability for the purpose
- availability of equipment, e.g. projector

Factors affecting design include the need for:

- a title
- clear labelling
- clear and adequate size of lettering
- simplicity
- use of colour
- up-to-date information

Unit 16 *People in the working environment*

Introduction

People spend about two-thirds of their waking hours at work. It is therefore not surprising that their morale is very much affected by their working conditions. If the surroundings are drab, equipment inadequate and furniture badly designed, morale is likely to suffer and affect productivity adversely. On the other hand, money spent on making working conditions congenial may well improve co-operation and lessen stress, resulting in greater output and improved quality of work.

When is a new office layout required?

A new office layout is needed when

- a new business is being set up
- an office is moving premises
- new systems and procedures are being introduced
- an improvement to the work flow is required
- there is an increase or reduction of staff
- physical conditions are inadequate
- health and safety provisions do not meet statutory requirements

If there is an O & M department, it will usually be responsible for designing the layout in consultation with departments and people affected. In organisations without this facility, administrative staff are usually given the task.

Planning the layout

Factors affecting design include

- type of layout
- flow of work
- type of work being carried out
- visual impression
- cost
- legal requirements
- physical conditions
- security

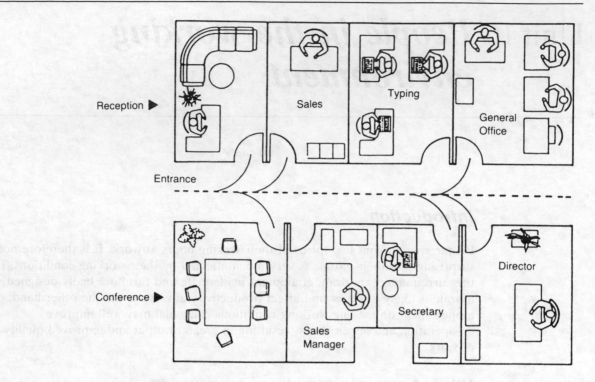

Figure 106 Cellular offices

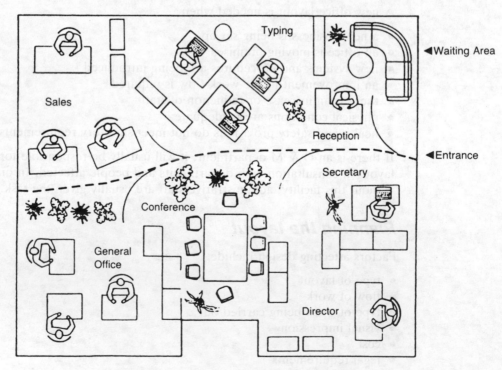

Figure 107 Open-plan office

Figure 108 Cellular office (prize-winning entry in the 'Office of the Year' award)

Figure 109 Open-plan office (prize-winning entry in the 'Office of the Year' award)

Type of layout

To some extent, this will be limited by the age and construction of the building in which the office is situated. The choice is between:

1 Cellular offices – individual offices for one or more people (up to about 5) (see Figs. 106 and 108).
2 Open-plan offices – several departments, or even the whole office, are accommodated in one large room. Groups of desks are separated by screens, filing cabinets or plants. Noise levels are reduced by the provision of carpets, sound-absorbent wall and ceiling tiles and muted telephones. The design may incorporate a few cellular offices for managerial staff and interview rooms are normally provided for confidential discussions (see Figs. 107 and 109).

Task 16.1

Compare the respective merits of cellular and open-plan offices by awarding a scale of 0–3 points for the following factors:

	Cellular (individual)	Cellular (shared)	Open-plan
Privacy			
Attractiveness			
Freedom from distraction			
Communication			
Work flow			
Space utilisation			
Supervision			
Economy of heating/lighting			
Economy of equipment			

Total the marks awarded for each type of office – the greater the score, the better is the result.

Flow of work

Whichever type of layout is used, the flow of work should be analysed to see that the movement of people and paper are reduced to a minimum. Therefore, departments and people who have frequent contact should be sited near each other.

Type of work being carried out

Certain departments have special requirements, e.g. reception needs to be located near the entrance; centralised office services should be accessible to all departments; drawing offices need, if possible, daylight conditions.

Visual impression

All layouts should be pleasing to the eye. Some offices, e.g. a head office, may be designed to impress visitors and will therefore incorporate more luxurious furnishings and equipment. This is considered to be part of a firm's 'image' as a prestigious office indicates financial stability and an air of efficiency.

Cost

The organisation is restricted to the amount of money available. When planning the office, therefore, the budget must be kept in mind, although often great improvements in layout can be made at very little cost.

Legal requirements

Employers' Liability (Compulsory Insurance) Act 1969
Employers must insure employees against injury and disease resulting from their work. A certificate of insurance must be displayed.

Offices, Shops and Railway Premises Act 1963
This covers

- space (3.715 m^2 (40 ft^2) per person
- temperature (at least 16°C after first hour of working)
- ventilation
- lighting
- provision of toilets, drinking water, washing and drying facilities
- cleanliness
- guarding of dangerous machinery
- design and construction of seats
- provision of lifting and transporting equipment
- first-aid provision
- fire precautions
- accident reporting

Health and Safety at Work Act 1974
This supplements the Offices, Shops and Railway Premises Act 1963 and requires an employer to provide

- a safe and healthy working environment
- information about safe practices
- safe storage and transport of goods
- training
- supervision
- properly maintained equipment
- safety equipment
- consultation for promoting health and safety

It requires an employee to

- follow safety practices
- co-operate with employer
- not endanger himself or colleagues
- not interfere with or misuse anything provided for safety

It has set up a Health and Safety Commission to

- monitor health and safety
- enforce legal requirements through Health and Safety Executive Inspectorate

Fire Precautions Act 1971/Fire Precautions Regulations 1976
An employer must obtain a fire certificate for premises.

Copies of these Acts will be available in your college library, the public library or in your own personnel department at work. Simple guides to the Acts and regulations are also obtainable from the offices of the Department of Employment and the Manpower Services Commission.

Task 16.2   Mr Frank Jones, safety officer at Domilux (UK) plc, has received the following complaints from staff about working conditions. In a memo to Mr Jones, you are required to advise him (a) whether or not the current law is broken in each of the situations; (b) what remedial action should be taken to improve the situation:

1 Tom Franks complains that the office is never warm enough – the temperature only reaches 17°C.
2 Betty Perkins says she regularly has a headache after spending the day keying data into the computer.
3 A deputation of staff met Mr Jones to express their dissatisfaction with the new open-plan office – they complain about lack of privacy and constant distractions from telephone bells.
4 Graham Lewis, the reprographics operator, complains that he has to carry large quantities of paper from the stores to the reprographics centre and they are very heavy.
5 Joan Clarke decided to 'have a go' at making the folding machine work (in the absence of the normal postroom clerk) and suffered an electric shock.
6 Mary Watts reported to the works nurse that she suffers from backache after spending a day typing. It was discovered that she used an ordinary chair.
7 Paul Turner objects to the other members of staff smoking in his office as he says it affects his health.
8 The staff in the drawing office complained about the inconvenient times selected for fire drills – on the last occasion it was cold and wet.

Physical conditions

Space
Overcrowding is not only prohibited by legislation, but is detrimental to morale. Open-plan layouts make the best use of space without crowding. Provision should be made for main gangways of at least 1 metre wide.

Heating
If people are too hot or too cold, productivity is affected. Although a minimum working temperature of 16°C must be achieved after the first hour of working, there is no stipulation on maximum temperature. Types of heating used include

radiators, ducted air or filtered air. Individual fires are not recommended for safety reasons.

Ventilation

A stuffy atmosphere causes lethargy, headaches and helps to spread illness. Natural ventilation from windows is usually sufficient in small offices. In larger offices, air-conditioning systems are often installed, eliminating the need for opening windows. Double-glazing ensures that the temperature is maintained evenly.

Lighting

Inadequate lighting, glare or shadows cause eyestrain. Daylight is best, but in large offices additional lighting is required, usually in the form of diffused fluorescent lighting.

Noise

Noise is stressful and disruptive. Internal noise can be reduced by installing carpets, acoustic wall/ceiling tiles, acoustic hoods for printers and telephones; and by segregating machinery from the main work area.

Cleanliness

A dirty office lowers morale and gives a bad impression to visitors. Most offices are cleaned daily, although the Offices, Shops and Railway Premises Act stipulates they need only be cleaned once a week. Windows should also be cleaned regularly, depending on the location, e.g. city offices will need more regular cleaning than out-of-town offices.

Decor

Colour schemes should be co-ordinated to form a total concept, i.e. walls, curtains/blinds, carpets, furniture. Staff need to be consulted, bearing in mind that some colours are restful, some create an illusion of warmth, some are drab.

Equipment

This should be positioned near to people who use it, e.g. filing cabinets, telephones etc.

Placement of desks

Close proximity to walls or heating units should be avoided.

The line of vision at a workplace should not directly face another's line of vision or a busy gangway as this is distracting.

Supervision

Supervisors should be accessible to staff. Observation should be possible without being obtrusive.

Choice of furniture

Furniture should be ergonomically designed with the job and the person in mind. Seating should be adjustable and designed to eliminate backache. Sufficient work surface should be provided to do the job or accommodate equipment. It should be easy to clean and move, and should blend in with the rest of the decor. Modular (linking) furniture should be considered. It should be safe (no sharp edges).

Toilet, washing and cloakroom facilities
These must be accessible and in the ratios stipulated. Provision of rest areas should be considered.

Security

Provision should be made for:

1 storage of information, with special provision for confidential records
2 keeping cash and cheques safely locked away
3 safeguarding items of equipment which could be stolen by coding or fixing them to desks
4 restricting access to certain areas, e.g. research and design, computer room, personnel records
5 protecting personal belongings of staff

Steps in planning a layout

1 Analyse communication flows between departments.
2 Plan location of departments.
3 Within departments, analyse the flow of work, taking special needs into account, e.g. noisy machinery, need for privacy.
4 Plan the overall groupings of staff and where they will be located in relation to each other.
5 Draw a scale plan and mark in permanent fixtures such as windows, radiators, doors, electrical points etc.
6 Make templates of furniture and arrange on a plan, allowing space for gangways, emergency exits etc. A special kit using models is illustrated in Fig. 110.
7 Make adjustments by consulting staff and considering safety, security and supervision aspects.
8 Draw in any extra power points required.

Changes imposed by new technology

The advent of the electronic office and the move towards working from home is changing many of the traditional methods of working, reducing the need for people and paperwork. Familiar items of equipment and machinery such as files, filing cabinets, duplicators, copiers etc. are gradually being replaced by microcomputers or terminals linked to a computer.

Screen-based information of all kinds is accessible by telecommunications links, reducing the need for conventional mailing equipment.

In the future, many executives will operate their own desk-top terminals, employing fewer staff. The emphasis will change from designing offices primarily

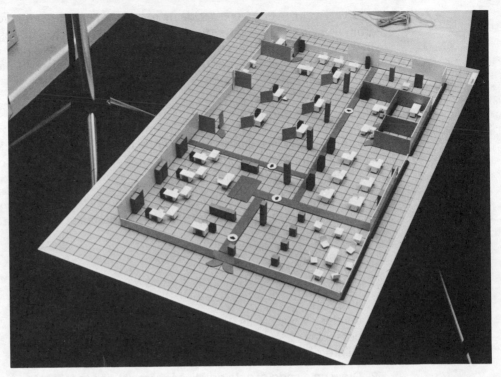

Figure 110 Office layout kit

for people to providing a problem-free environment for machines. An electronic office is illustrated in Fig. 84.

The main implications for office planning will be:

1 Design of workstations will incorporate ducting for cables, wells and platforms for computer peripherals, mobile filing units, slotted units for feeding paper through to the printer and linking units to provide extra work surface.
2 Provision will need to be made for increased cabling to be installed underfloor or in ducting with adequate power points located round the office.
3 An increase in power supply will be needed.
4 More air-conditioning will be required to create a dust-free environment and avoid a build-up of heat from the equipment.
5 Lighting provision will need adapting for work on VDUs, e.g. individual lighting to supplement ceiling lights.
6 Flexible grouping of furniture will allow project teams to work together on an *ad hoc* basis and cater for frequent changes in work patterns.
7 Care will be needed in the selection of computers, furniture and systems (see page 182) to avoid fatigue, eyestrain and stress.

Safety at work

Whilst it is the employer's responsibility to provide a safe and healthy working environment, it is the employee's responsibility to follow safe working practices.

Every year over 15,000 accidents in offices result in employees being absent from work for over 3 days; twice as many occur which requires less time off than this. Apart from the personal suffering and financial loss to the employee, the loss to the economy in terms of output and income is quite severe and, in most cases, could be avoided.

Causes of accidents

The majority of accidents are caused by falling or by lifting heavy loads; others are caused by bumping into, stepping on or dropping things; some are caused by fire, electrical shocks or machinery.

Task 16.3

1 Make a list of hazards commonly found in offices under the following headings:

equipment
floors, stairs
furniture
electrical
careless work habits
horseplay
failure of management to comply with legislation

2 Draw up a code of safe practice for employees to follow to ensure that accidents do not occur.

Accident reporting

All accidents and 'near-misses' must be recorded in an accident book accessible to employees. This enables remedial action to be taken if necessary and provides a written record in case of future queries. The accident book may be inspected at any time by the Health and Safety Executive Inspectorate (see below). There is a laid-down procedure for reporting various types of accident.

Safety representatives

The Health and Safety at Work Act provides for trade unions to elect safety representatives to consult with management on health and safety matters.

Safety officers

Many organisations appoint a safety officer who is employed in the personnel department to look after matters of safety throughout the organisation. Part of his job would be to make regular safety checks of departments, accompanied by the safety representative.

Task 16.4

Design a form which could be used as a checklist by the safety officer when he makes safety inspections. It should provide columns to indicate action needing to be taken and when it has been carried out, as well as providing a list of items to be checked.

Enforcement of health and safety legislation

The Health and Safety Executive appoint a team of inspectors who are entitled to visit offices or factories at any time to investigate safety matters. They have powers to serve notices on employers

- to improve existing unsafe practice within a certain time limit
- to prohibit use of equipment, machinery etc. until it has been made safe
- to prosecute for non-compliance with legislation

Task 16.5

This assignment relates to Jobline Personnel Agency.

Since the opening of the office services section on the ground floor, as described on page 33 in Task 2.1, the personnel agency have been asking for the office upstairs to be planned in an improved way.

The present layout is shown in Fig. 111.

The complaints which have been received are:

- The carpet on the stairs is frayed.
- A Betts complains he is too cramped but wants to stay near a window.
- The secretary does not get on with Gillian Lark.
- The receptionist complains she is in a draught and has too far to walk over to the personnel officers.
- Lorna Smith has fainted twice because of the heat and has requested air-conditioning to be installed.
- The printer attached to the secretary's WP is very noisy.
- There is no extractor fan for the fumes from the copier.
- There is no way out of the office apart from the front stairs and no instructions have been given or displayed about what to do in the event of fire.
- There is no privacy for interviewing or testing applicants.
- The accounts section cannot concentrate because of continual distractions and they would prefer to be near a window.

1 Advise Janet Keele on the legal position regarding these complaints and advise on remedial action to put the matters right.
2 Explain what action may be taken by the Health and Safety Inspector if she does not put matters right.
3 Replan the office layout taking into account flow of work, health and safety requirements and the views of staff.
   Note: Internal partitioning or screens can be erected, but no external changes may be made.
4 Design a notice to be laminated and displayed in the office giving staff instructions on procedures to be followed in the event of an emergency.

Task 16.6

After completing Task 16.5, Janet Keele has asked you to replan her office and provide an estimate for refurbishing it. She requires an executive desk with a return

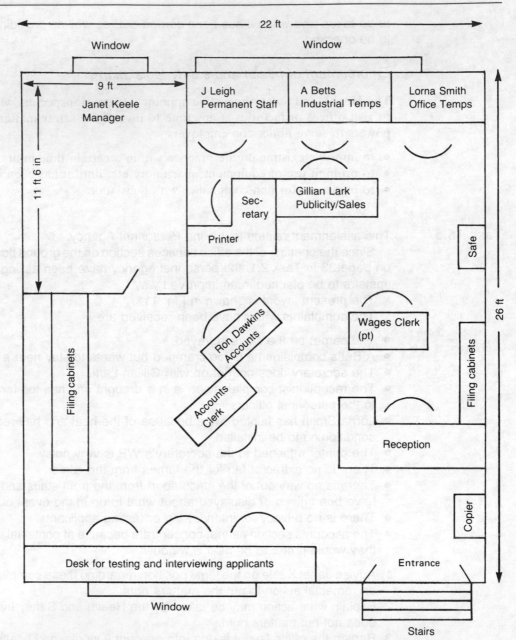

Figure 111

work surface to take a VDU unit. She also requires a filing cabinet and any other items of equipment or furniture you think necessary.

1 Prepare an estimate, including furniture and equipment, floor covering, decorating and window covering.
2 Prepare a layout plan.

Key facts   Office planning affects

- people
- the work being done
- the image of the firm

Factors to take into account include

- legal requirements
- physical conditions
- flow of work
- cost
- security
- type of layout required
- type of work being carried out

Health and safety at work is the responsibility of

- employers to provide a safe and healthy working environment
- employees to follow safe practices and co-operate with the employer

The Health and Safety Commission was set up to co-ordinate and improve health and safety provision at work.
     The Health and Safety Executive has the power to enforce statutory requirements through inspectors who may serve on defaulting employers

- improvement notices
- prohibition notices

or prosecute

Accidents must be reported to

- comply with legislation
- allow remedial action to be taken

Unit 17 *Organisation and methods*

Introduction

For many years, work study has been applied to discover the most efficient way of carrying out manual operations and making optimum use of material, labour, machines and factory space. Organisation and methods (O & M), in contrast, is a service provided to management to improve the effectiveness and efficiency of clerical work.

The objectives of O & M are as follows:

- to reduce costs of labour, office space, equipment and stationery and eliminate waste
- to standardise and simplify office procedures
- to increase output – but this is not always the case as other objectives may be paramount
- to improve accuracy – not always, although more volume may be handled
- to improve office conditions to relieve drudgery and effort
- to provide management with control information when it is needed
- to make staff efficiency-conscious

Work study, or O & M as we shall call it, consists of both method study and work measurement.

Method study is an analysis of existing and proposed procedures and includes paperwork, equipment and methods used. Work measurement involves the analysis of human effort and includes time and motion study. See Fig. 112.

Task 17.1
Situation: You are employed in the customer relations section at Domilux plc. There are rumours that an O & M investigation is to be made shortly and there is a general feeling that although work study is suitable for factory work, it cannot be applied successfully to office work. A meeting is to be held to discuss the matter.

For the meeting, think about the following aspects and prepare notes:

1 Reasons why it might be difficult to apply work study to office work
2 Types of office work for which work study would be suitable, giving reasons why.
3 Adverse effects on staff which an O & M investigation might cause.
4 Reasons why management may have asked for an O & M investigation, e.g. excessive overtime.

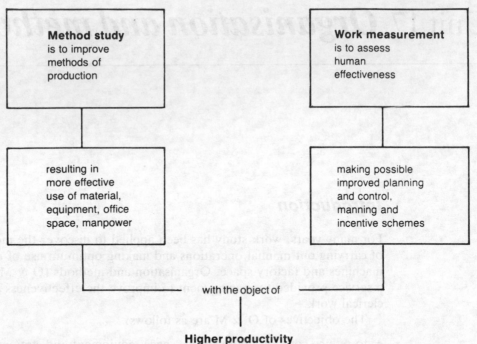

Figure 112

O & M staff

Why have O & M staff?

The main reason is that they can be completely objective because they are not part of the department they are investigating and are not influenced by established practices or personal relationships. They are also specially trained in O & M techniques, can test their ideas against similar work done elsewhere and can devote their whole time to the study (unlike a head of department who would be too busy with his own workload).

An O & M investigation may be carried out by full-time O & M staff in a large organisation like Domilux plc or by outside consultants in the case of a small firm. In both cases it will be necessary for O & M staff to be tactful and reassuring when they interview personnel in order to dispel suspicion and resentment.

O & M staff will also need to have up-to-date knowledge of office legislation; principles of office layout; office services; office technology; clerical routines; controls to prevent fraud and unauthorised access to information; reasons for clerical errors; human relations; methods of increasing accuracy.

Task 17.2   At the meeting of the staff of Domilux plc to discuss the O & M investigation (Task 17.1), the following points are raised:

1 'I already do 2 hours' overtime every night – how can they expect me to get through more work?'
2 'No wonder staff keep leaving – they expect miracles – I'm not only expected to answer the 'phone and deal with callers, but I have to take all the mail round

as well. I certainly won't have time to talk to this O & M chap.'

3 'How can they possibly tell how long it should take to find errors in the computer printout? And what about when people come on the 'phone with enquiries? I can't stop them talking!'

4 'We'd better save all our work until they come, so they won't think we haven't got enough to do.'

5 'I wish management would ask *us* what improvements are necessary. We know better than some outsider.'

6 'If the system's working OK as it is, why change it?'

7 'People are more important than productivity.'

8 'Make sure you don't work too fast, or we'll all be expected to work at the same pace.'

How would you answer them?

Procedure for an O & M investigation

An O & M investigation may affect one individual, a section, a department or a whole firm. The same procedures will be followed in each case:

1 determine objectives
2 investigate
3 record
4 analyse information and develop new system
5 report to management
6 implement new system
7 monitor and revise new system

Determine objectives

The objectives of the investigation must be agreed between the O & M specialist and the person requesting the study (usually a departmental manager or a more senior executive), e.g. improve the filing system because files cannot be found.

Facts	Primary questions (reasons behind facts)	Secondary questions (alternatives)
Purpose	WHAT is done? WHY?	What else is done and what *should* be done?
Place	WHERE is it done? WHY?	Where else *could* it or *should* it be done?
Sequence	WHEN is it done? WHY?	When else *could* it or *should* it be done?
Person	WHO does it? WHY?	Who else *could* or *should* do it?
Means	HOW is it done? WHY?	How else *could* it or *should* it be done?

Figure 113

Investigate

This involves examining the procedure in detail by looking at existing records; personal observation of people carrying out the tasks; interviews with staff; asking staff to complete timesheets showing how they spend their time; questionnaires.

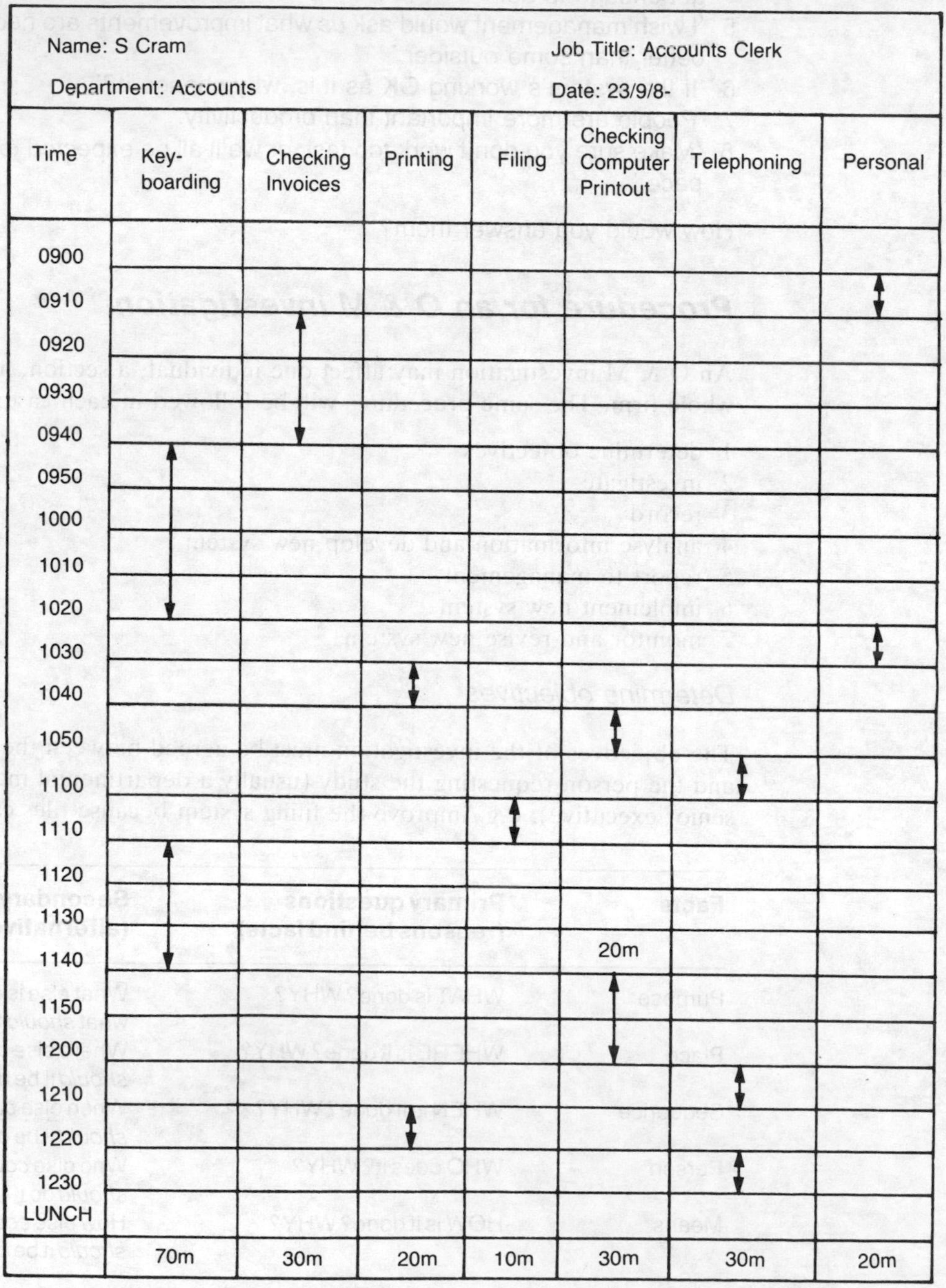

Name: S Cram					Job Title: Accounts Clerk	
Department: Accounts					Date: 23/9/8-	

Time	Key-boarding	Checking Invoices	Printing	Filing	Checking Computer Printout	Telephoning	Personal
0900							
0910							↕
0920		↕					
0930		⇃					
0940		↕					
0950	↕						
1000							
1010							
1020	↕						
1030							↕
1040			↕				
1050					↕		
1100						↕	
1110			↕				
1120	↕						
1130							
1140	↕				20m		
1150					↕		
1200							
1210						↕	
1220			↕				
1230						↕	
LUNCH							
	70m	30m	20m	10m	30m	30m	20m

Figure 114 Production study chart

Questions asked by O & M specialists are concerned with what? where? when? who? how? and why? (see Fig. 113).

Record information

Recording may be by means of:

1 Production study chart (sometimes called activity log sheet, time chart or diary sheet) (shows what is done by a person and how long it takes). See Fig. 114.
2 Multiple activity chart (shows how much time is spent by machines and people to perform certain tasks). See Fig. 115.
3 Procedure flow chart and document flow chart (show what happens with various documents). See Figs. 72, 116 and 117.
4 Process flow chart. See Fig. 69.

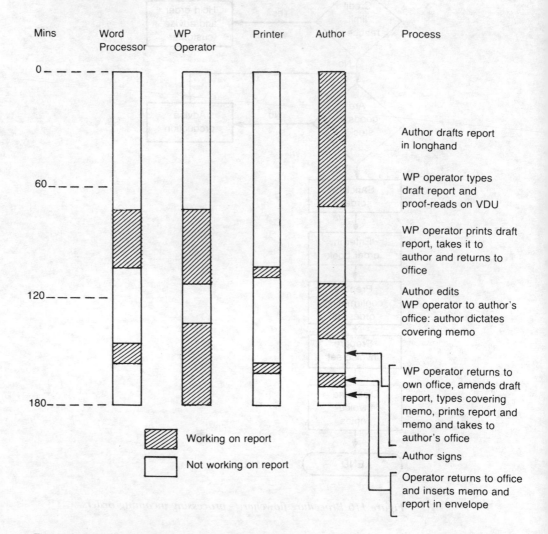

Figure 115 Multiple activity chart – preparation of a technical report

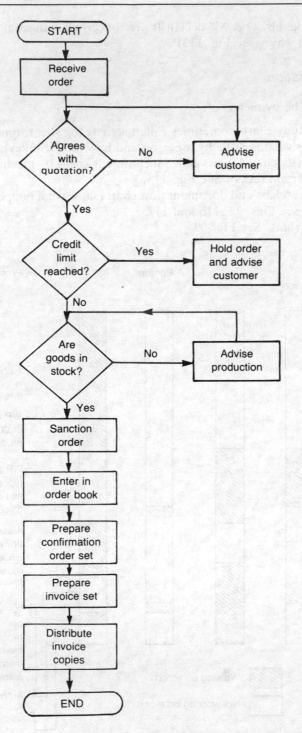

Figure 116 Procedure flowchart – processing incoming orders

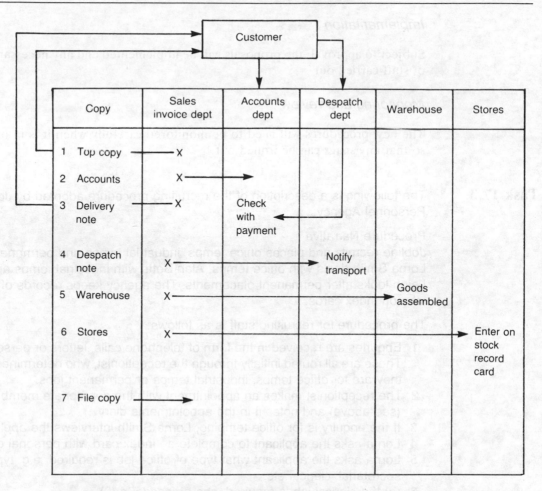

Figure 117 Document flowchart – distribution of invoice set

Analyse information and develop new system

Once all the information has been collected, it is analysed and alternative procedures, machines, office layouts etc. are considered to find the best system.

Report to management

A report is prepared for management comparing the present with the proposed system and giving details of any changes that may have to be made. The changes suggested could affect

- people – re-allocation of duties; work planning; pay incentives; design of workstations; new office layout; provision of better amenities such as restroom, better lighting etc.
- machines – installation of new technology; faster, more advanced machines
- forms – form redesign; flow of information; multi-recording; de-mechanising

Implementation

Subject to approval, the proposals will be implemented and any necessary training of staff carried out.

Monitoring and review

The new procedures will need to be monitored carefully when it is in operation so that any snags can be ironed out.

Task 17.3

The following is a description of the recruiting procedure adopted by Jobline Personnel Agency.

Procedure Narrative

Jobline recruits and places office temps, industrial temps and permanent staff. Lorna Smith deals with office temps, Alan Betts with industrial temps and James Leigh looks after permanent placements. The agency keeps records of available jobs on index cards.

The procedure for recruiting staff is as follows:

1 Enquries are received in the form of telephone calls, letters or personal calls. These are all routed initially through the receptionist, who determines whether they are for office temps, industrial temps or permanent jobs.
2 The receptionist makes an appointment with the appropriate member of staff (see above) and notes it in the appointments diary.
3 If the enquiry is for office temping, Lorna Smith interviews the applicant.
4 Lorna asks the applicant to complete an index card with personal details.
5 Lorna asks the applicant what type of office job is required, e.g. typing, secretarial, clerical etc.
6 (a) If a clerical job is required, she proceeds to (9).
   (b) If typing or secretarial, Lorna gives the applicant a typing/shorthand test.
7 Lorna assesses the test and enters the result on the applicant's personal card.
8 If the results are satisfactory, she consults the records to find a suitable typing or secretarial vacancy. If the results are unsatisfactory:
9 Lorna consults the records to find a clerical job where shorthand/typing is not required.
10 She asks the applicant if he is interested in the job selected.
11 If not, she selects another job.
12 If yes, she telephones the employer to arrange a starting date.
13 If the date is not suitable for the applicant/employee, she suggests an alternative.
14 If the date is convenient, she asks the applicant for form P45.
15 If the applicant has no P45, she completes form P46 and sends it to the Tax Office.
16 If the applicant produces form P45, she keeps one part and sends the other part to the Tax Office.
17 She completes the details on the applicant's card and employer's card, then

sends details to Ron Dawkins to prepare an invoice for the employer and pay applicant's wages.

18 The accounts clerk prepares the invoice and sends it to the employer, filing a copy.
19 The wages clerk completes the wages and sends them to the applicant.
20 Lorna telephones the employer after 3 days to check if the placement is satisfactory.
21 If yes, it is noted on the file.
22 If no, the applicant is replaced.

You are required to draw a procedure flow chart, using the proper symbols.

O & M interviewing techniques

Whether you are an O & M officer or a supervisor in an office, staff are likely to feel resentful or threatened if you carry out a study of their job. The way you approach staff and conduct the questioning will be crucial to the success of the study. If your tone and style is consultative and sympathetic rather than critical, interviewees are more likely to co-operate and make suggestions.

The interviewee's attitude may be

- defensive
- suspicious
- resentful
- uneasy
- tense
- aggressive
- unco-operative
- anxious

The causes may be

- fear of losing job
- fear of losing 'face'
- feelings of inadequacy
- fear of colleagues overhearing interview
- difference in status
- nerves
- inability to communicate
- frustration at disruption caused by O & M study

You can gain confidence and co-operation from the interviewee by

- reassuring him that the job is being studied, not him
- explaining the benefits to be gained
- setting an informal atmosphere
- asking for advice
- being sympathetic
- conducting the interview in privacy
- listening attentively and giving non-verbal cues, e.g. nodding, smiling etc.
- thanking him for his contribution and co-operation

Useful types of questions to ask are

- how do you manage to cope with all the background noise?
- I like your approach – how do you think it would be best to train someone on this job?
- you seem to have a lot to do – do you think there is any way we could simplify the work?
- what aspects do you think a trainee would find most difficult?
- if you had a free hand, how would you re-organise the work?

The important thing is to use open-ended questions, i.e. not questions that require a yes/no answer, and to be aware of the feelings of the interviewee.

Clerical work measurement

An O & M survey would not be complete without work measurement as the introduction of a better system or procedure needs to be carried out in the most efficient way if it is to achieve optimum results. The purpose of clerical work measurement is to establish standards which can be used as a basis for control. An increase in work output may be desirable, but it should not be at the expense of accuracy. In some situations, a certain tolerance of error may be acceptable – if so, then this must be established. On the other hand, if errors cannot be tolerated, e.g. on invoices, then it may be decided to accept a decrease in workrate to ensure accuracy. In other words, productivity is not just a question of quantity, but quality related to quantity.

What office work is measurable?

As you will have discovered earlier in this Unit, some tasks are easier to measure than others.

Easy to measure work	Hard to measure work
preparation of invoices	telephone calls
statements	thinking time
wages	problem-solving
typing	meetings
filing	receiving visitors
ledger posting	dealing with queries
completion of booking forms	
machine operations, e.g.	
calculating	
computer input	
copying	
franking	

Even though some office work cannot be measured, it is useful for allocating resources and planning workloads to know approximately how much time is spent on such activities.

Benefits of work measurement are that control is made easier because

- a standard or target can be defined
- actual performance can be compared with planned performance
- remedial action can be taken if there is a significant difference between the two
- work can be distributed evenly and fairly amongst staff
- manpower planning becomes easier
- incentives can be introduced
- errors should be reduced

Methods of measuring work output (quantity)

There are various ways of measuring output which are discussed in detail below. The method used will depend on the type of work being studied, the degree of precision required and the cost-efficiency of the O & M survey. Some of the simpler techniques could be used by any supervisor with a little training.

1 Diary sheets – these give precise details of how time is spent and are useful for recording non-measurable work, machine usage etc., e.g. an analysis of several diary sheets could indicate the need for a copier or WP terminal in an office (see Fig. 114)
2 Personal observation – this involves timing with a stopwatch and is unpopular with staff. Results are extremely accurate, but sometimes the person being watched reacts unfavourably by working differently than normal. Several staff would therefore need to be observed before a standard could be set.
3 Activity sampling – this means that work is observed at random times over a period and is cheaper than continuous observation.
4 Inspection and counting of tasks completed – this tends to be unpopular with staff and is not precise as it takes no account of interruptions, distractions etc.
5 Synthesis methods – these involve breaking a job down into small elements, each of which is timed to arrive at a standard time for each part of the task. Several organisations have published the results of their findings in manuals. The use of such data for routine clerical operations reduces the amount of direct observation and timing needed.

Relaxation allowance

No-one can work at peak performance all the time. It is therefore usual to add a 15% relaxation allowance to measured time to allow for fatigue, lapses of concentration and variations in the individual's work capacity during the day.

Individual productivity

When a person's output is being studied, he must be given a full quota of work to start with as he can only produce what he has been given to do. If he has slack periods during the day, then his productivity will be low through no fault of his own.

Task 17.4   1 How could the productivity of the following personnel be measured?

(a) a wordprocessor operator in the highways and planning department of Westleigh District Council
(b) an assembly-line worker at ALBEC
(c) a personnel officer at Westleigh District Council
(d) a purchasing officer at Domilux plc
(e) a salesman at Domilux plc
(f) a safety officer at Westleigh District Council

2 How could quality of output of the following be controlled?

(a) the wordprocessing centre at Domilux plc
(b) ALBEC's factory making electrical components
(c) the processing of planning applications at Westleigh District Council
(d) the council housing department at Westleigh District Council
(e) the reception/switchboard area of Jobline Personnel Agency

Task 17.5   For this task you are required to work in pairs.

Part 1
Individually:

1 keep a daily log sheet for a week, listing the tasks you carry out at work and the time you spend on each (if you only work part-time, log 5 days of your part-time job)
2 at the end of the period, make an analysis of the total time spent on each area of work

Part 2
In pairs, you should now interview each other to assess

1 your productivity and areas where your performance could be improved
2 how your jobs compare in terms of interest, difficulty, responsibility, contact with the public, routine/non-routine work, pay etc.

Part 3
Discuss any problems which occurred

1 when you were interviewer
2 when you were interviewee

Methods of controlling quality

Unless strict controls are kept on accuracy, an increase in output will not necessarily increase productivity. For example, if a price list is typed wrongly, reproduced and circulated, it will not only have to be retyped, reproduced and recirculated at extra time and cost to the organisation, but it may also affect the invoicing section (if they have to re-invoice the customer) and sales could be affected as well.

Methods of controlling work include

- checking of own work
- cross-totalling of vertical and horizontal figures
- 100% checking by supervisor
- partial checking by supervisor
- random spot checks
- checklists where each item is ticked off as it is completed
- control accounts which check accuracy of other accounts

Statistics can be kept of the number of errors made over a period to see if they fall within an acceptable tolerance level. If there are too many errors occurring, an investigation as to the cause(s) should be made and remedial action taken.

Main types of clerical errors

Errors fall mainly into the following categories:

1 Errors of accuracy caused through lack of attention or working under pressure, eg:

- figures transposed
- miscalculations
- mistyping
- misfiling
- information transferred wrongly
- wrong messages passed on
- times, dates wrong

2 Errors of principle caused through lack of understanding, eg:

- figures posted to the wrong column of an account
- information passed to the wrong person
- wrong decisions taken

3 Errors of omission caused through lack of organisation, eg:

- messages not passed on
- tasks overlooked
- appointments not kept
- deadlines not kept

Task 17.6

1 Consider some of the reasons why clerical errors may occur, taking into account such aspects as

environmental conditions
faults attributable to management
faults attributable to the worker

2 (a) What errors occur in your own area of work at your place of employment?
(b) What are the causes?
(c) What methods of controlling quality and quantity of output are or could be used?

Design and control of forms

In all administrative systems, the use of forms speeds up the flow of information and improves accuracy. Can you suggest reasons why this is so?

Even in the electronic office, forms are an integral part of record-keeping and communication systems. If the paperless office ever materialises, data will still need to be input on to a screen-based form so that information is organised, relevant and complete for computer processing.

Task 17.7   Think about forms you have filled in, e.g. application for a driving licence, passport, job, college course, booking forms, tax forms, forms used in connection with your job.

1 Make a list of things which have annoyed you about the forms.
2 Why do you think forms are necessary?

Design of forms

You may consider that many forms are badly designed, unnecessary or difficult to understand. It may be that the form was designed quickly without sufficient thought being given to the person who is to fill it in or the precise information required. Sometimes, forms are used for several years without ever being reviewed and information requested is out-of-date or irrelevant.

Before designing a new form, you should consider:

- whether it is needed at all
- whether an existing form could be adapted
- whether it would be simpler and better to buy standard forms from specialist printers, e.g. payroll forms, invoices, statements etc.

If, on balance, you feel a form is needed for a purpose, then it will help to observe the following guidelines.

Guidelines for good form design
Check that:

- the function and reference number of the form is clearly shown at the top, e.g. application form
- the name of the organisation appears at the top of the form if used externally
- the information is presented logically
- the wording is clear and concise
- sufficient space is allowed for completion
- instructions are clear and near the top, e.g. COMPLETE IN BLACK PEN ONLY
- the form allows for the minimum of information to be inserted, e.g. YES/NO answers or ticks in boxes
- the design and layout are pleasing to the eye
- important information is highlighted
- where copies are required, colour coding is used

- the print is easy to read
- the form meets the requirements for typewritten entries or computer output

Task 17.8

Each student is required to bring a form to class (preferably from their workplace or an outside source). The forms should then be numbered and passed round the class individually.

1 Award a maximum of 12 marks for each form, using the guidelines above, and deduct 1 mark for each rule not observed.
2 Total all the marks awarded for each form.
3 Redesign the form obtaining the lowest marks.

Control of forms

It is very common for people to hold larger stocks of forms than they actually need to avoid running out. This is very wasteful as it uses up unnecessary paper and space and there is the possibility that the forms will become obsolescent as requirements change.

Many organisations centralise the design and control of forms within the O & M department (if there is one) or within the office administration department. A specimen copy of all forms is kept in a register with details of date designed, purpose and type of paper, method of reproduction. They are reviewed regularly and a check is kept on issues so that departments do not overstock.

Benefits of centralised control include:

- well-designed forms
- standardisation of layout, e.g. title, date, reference number, margin allowance
- standardisation of size
- use of coding systems for various types of information, e.g. department codes, cost codes
- reduction in costs, e.g. bulk copying, bulk buying of paper
- regular review of forms to update or discontinue use
- monitoring of distribution of copies to reduce waste and to avoid stockpiles
- co-ordinated approach by facilitating flow of information between departments and consulting departments on their needs
- centralised buying of standard forms from specialist printers.

Task 17.9

Situation: You are an admin assistant in the O & M department.

Design a form which departments could complete when they require a new form to be designed.

You should include such details as purpose; how entries will be made, e.g. by hand, typing etc.; number of copies and type of paper, e.g. loose carbons, NCR etc.; usage: daily, weekly, monthly etc.; form distribution; whether an existing form can be modified; filing requirements; title; and any other details you think necessary.

Task 17.10

1 Carry out an O & M investigation into a procedure operating either at work or at college, using appropriate techniques and charts to illustrate your findings.
2 Produce a report setting out your findings and recommendations. Include any forms you have redesigned or plans of revised office layouts.
Suggestions for procedure to study:

emergency procedures
a clerical procedure
a communications procedure, e.g. informing the staffing officer of staff absences
a manual procedure, e.g. cleaning the office
security procedures
safety procedures

Guidelines on interviewing are given on page 259.

Key facts

O & M involves *method study* and *work measurement* with the object of achieving higher productivity.
O & M investigations consist of:

determining objectives
investigating } using charts: production study
recording multiple activity
procedure flow
process flow
document flow

analysing information
developing new system
reporting to management
implementing new system
monitoring and revising

Method study analyses systems and procedures.

Work measurement assesses: quantity } of work produced
quality

Efficient form control and design contributes to office efficiency and production.

Unit 18 *The needs of people at work*

Introduction

Throughout the book we have been examining the impact of various administrative and communication processes on people and their work. The main emphasis has been on ways of achieving maximum efficiency and productivity by installing systems and new technology which will get the job done most effectively. However, even the best system can only work in practice if the workforce – an organisation's major resource – is motivated to achieve optimum results.

What motivates people at work?

Several behavioural scientists have carried out research into why people work and what motivates them to work hard when they get there.

Economic needs

Clearly, an individual's first priority is to earn sufficient money to provide the basic needs – food, clothes and shelter – for himself and his family. It is important for the individual to have the security of knowing that he will be paid regularly, receive pay when he is off sick, be compensated if he is made redundant and have a pension when he retires.

Social needs

For most people, monetary reward is not sufficient to satisfy all their needs and they look for some kind of social acceptance as well. They like to feel part of a workgroup, to build relationships with colleagues and feel they are making a worthwhile contribution to the work of the team.

Personal needs

Some people are motivated by the ambition to achieve their potential or to gain respect from their superiors. Others are driven by the need for power or status in order to impress. There are, of course, those whose prime concern is satisfaction in the job itself, regardless of pay or conditions. These people are very lucky as they satisfy the need for self-fulfilment. Among these will be artists, craftsmen and people in the 'caring' professions.

In order to increase the commitment of employees, a manager has to be aware of their needs and their relative importance so that he can create the right conditions for a person to be motivated to work hard.

Task 18.1

When you are choosing a career for yourself, which of the following factors will count most? List them in order of importance.

status; power; challenge; promotion opportunities; 'perks', e.g. company car; salary; job security; recognition for work done; sense of achievement; job interest; responsibility; working conditions; creativity.

Job satisfaction

Research indicates that although people need to earn a basic salary to support a reasonable standard of living, many would prefer to do an interesting job with adequate pay rather than a monotonous one which is highly paid.

The factors which provide most satisfaction – and therefore motivation – are, in order of importance,

- achievement
- recognition
- the work itself
- responsibility
- career advancement
- personal growth

Good company policies, pay, working conditions and relationships all help to improve contentment but do not in themselves increase job satisfaction or motivate people to work harder. However, if these factors are lacking, employees are more likely to become extremely dissatisfied and their work will probably suffer.

Task 18.2

1 Consider the aspects of your own work experience. Which give you most/least satisfaction?
2 How do they affect your attitude to work?

Task 18.3

1 Research the theories of the following behavioural scientists:

W F Taylor
A H Maslow
F Herzburg
D McGregor

2 Discuss the ways in which they have influenced modern personnel management.

Making the job more worthwhile

Many jobs are monotonous and repetitive. The computerisation of routine clerical activities has removed the need for calculating, recording and transferring information which, whilst seen as a blessing by many, has taken away the interest and challenge for those who enjoy figurework. If you turn to page 184, you will be reminded of the fact that a production control clerk's job has been effectively degraded by automation as the computer has taken away the need for human decision-making and communication. Wordprocessing, whilst presenting many secretaries with new opportunities for broadening their skills, in other cases has the effect of deskilling by taking away the need for first-time accurate typing.

How, then, can organisations provide job interest for these office staff? The three main ways are:

1 *Job rotation* – where each member of the team takes it in turn to do each other's job. As all the jobs are often equally repetitive, it only increases job interest marginally, but at least has the merit of giving employees wider experience and cover during absence.
2 *Job enlargement* – where a person or team is responsible for a whole process rather than just part of it. In a factory, this could mean assembling a whole vacuum cleaner rather than just fixing, say, wheels on as it passes by on the conveyor belt.
3 *Job enrichment* – where a person is given greater responsibility and is involved in the design, processing and quality control stages. In an office, this could mean a secretary carrying out some of her boss's work such as drafting reports, dealing with correspondence and making decisions rather than just being a routine typist.

Task 18.4   How do you think the following jobs could be made more interesting?

1 A VDU operator processing incoming orders at Domilux plc.
2 A printroom operator working on the offset-litho duplicator at Domilux plc.
3 A filing clerk at Domilux plc Head Office.
4 A clerk processing council house applications at Westleigh District Council.
5 A bank clerk.
6 A sales assistant.

The working group

In most work situations, people have to work as part of a group or team rather than in isolation. Such groups may be determined by the structure of the organisation, department or section, or they may be formed by people who share workstations or have common interests. Sometimes people have to work with others from different departments on projects or committees and they will also develop close-knit relationships.

Each of these groups will normally exhibit similar characteristics:

1 It will breed friendship and a sense of belonging amongst its members and will choose who to accept or exclude.

2 It will establish norms of attitude, behaviour and discipline which it will impose on its members. For example, in a typing pool the group could determine at what rate the members will work, what attitude it will take towards smoking in the office or personal untidiness, and whether it will accept late or badly-written work from executives.

3 Members adopt roles such as leader, mediator, initiator etc. and will change roles in different circumstances.

4 The group judges situations from its own point of view rather than that of the organisation. For example, if a member of staff leaves unexpectedly and the group – or member – is expected to absorb that person's work indefinitely until a replacement is found, the group will resist this development in the fear that the vacancy will not be filled and their workload will be increased permanently. Management, on the other hand, will see it as being preferable to use competent staff to fill the gap (perhaps by offering some financial incentive) rather than employ a temporary person who will probably need training, make errors and cause problems for other staff.

5 The group has the ability to influence its members and will also influence other groups.

Needs of groups

Groups feel the need to be recognised, to be consulted when changes are taking place, to have provision made for their training, career development and social welfare.

Group conflicts

Relationships between members of a group sometimes suffer temporarily when changes occur. These changes may involve

- re-allocation of work
- promotion of a member to a position where he controls the rest of the group
- movement of workstations
- changes in responsibilities or duties
- provision of better facilities/conditions for certain members of the group, e.g. new equipment

Task 18.5

1 What effects do you think the changes outlined above might have on people?
2 Can you think of any other causes of conflict within groups?
3 In what circumstances might conflicts occur between different groups at work?

Fulfilling people's needs – the personnel function

Effective management involves getting work done through people. By helping to fulfil personal needs for security and job satisfaction, an organisation will get the best out of its employees. Personnel policies must be laid down at board level and should include

- sound recruitment procedures to fit the right people to the job
- staff appraisal, training and development
- provision of a safe and healthy working environment (see Unit 16)
- welfare facilities for staff
- participation and consultation in decision-making

These aspects are considered more fully below.

The recruitment process

In a small office, recruitment will be the responsibility of the office manager, whereas in a large organisation the personnel department will make all the arrangements in consultation with the department involved.

When a vacancy occurs, the following procedures should be carried out:

1 job analysis
2 job evaluation
3 attracting a field of candidates
4 interviewing
5 employment
6 induction

Job analysis

Job analysis is necessary in order to produce

- a job description (see page 44) or a job specification (see Fig. 118) which identify the components of the job and the skills and qualities necessary to perform it
- a personnel specification (see Fig. 119) which describes the main characteristics and qualities required by the person to perform the job to the required standard.

Job evaluation

The grade or salary can be determined from the job analysis. The aim of grading a job is to decide its worth compared with others. Methods used for job evaluation include:

1 A grading scheme for office jobs prepared by the Institute of Administrative Management (see page 45).
2 A points rating scheme where points are given for various factors such as:

    (a) skills required
    (b) degree of responsibility
    (c) qualifications or experience needed
    (d) difficulty of work
    (e) span of control

(f) physical discomfort
(g) monotony
(h) unsocial working hours
(i) availability of staff

The points are added up and the greater the total, the higher the grade given to the job.

Attracting a field of candidates

Most posts are advertised internally and externally. Care should be taken to balance recruitment from within and outside the organisation so that existing staff are rewarded for their ability and effort and new ideas are also brought in from outside.

Advertising
Internal methods of advertising include staff bulletins and noticeboards.

External methods include the press, recruitment agencies, schools/colleges, trade journals, personal contacts, local shops.

JOB SPECIFICATION   Date: 30 April 19–
Title of post: Wages clerk
Responsible for: –
Accountable to: Administration Officer

Job description	Task elements	Knowledge and skill requirements
1 Payment of wages to temporary staff	1.1 Checks timesheets	Familiar with details required
	1.2 Totals hours	Operation of calculator
	1.3 Checks hourly rates	Knowledge of rates for different types of job
	1.4 Calculates gross pay on an electronic print calculator	Operation of calculator
	1.5 Enters on P11 (employee record sheet), payroll and payslip	
	1.6 Calculates income tax and national insurance	
	1.7 Enters on P11, payroll and payslip	Knowledge of PAYE documents and reference sources.
	1.8 Calculates net pay	
	1.9 Enters on payroll, payslip and P11	
	1.10 Totals payroll	Ability to diagnose errors
	1.11 Prepares cheques, credit transfer slips and bank giro schedule	Knowledge of methods of payment
2 Preparation of salaries for agency staff	2.1 Selects previous P11	Accuracy in selecting records
	2.2 As 1.1 to 1.10 above	Knowledge of PAYE documents and reference sources
	2.3 Prepares cheques for signature	
	2.4 Passes to partner with payslip	Accuracy in completing cheques

---

Figure 118 Job specification

PERSONNEL SPECIFICATION

Post: Wages Clerk

	Essential	Desirable
1 Physical		
– age	–	20–40
– health	good record	
2 Attainments		
– educational	GCSE Mathematics and English or equivalent	RSA or BTEC first-level qualifications
– work experience	–	previous wages experience – especially computerised procedures
3 Aptitudes		
– skill with figures	able to calculate accurately and diagnose errors	
– skill with calculator	able to use competently	
– skill with VDU	able to use competently	
4 Interests		
– hobbies		normal social interests
– intellectual	interest in job	
5 Personality	acceptable to others dependable self-reliant honest discreet	
6 Circumstances		
– home location	within easy travelling distance	
– financial	no conviction for dishonesty	no heavy commitments
7 General Intelligence		
– problem-solving	able to deal with queries on tax	

Figure 119 Personnel specification

Sending out job information

The use of application forms speeds up the handling of applications. It is also useful to send applicants a full job description to reduce the number of unsuitable applications.

Pre-interview selection

The applications are matched with the job specification and personnel specification and a short-list is prepared. References may also be taken up at this stage.

Selection interview

Arrangements for the interview should be made well in advance.

Before the interview, it is necessary to:

- agree a date with the panel – usually one person from the personnel department and one from the department involved
- notify the selected candidate of the date and time and include directions on how to get there if necessary
- book a room

After the interview, it is necessary to:

- write to the successful candidate to offer the job
- write to the unsuccessful candidates
- arrange a medical examination, if necessary
- prepare a contract of employment

Interviewing techniques for the interviewer

Before the interview, the interviewer should

- familiarise himself with the job description and specification
- study the candidates' application forms and references
- plan the approach to be used at the interview in order to achieve the objectives
- decide on the questions to be asked

At the interview:

- welcome the candidates, arrange introductions and explain the interview procedure
- establish rapport by settling the candidate down and asking questions which are not crucial, e.g. 'What was the traffic like today? It's usually bad on Tuesdays.'
- acquire information by asking the candidate questions on his experience, knowledge and attitudes
- ask questions clearly and concisely, allowing the candidate to do most of the talking; listen carefully to what is said and note what is not said
- ask questions to discover the depth of knowledge and information which might otherwise be withheld
- do not make a judgement until a candidate has had a full hearing and all relevant facts have been established
- avoid excessive note-taking during the interview: brief, unobtrusive notes can normally be made without it being obvious to the candidate that everything spoken is being recorded; more detailed note-taking should follow immediately

after the candidate has left the room and, at this stage, an interview merit grading form can be completed to provide a score of the candidate's performance

- invite questions from the candidate and give answers
- finish the interview by thanking the candidate and agreeing subsequent procedures

Interviewing techniques for the applicant

Before the interview:

- research the organisation
- make a list of likely questions and prepare some answers
- think of some questions to ask on topics such as job prospects, the organisation's employment policies etc.
- find out how to get there in order to arrive in good time
- make sure that he is appropriately dressed

During the interview:

- be courteous, wait to be invited to sit down before doing so
- listen attentively and look at the interviewer
- think before speaking
- construct answers logically
- keep to the point, and try not to say either too much or too little
- try not to show nerves
- be pleasant – a smile always creates a favourable impression
- make the most of the subjects which you have experience or knowledge of
- be perfectly honest about your capabilities, drawing attention to any which support your application
- show that you are interested and enthusiastic by your attitude to the questions asked
- ask questions when invited or to clarify points
- at the end of the interview, thank the interviewer

Induction

A new employee should be given an induction course which includes a general introduction to the firm, its functions and structure, general conditions of employment, facilities, social activities, safety and security procedures, personnel policies as well as training for the job.

Task 18.6

For this assignment, divide into groups of four.

1 One pair is to prepare a job specification and personnel specification for a personnel assistant and the other pair is to prepare them for a supervisor in the sales office (both at Domilux plc).
2 Having prepared these documents, design an advertisement for the local press inviting applications for the jobs.
3 Each pair is now to apply for the job advertised by the other pair, enclosing a cv.

4 Each pair is to write to the other pair inviting them for interview.
5 Now hold the interviews, making a video if possible.
6 Select the best person for each of the two jobs and write suitable letters of appointment and rejection to the two candidates.
7 Analyse the performance of interviewers and candidates.

Staff appraisal

The aims of staff appraisal are

- to assess the performance of employees (this may be linked with pay)
- to utilise the abilities and strengths of staff and to help them achieve their potential
- to discuss problems and difficulties and ways of overcoming them
- to identify training needs
- to set targets for staff to achieve
- to prepare staff for promotion

As well as assisting the employee to achieve his potential and develop his career prospects through improving his performance and undergoing training, appraisal can also highlight deficiencies in work procedures or the need for a revised job description. Staff appraisal is also a useful means of identifying future manpower requirements.

Methods of appraisal which may be used are:

- periodic appraisal interviews by the superior
- merit rating where the employer assesses the employee on specific attributes such as punctuality, efficiency, co-operativeness, initiative, qualifications, accuracy etc.
- the employer and employee both complete an appraisal form on how they see the employee's performance and then agree a final version

Any form of appraisal should be followed up to ensure that any agreed action has been carried out.

Task 18.7

Situation: You are an administrative assistant at ALBEC Ltd. The board of directors has just agreed to introduce a staff appraisal scheme and have asked the office manager to try it out with office staff first. As the appraisal will also be linked with merit increments, the office manager has asked you:

1 to draft a merit rating form which will record an assessment of such attributes as productivity, accuracy, effort, experience, qualifications, punctuality, co-operativeness, initiative etc.
2 to inform him by memo of likely staff reaction to the scheme and counter-arguments he could make to any objections

Training and staff development

Benefits of training include:

- improved standards of work
- managers are able to delegate routine work to trained staff
- morale is improved and labour turnover reduced
- staff are motivated and developed for promotion
- safety standards are improved

Methods of training include:

1 *Induction* – includes information about the organisation, safety and security procedures, films, talks by personnel in various departments, tour of premises.
2 *On-the-job* – systematic training for the particular job should be developed and records kept.
3 *Off-the-job* – opportunity should be available for staff to improve their qualifications by attending local colleges on day-release courses.
4 *Special courses* – employees often need to attend short courses and seminars to update their skills, e.g. for new technology. Sometimes these are organised in-house.

Safety, health and welfare

Aspects such as regard for health and safety, flexibility in working hours, provision of appropriate 'perks' and pension schemes are all conducive to promoting good morale and a sense of security in employees.

Legislation relating to employment

Disabled Persons (Employment) Acts 1944 and 1958 – require employers of more than 20 people to employ a quota of 3% disabled.
Offices, Shops and Railway Premises Act 1963 – lays down minimum requirements for working conditions (see page 241).
Equal Pay Act 1970 – equal terms and conditions must be given to men and women where the work is broadly similar.
Health and Safety at Work Act 1974 – employer is responsible for providing a safe and healthy working environment; employee is responsible for following safe practices (see page 241).
Trade Union and Labour Relations Acts 1974 and 1976 as amended by the *Employment Acts 1980 and 1982* and the *Trade Union Act 1984* – lays down a code of industrial relations practice concerning 'no strike' clauses; trade disputes; picketing; collection of union dues; employee involvement in company affairs (over 250 employees); payment for ballots by government.
Sex Discrimination Act 1975 – this Act makes sex discrimination unlawful in full-time and part-time employment, training and related matters. Discrimination against married persons on the grounds of marriage is also covered.
Race Relations Act 1976 – a person discriminates against another if, on the grounds

of colour, race etc., he treats that other person less favourably than he treats others – it applies to employment, promotion, training, membership of trade unions and professional bodies, and advertising.

Employment Protection (Consolidation) Act 1978 as amended by the *Employment Acts 1980 and 1982* – all employees must receive

- a contract of employment within 13 weeks of commencing employment
- an itemised pay statement each pay day
- full pay for a maximum of 26 weeks if suspended on medical grounds
- maternity leave and maternity pay if certain laid-down conditions are met
- minimum periods of notice to terminate employment, i.e. at least 1 week's notice after 4 weeks' continuous service, at least 2 weeks' notice after 2 years' continuous service and thereafter 1 week for each completed year of service up to 12 weeks after 12 years' service
- a written statement of reasons for dismissal

An employee cannot be unfairly dismissed if he has been continuously employed for 2 years.

Social Security and Housing Benefits Act 1982 – introduced the statutory sick pay scheme in which employers are required to pay sick pay to their employees. Payment is dependent on the employee satisfying rules regarding periods of incapacity, periods of entitlement, qualifying days and notification of absence.

Data Protection Act 1984 – protects individuals from misuse of personal information held about them on computer files; lays down codes of practice for all who use or process data relating to personnel (see page 185).

Wages Act 1986 – governs the deductions which may be made from pay.

Task 18.8

1 Which of the following are contained in regulations governed by the Health and Safety at Work Act?

(a) cleaning of offices
(b) smoking in offices
(c) lighting of offices
(d) hours of work in offices
(e) the provision of first-aid boxes
(f) maternity leave
(g) design of chairs for office workers
(h) suspension from work on medical grounds

2 Pair the following Acts of Parliament with the years in which they were passed. Note that there is a surplus year included in the second column.

Act	*Year*
(a) Social Security and Housing Benefits Act	(a) 1986
(b) Wages Act	(b) 1970
(c) Race Relations Act	(c) 1974
(d) Data Protection Act	(d) 1976
(e) Health and Safety at Work Act	(e) 1978
(f) Equal Pay Act	(f) 1980
(g) Employment Protection (Consolidation) Act	(g) 1982
	(h) 1984

3 Name the Acts of Parliament which provide legislation on the following:

   (a) provision of running hot and cold water in offices
   (b) peaceful picketing to persuade employees to work or abstain from working
   (c) sex discrimination in the employment of staff
   (d) race discrimination in the employment of staff
   (e) security of computerised personnel records
   (f) statutory sick pay
   (g) contracts of employment

4 Which of the following statements are true?

   (a) Under the Health and Safety at Work Act, it is stated that a temperature will not be regarded as reasonable if it falls below 16°C after the first hour of work.
   (b) Regulations relating to fire precautions are stated in the Employment Protection (Consolidation) Act.
   (c) Employees on 15 hours or more a week must, not later than 13 weeks after their employment began, be given a written statement of their contract of employment.
   (d) The Employment Protection (Consolidation) Act states that employers must give employees on or before pay day an itemised statement of pay.
   (e) An employer must give his employees at least 4 weeks' notice after 2 years' continuous service.

Key facts	Needs of people at work:	economic social personal (including job satisfaction)
	Interest in work is created by:	job rotation job enlargement job enrichment
	Working groups:	people need to work with others as part of a team or group
	Fulfilling people's needs:	allocating them to the right job appraisal, training and development safe and healthy working environment welfare participation/consultation in decision-making
	Legislation relating to employment	Employment Acts 1944 and 1958 (disabled persons) Offices, Shops and Railway Premises Act 1963 Equal Pay Act 1970 Health and Safety at Work Act 1974 Trade Union and Labour Relations Acts 1974

and 1976 as amended by the Employment Acts 1980 and 1982 and the Trade Union Act 1984
Sex Discrimination Act 1975
Race Relations Act 1976
Employment Protection (Consolidation) Act 1978 as amended by the Employment Acts 1980 and 1982
Social Security and Housing Benefits Act 1982
Data Protection Act 1984
Wages Act 1986

Unit 19 *Management of people*

Introduction

In Unit 18 we examined the needs of people at work and the factors which motivate staff or give them cause for dissatisfaction. The office manager or supervisor can do much to improve motivation and morale by being aware of these factors and taking practical steps to meet people's needs in his day-to-day leadership.

What is leadership?

Good leadership involves

- building a team and making sure everyone works together as a team
- developing people as individuals and recognising their different needs and values
- ensuring the job is done properly

Task 19.1

1 Select three leaders whom you admire from different walks of life (e.g. captain of a sports team, someone at work, someone in public life).
2 List the qualities each one has which makes him a good leader. Are they the same qualities in each case?
3 Do leaders require different qualities in different situations? If so, give examples.
4 Are leaders born or made? Discuss.

Selecting a supervisor or manager

The leadership qualities you listed probably included the ability to control people, think problems through, make decisions, treat people firmly but fairly, have a sense of humour, be willing to work as part of a team, get on with people and be interested in them.

You may also have mentioned technical ability, and it is true that in order to gain the respect of subordinates, a supervisor must be able to offer the advice, practical training and instruction required for them to carry out their work. However, as a person progresses up the career ladder, he cannot be expected to have detailed knowledge of all the work his subordinates carry out: the main criteria is whether he has sufficient knowledge of what is involved in the work being supervised to enable him to assess performance, diagnose problems and suggest solutions.

One of the key qualities a supervisor needs is the ability to communicate with people as unless his subordinates are properly informed, properly instructed and have access to constructive counselling and advice when necessary, morale and motivation will suffer.

A good supervisor, then, is a person whose combination of leadership qualities, technical expertise and communication skills inspire staff with the will to give of their best.

Styles of leadership

Styles of leadership range from the authoritarian to the democratic. The style a person chooses to adopt is very much influenced by his own personality, the personalities of the people with whom he is dealing and the policy of the organisation. Most people favour a particular style, but the good leader will be flexible and adapt his approach to different situations. You will probably know people who fit all of the descriptions given below.

Authoritarian style

This type of leader likes to make the decisions and impose them on the group; he expects obedience and is reluctant to delegate. Whilst this style works in situations where staff are inexperienced or where quick decisions need to be made, it causes resentment where consultation is needed or where the leader is dealing with experts.

Paternalistic style

The paternalistic leader does ask for opinions but then makes the decision himself and persuades the team to accept it. Although he delegates some of his work, he does not always delegate the necessary authority with it. This approach works with staff who have limited experience, and enables decisions to be made quickly, but it should not be used when competent and expert staff are available as they become frustrated because their abilities are not being fully utilised.

Democratic style

The democratic leader involves the group in decision-making by explaining the problems and the factors involved and then asking them to arrive at a decision; he may even ask them to investigate and define the problem. He is prepared to delegate and to modify his views. This style is appropriate when negotiating, dealing with complex problems, where consultation is needed and where expert staff are available and willing to take responsibility. It is not appropriate for use with

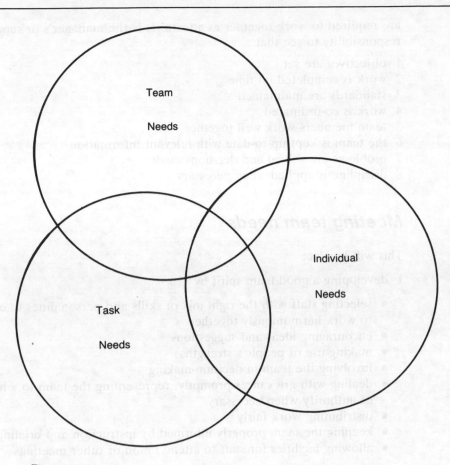

Figure 120

inexperienced staff, where procedures are already laid down or where quick decisions are needed.

There is no 'best' style of leadership which will result in high work performance or maintain long-term morale. Democratic styles tend to increase job satisfaction and group cohesiveness, but some subordinates prefer more direction and do not wish to be involved in decision-making.

Whatever style is adopted for the situation, the leader must ensure that he balances the need of groups, individuals and the task itself (see Fig. 120). If he merely concentrates on the task in hand without considering the needs of people, morale will fall. Similarly, if individuals cannot see the results of their efforts, there will be no sense of achievement.

Building a team

Organisations usually employ specialists to carry out specific jobs such as wordprocessing, printing, accounting etc. In order to get the job done, these people are required to work together as a team. It is the manager's or supervisor's responsibility to see that

1 objectives are set
2 work is completed on time
3 standards are maintained
4 work is co-ordinated
5 team members work well together
6 the team is kept up-to-date with relevant information
7 problems are solved and decisions made
8 discipline is applied when necessary

Meeting team needs

This will involve:

1 developing a good team spirit by

- selecting staff with the right mix of skills and personalities to enable them to work harmoniously together
- encouraging ideas and suggestions
- making use of people's strengths
- involving the team in decision-making
- dealing with grievances promptly, representing the team to a higher level of authority when necessary
- distributing work fairly
- keeping the team properly informed by instruction and briefing meetings
- allowing facilities for staff to attend union or other meetings

2 creating a safe and healthy working environment by

- making adequate safety and first-aid provision
- training
- consulting on safety matters
- regular safety checks of equipment, plant, buildings
- carrying out emergency drills
- encouraging good practices

Meeting individual needs

This will involve:

1 ensuring each team member knows

- what the team is trying to achieve
- what is expected of him
- to whom he should report and for what he is accountable
- the level of performance expected
- the progress he is making

2 treating people as individuals by

- listening to problems
- counselling
- visiting them on the job
- appraising individual performance

3 motivating staff by

- consulting for opinions and advice
- giving constructive criticism
- giving them credit for good ideas and using them
- being fair and impartial
- training and developing them for promotion

Meeting task needs

Work planning

An important aspects of leadership is planning the job – what, why, when, where and how it is to be done and who will do it. This is discussed fully in Unit 13 (page 199).

Monitoring performance

This has already been discussed in Unit 17 (see page 260).
A good manager will ensure that monitoring takes place on a continuous basis and that records are kept of variation in output, breakdowns, delays, bottlenecks, errors, wastage, successes etc.

Informal methods of monitoring will include

1 talking to people on the job
2 observation
3 walking round

Formal methods will include

1 Sampling of output for quality
2 manual or computerised logging of quantity produced, e.g. telephone calls, typed output, items of data entered into computer
3 staff appraisal (see page 276)

Results obtained can be used to:

1 improve systems and procedures
2 distribute work evenly
3 identify needs for training or new machinery

Attitudes to work and relationships

Personal attitudes to work vary considerably. Some people can be relied upon to produce work which is always of a high standard and completed within the time stipulated. Others are over-conscientious and whilst their work contains very few errors, it takes them too long to do it and slows down production. Some people get a sense of achievement from completing as much as possible; they get through a large volume of work and speed up the general pace, but often make errors in the process which have to be checked and corrected.

Attitudes towards other people also vary. Some people work happily in a team, doing their share and lending a hand when others are overloaded; they are willing to work late to get jobs finished and make sure no-one else's work is held up. Others prefer to work independently and whilst their work may be of an excellent standard, they resent being tied to the pace and needs of other workers and often resent authority as well, sometimes making decisions beyond their terms of reference. Just as difficult to cope with are the people who refuse to display any initiative and only do what they are asked to do or are lazy and do as little as possible.

A manager or supervisor must recognise that all individuals are unique and that just because they work together does not necessarily mean they share the same needs, ambitions, attitudes or outlook. Personality traits which cannot be changed must be accepted and used to the advantage of the group. The group itself will, in any case, exert its own pressure on members who do not conform to its code of behaviour, and this often proves more acceptable and effective than intervention by the superior.

Task 19.2

1 What attitudes towards work do you think are desirable?
2 In what ways do you think superiors can generate such attitudes in subordinates?

Dealing with problems

Imagine that you have been promoted from the post of computer operator to the post of supervisor of the office services section of Jobline (see information supplied in Task 2.1, page 33). Morale had been very low since Wendy Jones was dismissed two months ago. Tasks 19.3 and 19.4 refer to this situation.

Task 19.3

The sales assistant has been very unco-operative since your promotion and you suspect that the other staff are not inspired with confidence in you. You knew that things might be difficult at first but expected the situation to have improved by now. Instead, you seem to have work piling up waiting to be done, Mary Webb (the manager/partner) is anxious because orders are taking longer to complete, the reprographics operator has threatened to hand in her notice because she is overworked even though the part-time sales assistant often doesn't have anything to do, and you are trying to man the computer as well because the person you appointed three weeks ago is now on 2 weeks' holiday. Mary Webb has asked to see you later today to discuss the problems and you anticipate she is having second thoughts about promoting you.

1 Why do you think you are in this mess?
2 Do you think you were properly prepared for promotion?
3 Do you think Mary Webb should have done anything about this?
4 Why do you think you were chosen for the job?
5 What training do you think you needed?
6 Do you think internal promotion is a good idea? Give reasons for your answer.
7 What action will you take to improve your situation?
8 What can you learn from your mistakes?

Task 19.4   You are required to deal with the following problems, using appropriate management styles and techniques:

1 The reprographics operator has been persistently late recently, despite several warnings. Simulate a disciplinary interview with this member of staff.
2 The telex/wordprocessor operator and the computer operator have always been allowed to go to lunch at the same time, leaving no-one to deal with urgent telex messages. Conduct an interview with both members of staff in which you must persuade them to stagger their lunch break to provide cover for each other in spite of their vociferous objections.
3 In order to improve the job satisfaction of the reprographics operator who, despite her complaints, is an excellent worker, you have decided to train her to use the telex and wordprocessor so that she can cover during the lunch hour or staff absence. Draw up a training programme which will be 2 hours a day spread over 3 weeks. The training scheme should include instruction on composing and sending telex messages and distributing incoming messages; procedures for using the wordprocessor for form letters and typing reports; housekeeping of discs and routines for copying.

Participation and consultation

The modern approach to improving management/employee relations is to involve employees in decision-making. This can take various forms, including

- briefing meetings of workgroups and departmental meetings
- consultative committees between staff and management on matters such as safety
- suggestions schemes (sometimes with a cash incentive)
- management by objectives, where staff are allowed to share in decisions affecting their own work
- negotiations between management and unions on pay and productivity deals

The benefits of this style of management are that morale and output are improved because staff are more committed to the success of the policies which have been decided by them.

Level	Types of decision	Examples
Executives	Policy; setting objectives and targets; division of work; budgeting; staffing; settlement of disputes; financial decisions	Reducing number of staff employed; plans for expansion
Middle management/ supervisors	Work planning; allocation of tasks to staff; authorising purchase, movement and use of resources; day-to-day discipline; safety matters; quality control; work methods and systems	Adjusting production to meet demand; deciding standards of work acceptable
Operatives/ clerks	Routine, task-related decisions, e.g. procedure, method, sequence, speed of working	When to collect and frank mail; layout of typing

Figure 121

Decision-making

Examples of types of decision associated with various levels of responsibility are illustrated in Fig. 121.

All decision-making, at whatever level, involves choice, a degree of initiative and an element of risk. Errors of judgement can be costly, e.g. a decision to expand at the wrong time can bankrupt a firm; the appointment of an unsuitable candidate to a post can cause inefficiency, bad staff relations and lower productivity.

Sound judgement is usually the result of experience, instinct and expertise. However, even the inexperienced employee can learn the art of good decision-making by approaching problems systematically.

Guidelines for decision-making

1 gather all the facts
2 compare possible consequences of alternative courses of action
3 refer to company policies, procedure manuals and codes of practice when appropriate
4 make use of precedent, i.e. previous decisions made in similar situations
5 ask superior for advice
6 consult with colleagues, experts and other people affected
7 above all, apply commonsense, i.e. what is reasonable and practicable in the circumstances

Key facts

Leadership styles may be

- authoritarian
- democratic
- somewhere in-between

Management of people involves balancing

- team needs
- individual needs
- task needs

A good team spirit can be encouraged by

- selecting staff who will work well together
- keeping the team properly informed
- making use of people's strengths
- involving the team in decision-making
- allocating work fairly
- providing a good working environment

Individuals can be motivated by

- treating them as individuals
- ensuring that they know what, why, when, where and how to do the job
- developing and training them
- making use of their ideas and suggestions

Getting the job done involves

- planning and allocating work
- monitoring progress and performance
- developing good work systems

Attitudes of people to work affect

- quality and quantity of output
- staff relationships

Making decisions involves

- gathering facts
- comparing alternatives
- communicating to staff

Unit 20 *Introducing change*

Introduction

No organisation can afford to remain static for very long if it is to remain competitive. It must constantly review its policies, systems and procedures to ensure they are efficient and cost-effective. It must also adapt to meet external requirements imposed by changing legislation, markets, technology and social attitudes.

Much of the change taking place in offices at the moment is associated with new technology and we will therefore give particular consideration to this aspect.

Why people resist change

As we have already discovered, people work to fulfil certain economic, social and personal needs. Provided these are met, morale is high. When changes are made to existing systems or procedures, individuals may feel that some of their needs will no longer be met and may therefore feel threatened.

Let us take, for example, the proposed introduction of a computer at ALBEC Ltd, and consider how it might affect the economic, social and personal needs of staff.

Economic fears

The computer will be able to produce an invoice, update the customer account and print a statement automatically, from one input of information; the payroll will be completed in one-third of the time it takes at present; stock records will be linked to purchasing, eliminating the need for several clerical operations. This could make staff fear redundancy or reduction in pay because work will be completed in less time and lower-level skills will be required.

Social fears

The installation of new workstations and possible reduction or redeployment of staff could mean work groups being broken up or changed in composition. Many employees get very upset when the balance of a working team is changed, particularly if the change results in working in new surroundings, being isolated or getting used to new people.

Personal fears

Individuals take pride in the skills they have acquired and may see the new job as demeaning or less interesting. They may even feel that new technology has been introduced because their work was inadequate. Their status could be affected as they may be controlling less staff, and their job prospects may worsen.

Reactions to change

People react to change in different ways depending on what they expect from a job, their age, whether they fear the change, see it as a challenge or feel it is an opportunity for self-development.

Reactions may take the form of

- aggression by staff who see it as being a way of cutting costs, getting more work out of them and reducing their own job satisfaction
- apathy from staff who think nothing they say matters anyway
- unco-operativeness from staff who feel inadequate and are afraid they may not be able to cope with the new system or may lose their jobs
- enthusiasm from staff who see change as the chance to widen their experience and improve career prospects

Sometimes, feelings may be so strong that the group will take united action against management by refusing to use new technology or even withdrawing their labour in exceptional cases.

Recently, a typing pool in a large organisation agreed to try out wordprocessors for 6 months on the understanding that they would be involved in making the final decision at the end of the trial period as to whether or not to install the equipment permanently. At the end of the 6 months they discovered that management had already taken the decision and purchased the equipment. The typists refused to use the wordprocessors and the equipment was locked in cupboards for a year until consultations had taken place to agree revised work conditions and pay. The cost in terms of relationships between management and workers was very high, apart from financial considerations.

Task 20.1

1 What do you think might be the fears and reactions of staff in the following circumstances?

    (a) The secretary to the home sales manager at Domilux is to be transferred to a wordprocessing centre. She will still work for the home sales manager, but will also work for the regional sales managers as well (five in all).

    (b) Westleigh District Council have decided to do away with the offset-litho duplicator in their printroom as all colour work for district councils in its area will now be undertaken by the County Council's printing section. The staff will now only be required to produce black and white copies using plain paper copiers. There is likely to be a reduction in staff.

(c) ALBEC Ltd are looking for larger premises and there are rumours that the board is considering moving to a development area in another part of the country.

(d) Domilux sales representatives are to be provided with a computer terminal so that they can work from home and communicate with Head Office via the VDU linked to telephone lines. They will only need to visit Head Office about once a week.

2 How do you think these fears and reactions could be overcome?

Task 20.2

Situation: You are employed as a trainee assistant in the chief executive's department of Westleigh District Council (see Task 1.6, page 28).

Recently, the work study section introduced a new bonus scheme for refuse collection based on 'Task and Finish'. This means simply that instead of workmen completing a set number of working hours, they are allowed to finish work as soon as their set task (i.e. collection of refuse from a particular number of roads) is finished.

This resulted in a change in collection times from those traditionally established as workmen were working faster and therefore finishing earlier.

1 Reply to the letter in Fig. 122 from Mrs Page.
2 Draft a memo to the work study officer explaining the situation and advising him how to avoid such an occurrence in the future.

Winning people round

The best way to minimise resistance to change is to secure the co-operation of staff by consulting them at all stages – before, during and after the implementation of the new system.

Don't

1 spring change on people
   • it isn't fair
   • it breeds mistrust
   • there is no time to build positive attitudes
   • there is no time for revising plans

2 expect too much too soon
   • it isn't fair
   • staff will feel pressurised and inadequate
   • there are snags in any new system which cause delays or errors
   • it is better to introduce change gradually

2 Kingsway

WESTLEIGH

Midlandshire

WM4 2FQ

14 February 198–

Dear Sir

I am writing to complain about the poor service given by the refuse disposal men.

Last Tuesday, I put my refuse bags outside the front gate, expecting them to be collected at around 12 o'clock as usual. I then went to work.

When I got home at 4 pm the sacks were still there so I telephoned the Technical Services Department to enquire why my refuse had not been collected. The girl who answered said the rubbish had been collected from Kingsway on Tuesday and that I would just have to wait until next week now as my sacks were obviously not there when the dustmen called.

This really isn't good enough! As a ratepayer I expect to have my rubbish collected every week – not just when it suits the men to pick it up.

Perhaps you would be good enough to give me an explanation as to why this occurred and give me your assurance that it won't happen again.

Yours faithfully

Sandra Page (Mrs)

Figure 122

Do

Before investigating the old system, give reasons (to secure co-operation). Before planning the new system, consult staff:

- ask for suggestions and advice (it boosts morale)
- incorporate their good ideas (the person on-the-job often knows best)
- find out their worries and requirements (to forestall problems)

Before installing the new system:

1 brief staff well in advance
  - it gives time for adjustment to change
  - it enables questions to be answered
  - it helps to develop positive attitudes and reassures them
  - it allows them to put forward ideas

2 give staff adequate training and instruction

During installation, support staff when the system is being installed by:

  - being available for advice
  - giving encouragement
  - dealing constructively with problems
  - making decisions
  - understanding difficulties and delays

After the trial period

1 consult staff by
  - asking for comments and ideas
  - making a note of problems so that you can

2 make remedial changes such as repositioning of equipment or furniture, changing workloads, modifying software, installing noise-absorbent furnishings etc.

While the new system is settling down, it is better not to dispense with the old one until all the snags have been ironed out.

Patterns of employment

In many cases where new technology is introduced, it results in a reduction in staff, relocation or redeployment. In some cases, staff may find themselves working mainly from home, communicating with Head Office and external contacts via computer terminals. Within the office itself, workers are becoming more isolated and desk-bound as screen-based communication systems replace the need for face-to-face contact. They are being required to take on larger workloads as computers can process information far more quickly – in some cases, this may bring additional responsibilities and in others turn people into machine-minders.

Skills and attitudes

All levels of staff will need keyboarding skills, the ability to analyse and interpret data from computer printout, and a knowledge of basic concepts and applications of new technology.

Many existing staff will find they have to change their attitudes, for example:

  - managers who consider that keyboarding is demeaning will have to recognise it as an essential skill

- secretaries who are used to being a personal assistant to one boss may have to adapt to working for several people and having less personal contact with each
- staff who are used to the social contact and support brought about by working in a group may be required to develop the self-reliance and initiative needed to work on their own

Job design and job evaluation

It is the responsibility of management to ensure that jobs are made as interesting as possible either by enriching or enlarging them (see page 269) to provide challenge and job satisfaction. Remuneration should reflect not only the job responsibilities and skills, but should also compensate for the unsatisfactory elements such as monotony and lack of social contact.

Coping with expansion

Expansion or diversification will inevitably bring about changes in the organisation structure and may involve moving premises. Particular problems faced by staff may be concerned with

- enhancement or relegation of status
- changes in methods of working
- changes in composition of work groups
- need for retraining
- upheaval and expense of moving house

Task 20.3
Refer to the organisation chart you completed for ALBEC in Task 2.1, page 33.
Situation: You are a trainee at ALBEC Ltd.
After 2 successful years of operation, ALBEC Ltd had more orders than it could cope with and it was ready to re-organise and expand. It took over an adjoining factory unit to cope with increased production and bought out a partnership, White and Monk, which owned five retail electrical shops in Midlandshire. The staff employed by the partnership were as follows:

Colin White	In charge of sales
Edwin Monk	Office manager and buyer
Pam Brown	Secretary to both partners
One accounts clerk	Dealing with wages, purchases and credit control
One general clerk	Dealing with invoicing and the sales ledger and filing, liaising with both partners
One storeman	
Two drivers	
Five shop managers with two assistants in each shop	

As part of the deal, White and Monk were made directors of the new company, renamed All British Electrical Components Ltd. The logo ALBEC would now appear on all its products. It was agreed that none of the existing staff in either firm should be made redundant.

The new board of directors is as follows:

Bob Jones	Managing Director
Andrew Baxter	Chief Accountant
Colin White	Marketing Manager
Edwin Monk	Office Manager and Buyer
Larry Symonds	Research and Design Director
Kevin Adams	Distribution Manager
Dave Parkes	Production Manager

1 Prepare a new organisation chart ready for the staff handbook.

To help you with the chart, the following information may be of use:

Miss Smith will now become secretary to Bob Jones and Andrew Baxter. She will also be in charge of personnel records.

Mrs Brown will do secretarial work for Ed Monk and Colin White. A new secretary, Miss Jill Bland, will carry out secretarial work for the other directors.

The clerk/typist will be accountable to Miss Smith, but will also do work as required for Mrs Brown, Miss Bland and for the general clerk. She will also type invoices and statements.

The general clerk will no longer deal with the sales ledger, but will do filing and take details of incoming orders. She will be accountable to Miss Smith.

One accounts clerk will deal with wages, purchase and sales ledgers and day books liaising with clerk/typist doing invoices.

One accounts clerk will deal with credit control, costing, purchase and sales control accounts, and act as cashier.

The warehouseman will be in charge of the finished goods in the warehouse. The storeman will be in charge of stores in the production department but will be accountable to the warehouseman in distribution.

Five more factory workers will be taken on and two of the existing assembly line workers will be made supervisors in charge of Workshop A and Workshop B.

2 Write a covering memo to Edwin Monk with the chart suggesting any improvements which you think could be made in the allocation of duties or lines of communication.

Task 20.4

This assignment relates to ALBEC Ltd.

It is now 6 months since ALBEC expanded and the office manager is carrying out a review of the working arrangements within the company. As a result of his investigations, the following problems of co-ordination have come to light:

1 Production department staff complain that they cannot complete some of the current orders because of shortages of materials.
2 Shops complain that although, according to their stock lists, products are available, there are often long delays before goods are delivered to customers. They say this is having a bad effect on sales.

3 Sales departments staff complain that they cannot always get through to the switchboard to 'phone their orders in and that the details are often taken down wrongly when they do.

4 A large contract was lost recently because the quotation was not received in time by the customer.

5 Time was lost recently when a new computerised machine was introduced into the factory. The men refused to use it for 2 weeks and management eventually persuaded them to accept it by offering a cash incentive.

The office manager has asked you, the trainee, to suggest ways in which these problems could be avoided in future. Set out your suggestions in the form of a report. No more than a paragraph is needed for each problem.

Task 20.5   **Integrated Assignment**

Situation: You are employed at ALBEC Ltd.

Refer to the information concerning the expansion of ALBEC Ltd in Task 20.3 (page 296).

The existing premises soon prove to be inadequate for the company's increased production and Mr Bob Jones, the managing director, wishes to consider relocating the factory and head office to new premises out of town.

You are asked to make enquiries and supply the managing director with a report containing the following information:

1 the factors which will need to be considered when choosing new premises
2 the advantages and disadvantages of moving the firm to a new location out of town
3 the effects of such a move on staff, customers, suppliers and the local community
4 items of expenditure incurred in moving to new premises
5 consultative procedures necessary when contemplating the move

Key facts   People resist change for

- economic
- social
- personal reasons

Reactions to change may take the form of

- aggression
- apathy
- unco-operativeness
- enthusiasm

Ways of helping people to accept change:

- give reasons
- consult
- brief well in advance

- provide training and support
- make remedial changes in the light of experience

Changes in patterns of employment:

- additional skills/jobs required for new technology
- new office procedures
- new relationships
- different attitudes
- different organisational structure to cope with expansion and speedier work flow

Index